MATTERS OF LIFE AND DEATH

MATTERS OF LIFE AND DEATH

10 QUESTIONS NO SERIOUS CHRISTIAN CAN AVOID

ERWIN W. LUTZER

MOODY PRESS
CHICAGO

All Scripture quotations, unless indicated, are taken from the *New American Standard Bible,* © 1960, 1962, 1963, 1968, 1971, 1972, 1973, 1975, and
1977 by The Lockman Foundation, and are used by permission.

The use of selected references from various versions of the Bible in this
publication does not necessarily imply publisher endorsement of the versions in their entirety.

ISBN: 0-8024-5292-2

1 3 5 7 9 10 8 6 4 2

Printed in the United States of America

*To those who share the
pastoral ministry with me
at Moody Church*

*Doug Bastian
Paul Craig
Gerald Edmonds
Mike Milco
Mark Taylor
Daryle Worley*

Contents

Preface

O h, God," a friend of mine prays each morning, "please keep me alive until I die!"

All of us should have the desire to live life to the fullest, to live each day as if it were our last. For all of life is but preparation for the life to come. And only those who know how to live will know how to die.

This book is an exposition of ten topics that no serious Christian can avoid. We pass this way but once; either we face the issues that relate to our life on earth and our future with God, or we squander opportunities that will affect our role for all of eternity. Make no mistake: The attitudes we adopt, the moral choices we make, and the spiritual values we avow will have eternal repercussions. That's why these are indeed matters of life and death.

Of course I make no claim that these are the only issues we must face, but they certainly are among the most important. Part 1 of this book, "Confronting the Perplexities of Life," deals with the choices we must make in serving God in our vocation and how God deals with us when we opt for our will rather than His. Unless we understand the mystery of un-answered prayer and the pitfalls Satan has laid out for us, we might not be able to navigate between the rocks as we wend our way through the danger zones of life.

Given the moral climate of our culture, part 2 of this book, "Confronting Questions of Sexuality," might well be the most relevant. Sex, as we know, has the power to bond a man and a woman in a loving union or to destroy one's dignity and the possibility of emotional wholeness. The chapter dealing with a sexual past is a message that needs to be preached from the housetops. Here is hope for our permissive generation, where failures of the past often mar the future. We must comprehend both the scars of sin and God's ability to cleanse and forgive.

Homosexuality is a topic that must be treated with integrity and compassion. Unless we understand why God can offer homosexuals hope, we may miss our opportunity to be healing agents in our hurting world.

Given the many unhappy marriages, it is essential that we understand the role of conflict within marriage. We must move beyond the notion that marriages can be saved merely by offering advice on how to improve communication and enhance understanding. Unless we identify the roots of conflict, we will always deal with symptoms and not the underlying causes of marital unhappiness.

If sections one and two of this book deal with matters of life, the third section, "Confronting Eternity," confronts the ultimate issues: death and dying, hell and heaven. Death and dying is in the news today for many reasons, but we must remember that only God who sees the future can speak with authority about what lies on the other side of the parted curtain.

Some will wish to read this book from beginning to end; others will want to turn first to those chapters that are of particular interest. But I hope that eventually all of the chapters will be digested because each contributes to our understanding of what is truly important. There is more to life than earning a living; there is more to fulfillment than sexual gratification; and there is more to salvation than going to heaven when we die.

If it is true that he who lives well dies well, we had better examine the bigger questions of life. My prayer is that this book will help all of us pass the tests God gives us *here* so that we might have a joyous welcome *there*.

Life and Death; Sin and Grace; Time and Eternity. These are issues no serious Christian can avoid.

PART ONE:

Confronting the Perplexities of Life

CHAPTER 1

How Can I Be Content with My Job?

When I'm at home I'm one person. When I am at work I'm another," Del said, complaining about the pressures that his job put upon him.

"When I'm with Christians I act like them; at work nobody even knows that I'm a church-goer, much less a born-again believer."

Del was working seventy hours a week trying to please a demanding boss who expected ever more from his employees. To quit meant that he would be without a job in a competitive market. To continue meant that he was cheating his family and jeopardizing his health.

His wife's critical attitude toward his long hours of low-paying work drained whatever romance was left from their relationship. Now he was tempted to seek fulfillment with a woman who adored him, a woman whose friendship would be free of the tensions that existed in his home. He began to consider an affair with this woman co-worker.

Del knew that with his job dilemmas there were no easy answers, perhaps no answers at all. To quit after two years of training and heavy time investments was unthinkable; to continue was to be pulled even further away from his family. Now even sexual temptation lurked on the job. He was convinced that there were no reasonable options.

What should he do?

As Americans earning a living in the late twentieth century, we face a set of challenges unknown to previous generations. With the proliferation of knowledge and inventions, we are told that there are perhaps 50,000 different kinds of possible jobs, demanding a wide range of training and aptitude. Many of these responsibilities are highly specialized and require years of training. Finding the one that best matches our abilities, temperament, and pocketbooks is indeed a difficult task.

Millions of jobs also demand intense interpersonal relationships that spark conflict and force individuals to make decisions with unclear ethical guidelines. Whereas previous generations faced rather simple day-by-day responsibilities, our technological and informational explosion has created a whole new set of problems. Stacks of books on such topics as tension, managing conflict, and workaholism testify to the pressures of the workplace.

If you are dissatisfied with your career, you have plenty of company. Even as early as 1976, researchers in New Jersey reported that up to 80 percent of Americans are in the wrong jobs![1]

Nevertheless, the pressure-packed working world is a great place for personal and spiritual growth. In fact, *the complex demands of the twentieth century workplace form the best laboratory to prove the reality of God.* Right in the midst of corporate America, with its ever-crumbling ethical structure, is one of the best opportunities to prove that Christ can make a difference.

The purpose of this chapter is to challenge Christians to bring God from the sidelines to the very center of the workplace. It is a wake-up call to hear the voice of Christ telling us that every single day on the job is a day of eternal significance.

Specifically, this chapter will show that:

- Christians in the workplace are strategically placed there by God.

- Most of the biblical heroes were not in full-time ministry but had regular jobs that they shared with the unbelieving world of their day.
- The ethical pressures of the marketplace are tests given to us by God to let us prove that our love for Him is stronger than life itself.
- God often uses our dislike of a particular job to teach us lessons we could never otherwise learn.
- To "let our light shine" in the workplace means that we have earned the right to be heard.

Our vocations are an entrance exam to see where we should be slotted in the coming kingdom. Christ told several different parables, each emphasizing the same point: Those who are faithful with what God has given them will receive a reward in heaven; the careless will suffer loss. Not everyone who enters heaven will hear, "Well done, good and faithful slave; you were faithful with a few things, I will put you in charge of many things; enter into the joy of your master" (Matthew 25:23).

The purpose of the judgment seat of Christ is not to berate us but to assign us a responsibility that corresponds to our degree of faithfulness, including our diligence at work. All believers will be fulfilled in the kingdom, but some will have more responsibility than others.

Is God interested in your work? It may come as a surprise that God Himself is a worker. After creation we read, "And by the seventh day God completed His work which He had done; and He rested on the seventh day from all His work which He had done" (Genesis 2:2). God created the world, and it is described as work. He upholds creation, and that is work. Because we are created in the image of God, we also were created to be workers.

Created to Work

Most of us suspect that work came about as a result of the curse. In truth, God intended that we work. Even before Adam and Eve sinned we read, "And the Lord God planted a garden toward the east, in Eden; and there He placed the man whom He had formed. Then the Lord God took the man and put him into the garden of Eden to cultivate it and keep it" (Genesis 2:8,15). Sin makes work harder, but by no means was it the cause of work.

We were created to work; indeed, work is man's lot by virtue of the design of God. Through work we affirm our partnership with God in governing the world. Ecclesiastes 3:13 teaches that work is a gift of God.

Tragically, with few exceptions, God has been shut out of the workplace. The chasm between Sunday and Monday seems too wide to span. Keen observers tell us that very little that happens in a person's religious life profoundly affects his job.

The Princeton Religion Research Center found "little difference in the ethical views and behavior of the churched and the unchurched" in a recent study of the impact of religion on day-to-day work. Comparing "churched" workers with those workers who do not regularly attend church, the Princeton center surveyed a wide range of behaviors, such as pilfering supplies (stealing), overstating qualifications on résumés (lying), calling in sick when not sick (lying and cheating), and overstating tax deductions (lying, stealing, and cheating). The center concluded that any differences are of marginal significance.[2]

Full-time Christian Work

Often we speak about ministers and missionaries as being in "full-time Christian work." That simply means that some people are paid for using their specialized gifts of ministry full time. Unfortunately this terminology often perpetuates the mistaken idea that these people are serving the Lord more "fully" than those in a "secular" vocation. Some Christians in the workplace see themselves as second-class citizens in the kingdom, not truly serving God. As a result, they don't even seriously consider the scope of their opportunity to serve God. They confine His demands upon their lives to one day a week. Call to mind the person whom you consider to be most devoted to doing the will of God. If you are like most Christians, you probably thought of a missionary or pastor. Although such are exercising their special gifts of God, many people in other vocations are equally faithful and have just as great a spiritual impact.

What does the Bible teach about the role of believers in the workplace? And what is the divine perspective on work? Christ answers that question by demonstrating the compatibility of a vocation and spiritual ministry.

Christ in the Workplace

When Christ came to His hometown, Nazareth, the people were astonished that He could teach with such wisdom. They asked, "Where did this man get these things, and what is this wisdom given to Him, and such miracles as these performed by His hands? Is not this the carpenter, the son of Mary, and brother of James, and Joses, and Judas, and Simon? Are not His sisters here with us?" Mark adds, "And they took offense at Him" (Mark 6:2–3).

Not this teaching from a carpenter! Christ offended them because He did not follow the expected cultural pattern. He was not a full-time religious worker and yet He was doing spiritual ministry.

He is neither a scribe nor a Pharisee and yet had the nerve to perform "religious" duties! they thought. *How can this common carpenter speak for God? A man with splinters in his hands and calluses should stay in the pew where he belongs! Full-time carpenters are not supposed to teach in a synagogue. They don't know God well enough to do miracles.*

Apparently they were not offended by what Christ said, but by His occupation. "Is not this the carpenter, the son of Mary?" And they wonder what right He had to teach. *He is the son of a common laborer. Spiritual leaders do not arise out of secular professions.*[3]

Yet here, for all time, Christ demonstrated both the dignity of work (in His case being a carpenter) and the compatibility of such vocations with spiritual ministry.

What about the other spiritual leaders of the Bible? Were they full-time religious workers, or did they also have "secular" vocations?

Saints in the Workplace

Pete Hammond has done a study of forty leading characters of the Bible who are held up to us as examples of spiritual commitment. He calls these people "Surprising Saints" because of the conclusions he reached in his study.[4]

Of these forty leading characters, Hammond discovered three out of every four (75 percent) never had a religious job. They didn't leave the business world to go into "full-time ministry." They held what we call secular jobs all of their lives. Whether it be Joseph, David, Luke, or Paul, they all had their own professions and never did leave these responsibilities so that they could "really" serve the Lord.

If they lived today, they would possibly be treated as second-class citizens, spiritually speaking. With the false dichotomy between those who are in full-time service and those who aren't, they would be told, "All that you can do is pray and pay."

Recently I visited an Islamic country that will not allow missionaries within its borders. At a conference, I met more than 120 believers from the United States and Europe wholly committed to sharing the gospel as witnesses for Christ in this hostile culture. Every one of them had his own job: computer operator, English teacher, businessman, writer, etc. Clearly these people are as important to the kingdom as full-time pastors and missionaries.

In fact, these people told me that their vocations gave them an authenticity that they could not have if they had been allowed to be full-time missionaries. After all, if Christ is credible, He must be proved to be so in the very fabric of everyday life. The pressures of the workplace give Christians the greatest opportunity to prove the authenticity of the gospel.

To make the light shine in a religious gathering is easy enough. However, God wants our lights to shine much farther—in hospitals, the courts, government, schools, factories, and the offices scattered throughout the land. Light must shine in darkness.

The distinction between the clergy and laity is understandable (I myself belong to the first group), but it has led to the crippling impression that those who are in secular vocations cannot serve Christ as fully as those who have chosen religious careers.

Ten of those forty Bible characters had prison records, Hammond notes. Joseph, Daniel, Jeremiah, Peter, Paul, and others had been incarcerated for one reason or another. Today such people (with few exceptions) would likely never be welcomed by the average evangelical church.

We might also add that many of those whom God used had a past blot on their lives that needed the forgiveness and restoration of God. Moses was guilty of manslaughter, David committed adultery, and Paul the apostle had spent his preconversion days rounding up Christians and having them thrown into jail. Thankfully, God still uses imperfect people today. One of my friends says, "Have you ever noticed how often God puts His hand on the wrong man!"

How many vocations are mentioned in the Bible? Hammond counted eighty-six different jobs among those forty people. Apparently the idea that only the priests were really servants of God did not occur to them. They wrestled with virtually all the pressures that dominate the marketplace today: unreasonable demands from a superior, competition, unfairness, prejudice, job insecurity, and being fired.

Hammond says that for the faith of a believer to be trapped into one day a week (Sunday) is an embarrassment to the work of God. Clearly you can do the will of God without leaving the marketplace. Christ must be Lord not just on Sunday but from Monday through Saturday too.

The church will not have a significant impact on the world until there is a revival among the laity. Only when believers everywhere are willing to see their vocations through the eyes of Christ (whatever the cost) will the authenticity of the gospel make its mark in our society.

Regardless of your vocation, someone has faced the same pressures as you and has done so successfully. Someone has used the struggles and temptations you face to prove the reality of Christ. Our task is to see that the God who ordained that man should work is available to use every believer in almost every vocation as a powerful witness for His glory.

Ethics in the Workplace

Whether on Wall Street, Capitol Hill, or in Christian ministries, our ethical standards have eroded. As I write, one television network news show has just shown a documentary on how service stations pad their bills and how small investors lost their money in a "scam." On another station, a video clip tells how a public school principal told her teachers to help students cheat on test scores so that the school (and her leadership) would look good. Meanwhile, the hidden lifestyles of religious leaders are being exposed to a cynical world. Quite literally we have to ask whether anyone can still be trusted.

We can't insulate ourselves from participating (at least in some way) in the ethical dilemmas of our fallen world. I have a friend who will not go to a restaurant that has a bar, believing that patronizing such an establishment supports the liquor industry. I can respect his conscience, but no amount of separation will keep us from becoming a part (at least indirectly) of the evil network within the world's system. I may buy a car that was assembled by employees who will use their incomes for drinking and immorality. I pay taxes to a government that will squander its resources on destructive social legislation and overpriced defense technology. Like it or not, we are a part of the fabric of this fallen society.

Paul told the Christians in Corinth not to associate with someone who claimed to be a believer but lived an immoral or dishonest life. But he affirmed that such associations are necessary with people of the world. "I wrote you in my letter not to associate with immoral people; I did not at all mean with the immoral people of this world, or with the covetous and swindlers, or with idolaters; for then you would have to go out of the world. For what have I to do with judging outsiders? Do not you judge those who are within the church? But those who are outside, God judges" (1 Corinthians 5:9–10; 12–13).

How should Christians relate to this sinful environment? To live and work in an immoral world without compromising our convictions is the challenge that every working person faces. How do we remain ethical in a competitive, unethical workplace?

PERSONAL HONESTY

One day while shopping in Hong Kong, I visited an electronics shop owned by a Christian man. We got into a discussion about the widespread "price gouging" that took place in virtually all the stores along his busy street. Then, in a candid moment he surprised me by saying, "I cannot operate this business and be totally honest. If I wouldn't play at least some of the games of the trade, I'd be out of business because of the competition."

I was struck both by his honesty (to me, if not to all of his customers) and the evident pressure he felt to remain competitive. He didn't exactly enjoy being dishonest, but he thought he must be in order to survive.

Is dishonesty excusable if it is necessary for economic survival? I told this man (though too feebly, I fear) that God had confronted him with a wonderful opportunity. He was given a clear mandate to see whether God was trustworthy or not; here was a well-defined trial that could either prove God or disprove Him.

What if he were to run his business honestly and entrust the success or failure of it wholly to God? If it failed, would not his obedience be even more precious in the sight of God? Are there not times in all of our lives when we prove that our relationship with God means more to us than life itself?

George Mueller, who founded several orphanages in England in the last century, said that the care of children was the secondary purpose of these ministries. His first objective, he said, was to prove that God was trustworthy. Businessmen were compromising their principles for economic survival. They would not believe Mueller when he asserted that God could take care of them if only they would trust in His promises. So he began these orphanages determined he would never ask for funds but trust wholly in God for daily support. One miracle after another was documented as God provided food and money, often just in the nick of time. We desperately need people today who develop our confidence in the trustworthiness of God.

Not everyone is called of God to begin orphanages by faith. But we are all called upon to be honest, even in the face of economic disaster. How else can we show our fundamental belief that God is trustworthy and can take care of His children? The Almighty does not need our dishonesty to keep food on our table; He meets the needs of those who trust Him in other ways. Dishonesty is always proof of distrust.

Stuart Briscoe tells the story of how he was expected to be dishonest when he worked for a bank in England. He replied to his boss, "If you expect me to steal *for* you, what makes you think that I will not eventually steal *from* you?" Whether the boss appreciated his honesty or not, Briscoe said no when asked to violate his conscience. And it was God's responsibility to take care of the consequences.

We must also remember that dishonesty is more than simply stealing money from the cash register. Theft can take many forms. Workers may steal time by taking extralong lunch breaks or making personal telephone calls at the company's expense. In these and a dozen other ways, dishonesty cuts into the very lifeblood of the business world. Again the Scriptures are clear: "Let him who steals steal no longer; but rather let him labor, performing with his own hands what is good, in order that he may have something to share with him who has need" (Ephesians 4:28).

In those gray areas where we are not sure whether complete honesty is required, we can follow this simple rule: I will treat others the way I would like to be treated if I were in their shoes.

What about the negative fallout a commitment to honesty might have? Remember Shadrach, Meshach, and Abednego? They refused to compromise their commitment to God even at the pain of death. When told that they would be thrown into the fiery furnace, they affirmed their faith that they would be delivered, but added that even if God did not deliver them, they would never worship a false god (Daniel 3:17–18).

As Christ's witnesses we should be willing to do what is right whether the earthly outcome is positive or negative. Honesty does not have to pay in this life to make it worthwhile; it will bring a windfall in the life to come.

To first-century Christians who faced severe persecution for their faith, Peter said that suffering for Christ should not be thought of as strange. The apostle wrote, "Beloved, do not be surprised at the fiery ordeal among you, which comes upon you for your testing, as though some strange thing were happening to you; but to the degree that you share the sufferings of Christ, keep on rejoicing; so that also at the revelation of His glory, you may rejoice with exultation. If you are reviled for the name of Christ, you are blessed, because the Spirit of glory and of God rests upon you. By no means let any of you suffer as a murderer, or thief, or evildoer, or a troublesome meddler; but if anyone suffers as a Christian, let him not feel ashamed, but in that name let him glorify God" (1 Peter 4:12–16).

Peter says the world is largely hostile. But our enduring such persecution is precious to Christ. In our endurance we are believing that in the end Christ will have proved Himself totally trustworthy.

SEXUAL ETHICS

When Judge Clarence Thomas faced Anita Hill on national television during Senate hearings to confirm him to the Supreme Court, the issue of sexual harassment sailed into the public eye. Recently, a celebrated court case in Texas raised the question of whether freedom of speech gives men the right to make sexual innuendoes in the presence of women.

For the Christian the answer is clear. "Do not let immorality or any impurity or greed even be named among you, as is proper among saints; and there must be no filthiness and silly talk, or coarse jesting, which are not fitting, but rather giving of thanks. And do not participate in the unfruitful deeds of darkness, but instead even expose them" (Ephesians 5:3–4, 11).

Sexual temptations, both to harass and to seduce, will exist whenever men and women are in the same environment. But there can be no compromise for Christ's followers, either in speech or in actions. Immorality is the surest way for a Christian to ruin his or her witness, and it can destroy an entire family at the same time.

One day a man confided to me that he was falling in love with a co-worker and had a strong feeling that they would soon be having an affair. I told him that he should quit his job.

"But," he protested, "I have a wife and children to support." He apparently didn't realize that if he acted out his fantasies he would have brought more harm to his family than resigning from his job could ever have done! Better to live in poverty and be acceptable to God than commit immorality and incur the displeasure of the Almighty (Hebrews 13:4).

Again, I must stress that honesty and sexual fidelity don't always pay immediately. When Joseph said no to the sexual advances of Potiphar's wife, she lied about him and he was thrown into prison. So much for the notion that serving God is always a sure route to vocational advancement. But the God who was with Joseph in his promotion was now with him in his demotion too. Eventually, God turned it around for good (see Genesis 39:20–23; 41:38–44).

Thousands of believers have been fired because they will not accept the unethical practices of their bosses or companies. Others have had to voluntarily resign, having to choose between God and their jobs. An employee of a company that specializes in pornography put it this way: "When I finally made Christ Lord of my life, I decided it would be better to go hungry than to work for a firm dedicated to promoting what God hates."

Remember, when we suffer injustice because we have sought to do good, we are especially pleasing to God. Servants, Peter says, should be submissive to their masters, even if those masters are unreasonable. Then he continues, "For this finds favor, if for the sake of conscience toward God a man bears up under sorrows when suffering unjustly. For what credit is there if, when you sin and are harshly treated, you endure it with patience? But if when you do what is right and suffer for it you patiently endure it, this finds favor with God" (1 Peter 2:19–20). To suffer unjustly attracts the favor of the Almighty.

Earning a living is very important, but is it more important than obedience to God? If obedience cost Christ His life, should we be surprised when the obedience of one of His followers costs him a job?

FINANCIAL FAIRNESS

If you are giving your best to your boss and to the company, you would expect to be compensated fairly. But the word *fairness* sometimes means one thing to employees and another to management.

The book of James has some very pointed words for managers or employers who cheat their workers; it also has some words for those who are the victims of unfair compensation.

As for those employers who exploit the poor, James says that they should weep and howl for the miseries that will surely come upon them. The gold and silver they stored up will actually be evidence held against them in the day of judgment. Then he continues, "Behold, the pay of the laborers who mowed your fields, and which has been withheld by you, cries out against you; and the outcry of those who did the harvesting has reached the ears of the Lord of Sabaoth" (James 5:4).

Imagine working in the fields all day making your boss rich and yet not being paid! Employers can be smug about their selfish misuse of their employees because they think that no one will ever even the score. They forget that every transaction they make will eventually be meticulously reviewed by the Judge of all the earth.

I've even known Christians who were unfair to their employees by underpaying them and making unreasonable demands. If such employers are doing well financially because of the exploitation of others, they have a covetous heart. This too shall be revealed in the last day.

What does James say the poor should do about this unfairness? Obviously they could not appeal to a labor relations board. In those days they had no court of appeal, no grievance committee that would listen to their outcry. But there was one thing they could remember that would satisfy their desire for justice. "Be patient, therefore, brethren, until the coming of the Lord. Behold, the farmer waits for the precious produce of the soil, being patient about it, until it gets the early and late rains. You too be patient; strengthen your hearts, for the coming of the Lord is at hand. Do not complain, brethren, against one another, that yourselves may not be judged; behold, the Judge is standing right at the door" (5:7–9).

God, he says, monitors all business transactions and in the end will personally address all of the injustices that have ever taken place in employer-employee relationships. Obviously, the oppressed should do all they reasonably can to get what is their due. But the painful fact back then as now is that many of these grievances will never be rectified in this life. But rectified they will be by a Higher Court.

Of course today we can use every legitimate avenue to make our complaint known. But if we reach an impasse we must realize that injustices are used by God to test our faith. Do we believe that we eventually will be adequately recompensed for our faithfulness despite the unscrupulous actions of our employer? Can we not only receive good from the hand of God, but also adversity? Can we put our complaint before the Lord and leave it there? And, can we trust God to meet our needs in other ways?

To the person who has been defrauded of money that is his due, James assures us that the cry for justice has reached the ears of the Lord of Hosts. During this waiting period the wronged person should turn his grievance wholly over to God. Once that transfer of responsibility is made, the oppressed can rest assured that God will do right. And God will walk with the person through it all.

SOUND SPEECH

Our words on Monday, not what we sing on Sunday, best reveal our hearts. Christ said, "The good man out of his good treasure brings forth what is good; and the evil man out of his evil treasure brings forth what is evil. And I say to you, that every careless word that men shall speak, they shall render account for it in the day of judgment. For by your words you shall be justified, and by your words you shall be condemned" (Matthew 12:35–37).

Here perhaps more than anywhere else, a Christian can gain the credibility that is so important in communicating the Christian faith. Three rules must be followed to assure wholesome conversation in the workplace.

First, we must steadfastly *refuse to join in critical gossip* even if the person spoken about deserves all the unkind things said about him. Second, *speak positively about everyone,* even those who may be cruel and demanding. Jesus taught that if we love only those who are lovable, we are no better than the world. Only when we love our enemies are we "God-like" (Luke 6:32–35). Third, *discuss criticism only with those who are either a part of the problem or part of the solution.*

James reminds us, "And the tongue is a fire, the very world of iniquity; the tongue is set among our members as that which defiles the entire body, and sets on fire the course of our life, and is set on fire by hell. But no one can tame the tongue; it is a restless evil and full of deadly poison" (3:6–8).

If "tongue control" seems impossible, let us remind ourselves that the Holy Spirit indwells us so that we might be able to control the uncontrollable. Our speech will soon reveal the extent of our commitment to the God whom we claim to love and serve.

We cannot control our circumstances, but we can control our reaction to them. To contain our anger, to speak words that help rather than hurt, is a distinguishing mark of Christian conduct. Against the backdrop of our depressing crisis in ethics, Christians have the opportunity of displaying the character of Christ. Such conduct will attract the attention of the world.

Your Attitude in the Workplace

Ideally, each person should match his or her abilities with the right vocation. Each of us was made by God with a unique combination of aptitudes and gifts that cry for expression. You may desire to be a teacher, while your brother wants to be an attorney or go into medicine. Many workers are content with common labor or one of the many helping professions. Books have been written to help us find a job we can love. I have a vocation that fits my gifts and temperament; I know many others who do not.

What if it doesn't happen, and you now work at a job you don't enjoy?

If being a Christian cannot transform a person's attitude toward a job he dislikes, then the promises of the New Testament are largely empty and Christ's credibility is tarnished. If the reality of God is best proved in the workplace, it must be proved also in the life of a Christian who has a job he or she dislikes.

The painful fact is that many people simply never find the right job/gift mix. Multitudes—perhaps the majority of the work force—dislike what they are doing. But the need for money forces them into jobs that ignite frustration, boredom, and ethical conflict. Many play a state lottery hoping that hitting the jackpot will extricate them from the daily grind they endure but don't enjoy.

Good news is available: If we yield ourselves to God and see our work from His perspective, we can have our attitude changed so that we can find fulfillment even in a job we don't enjoy. Or to put it differently, we can find a source of satisfaction that comes from a world that exists beyond the daily grind.

Christ Himself was given a painful assignment when He stepped out of eternity into time at Bethlehem, an assignment that was far from enjoyable in human terms. His job description was infinitely beneath His dignity: an itinerant evangelist without a home, delivering a message that was rejected by the religious establishment.

He began in the glories of heaven, sharing the same nature and grandeur as His heavenly Father. From there He went to the humiliation of being unrecognized among His own creation. He accepted insults without reminding anyone that He had the power to crush them with a word from His mouth. He began higher and ended lower than any of us could possibly imagine.

Consider the irony: "For by Him all things were created, both in the heavens and on earth, visible and invisible, whether thrones or dominions or rulers or authorities—all things have been created by Him and for Him" (Colossians 1:16). Yet Christ chooses to wash His disciples' feet. He who created their feet now stoops to wash them!

We chafe at the thought of being asked to do something beneath our dignity. Imagine a Ph.D. in mathematics consigned to teach second grade arithmetic; or the president of General Motors asked to manage a hot dog stand.

DOING GOD'S WILL

What was the secret of Christ's being able to adapt to His assignment? He had the confidence that He was doing the will of God. "For I have come down from heaven, not to do My own will, but the will of Him who sent Me" (John 6:38). Before He left heaven, He knew that His daily assignments had been meticulously organized. He would teach, perform miracles, and eventually die at the young age of thirty-three. This ignominious end would purchase salvation for the people whom the Father had given Him.

Most of us think that obedience was easy for Christ. But His divine nature was united with a human nature subject to all the emotional and spiritual stresses that we face. On the human level Christ was not doing what He pleased. The cross and all that led up to it was tough and painful. He learned obedience by these things that He suffered

(Hebrews 5:8). The will of God was not a path of uninterrupted tranquility.

One fact sustained Him: *Heaven would make up for the pain of earth.* So He served with one eye on the Father, always mindful that no circumstance on earth could counterbalance the ultimate bliss of obedience: "Who for the joy set before Him endured the cross, despising the shame, and has sat down at the right hand of the throne of God" (Hebrews 12:2).

Christ endured because He knew that it's not what you do but who you do it for that makes the difference.

This perspective worked for Christ, but is it realistic? Could we actually serve that way? Could we actually work for Him as He worked for His Father?

BEING A SERVANT

Put yourself in a time machine and go back 2,000 years and imagine that you are one of 60 million slaves in the Roman Empire. You don't have any recognizable rights. (Aristotle said, "A slave is a tool with a soul.") There are no opportunities for you to choose a vocation in line with your gifts and aptitudes. You have no chance for a promotion and, if abused, you have no court of appeal. This, humanly speaking, is simply the card you have been dealt.

When Paul wrote to Christian slaves he said, "Slaves, be obedient to those who are your masters according to the flesh, with fear and trembling, in the sincerity of your heart, as to Christ; not by way of eyeservice, as men-pleasers, but as slaves of Christ, doing the will of God from the heart. With good will render service, as to the Lord, and not to men" (Ephesians 6:5–7).

Paul has often been criticized for supposedly condoning slavery. Some prefer that he would have agitated for organized rebellion among the slaves so that they could have been freed. Instead, he says in effect, "Be a good slave."

Paul was not insensitive to their plight. He addresses the masters also, urging them to be kind and reasonable (v. 9). He fought slavery through the only way available to him, namely, by the preaching of the gospel. This would transform both slave and master so that there might be mutual respect and equality. As the years progressed, Christianity was the force that eventually brought an end to slavery in the civilized world.

Thankfully, slavery, at least in the Western world, does not exist today. No employer has the right to treat his employees as slaves; workers do not *have to* work for any employer, business, or company. Yet despite the cultural changes, Paul gives three revolutionary principles that remain valid in the workplace today. His teaching will help all of us change our attitude in the workplace as we serve Christ.

1. *Don't work for men, but for Christ.* Just as Christ served the Father, Paul taught that the slaves should in turn serve Christ. They should switch masters without changing jobs. They were to see their master as the one whom Christ had personally assigned to them. They were to be obedient "as to Christ; not by way of eye-service, as men-pleasers, but as slaves of Christ."

As every manager knows, there is a big difference between a man-pleaser and someone who serves with single-mindedness. Eye-service means that a person works only when the boss is looking. Think of all the eye-service that goes on in today's marketplace, where work breaks are needed to offset coffee breaks.

Second, they were to serve in "fear and trembling," knowing about their accountability to God. Millions today work with the fear of being harassed, the fear of being humiliated by an irate boss, and the fear of being fired. But to "fear Christ" means that we are aware of our personal accountability to Him.

Would we cheat Christ by taking extended coffee breaks? Would we tell a lie to Christ to make ourselves look good? Would we demean Him to others? I think not. Paul told the slaves that they should treat their masters as if they were Christ.

But what if the master was mean and unfair? Again, in the absence of any court of appeal, Paul says that Christian slaves should remember that the sufferings of this present life are but a sliver of time in light of eternity (see principle #3, page 35). Any one of us could put up with a mean slave owner if we knew that within six months we would receive a large inheritance and live in uninterrupted bliss. A reward awaits the faithful; a reward that will last infinitely longer than any abuse on earth. Can we believe God like that?

To Titus Paul wrote that slaves were to be subject to their own masters, to be "well-pleasing, not argumentative, not pilfering, but showing all good faith that they may adorn the doctrine of God our Savior in every respect" (Titus 2:9–10). To serve their master well would make the gospel attractive to all who cared to notice. This should be the priority of every worker.

2. *Don't work for advancement but for fulfillment.* Among the slaves were those who had special gifts for drama, music, and the various trades. Some, if they had had an opportunity, would have been great writers and artists. But few, if any, of these people would ever have the opportunity of fulfilling those dreams.

Work can bring wonderful fulfillment to our lives. The craftsman, the attorney, the writer—all of us know the exhilaration of having completed a project, doing our best. But the slaves in Paul's day were locked into their routine without vocational freedom. Yet Paul exhorted them to consider themselves as slaves of Christ "doing the will of God from the heart" (v. 6). Though they would never know vocational fulfillment, they would have a sense of spiritual fulfillment, serving Christ even though their work was arranged for them by their masters.

What happens if we don't get that promotion? What happens when we work hard and someone else gets the credit? What happens when we don't get to do the very thing we think we were born to do? Is fulfillment dependent on our finding the right job?

Unfortunately, many people think it is. In our culture so much of who we are as individuals is determined by our vocation. Our achievements are often the ticket to acceptance and a healthy self-image. We want to achieve something so that the world will notice. The man who is a failure at home will be tempted to spend extra hours in the office where he is perceived as being a success. Workaholism is often a refuge from having to face the reality of failed relationships. It is a sign of insecurity.

How different it would be if we saw our vocations as an opportunity to "do the will of God from the heart." We would be much better equipped to handle disappointments in the workplace. Our identities would not be as closely tied to promotions, achievements, and salary. We would not sacrifice our families on the altar of success; we would accept every day as a gift from God, the blessings and the blahs.

I have yet to meet a person who was fired from a job who believed that he or she deserved it. Like a child in a house of mirrors, most of us spend much of our time finding a mirror that will make us look good. I do not minimize the pain, anger, and sense of loss that comes with a pink slip of dismissal. But if we can accept demotions as well as promotions as God's will, then the harsh reality of the workplace can be made bearable.

Our identity as a child of God remains secure no matter what happens in our vocations. Our relationship with Him can do what a promotion cannot; it can make us see a silver lining even in swirling, unpredictable clouds.

The bottom line: what does God think? Ask yourself, "Have I served Him to the best of my ability? The opinions of others, though important, cannot make me a victim of the workplace. I refuse to have my dignity made dependent on the evaluation of men whose opinions will not be asked for at the judgment seat."

There is a legend that when Christ was on earth he asked each of His disciples to pick up a stone and carry it. After a few days, He turned these stones into bread. Then He asked each disciple to pick up another stone, and each chose a larger one. They carried their burdens for many days without any instructions. Finally they came to a river. Then Christ told them, "Throw your stones into the water." They looked at each other in astonishment, wondering what their hard work had accomplished. But Christ answered, "Why do you wonder? . . . For whom do you carry the stones?"

If you have to carry stones at work, carry them for Christ. No matter what the task, if Christ gives you a job, it has value.

If you have a boring, routine job in a factory, let every turn of the wheel be done for Christ. If your boss asks you to do the lesser task, do it for Christ. "And whatever you do in word or deed, do all in the name of the Lord Jesus, giving thanks through Him to God the Father" (Colossians 3:17).

3. *Don't work for time but for eternity.* Paul again encourages the slaves by reminding them that whatever good each one does, "this he will receive back from the Lord" (Ephesians 6:8). Eternity puts time in perspective.

Maybe you have seen a truck stacked with flattened cars on their way to the recycling shop. At one time somebody actually had borrowed money to buy one of them; somebody actually became irate when the first dent occurred on the vehicle. But all that doesn't matter now. If time can put the past in a different perspective, think of what eternity will do.

"Since all these things are to be destroyed in this way, what sort of people ought you to be in holy conduct and godliness, looking for and hastening the coming of the day of God, on account of which the heavens will be destroyed by burning, and the elements will melt with intense heat" (2 Peter 3:11–12).

All that will be left from our hard work is the approval we receive from Christ for having served Him. The people whose lives we touched, the attitude with which we accomplished the routine, the love we demonstrated—only these things will survive the flames.

God is generous. He will overcompensate the losses our faithfulness cost us on earth. But only those who serve with the right motivation will hear the commendation "well done."

Three kneeling men were asked what they were doing. The first said that he was chiseling stones; the second said that he was earning a living; and a third said that he was building a cathedral. It's all a matter of perspective.

A Witness in the Workplace

I've known Christians who have quit their jobs because there were no other Christians in their firm or office. Apparently they did not realize that they had been planted there by God for the express purpose of being Christ's exclusive representative. Such a person should no more leave because of a lack of Christian influence than a missionary should quit serving in a culture hostile to the gospel. Both are equally called to let their "lights shine."

What gives you as a Christian the right to be heard in the workplace? In a word, it is *credibility*. Christians can easily turn their candle into a smudge pot by having a witness that is forced, hypocritical, or "supersaintly." We've all met believers who make us feel uncomfortable because of their sanctimonious piety that reeks of crafted dishonesty. They leave tracts lying around, they squelch laughter, and in general they make their religious commitment obnoxious. They think that they would be betraying Christ if they were to admit to personal faults, so they appear to lack genuine understanding of the problems of others.

How can one have a clear witness for Christ that is credible? Peter's prescription still stands: "Sanctify Christ as Lord in your hearts, always being ready to make a defense to every one who asks you to give an account for the hope that is in you, yet with gentleness and reverence" (1 Peter 3:15).

Witnessing must be done with humility, an attitude that respects others even if they belong to a false religion or no religion at all. Nothing turns people off more quickly than someone who believes that because he has the truth (and Christians do) he has the right to disparage others. Given the skepticism that exists about Christianity, we must win a hearing among unbelievers.

Second, a credible witness is one who can give reasons for the hope within himself. Many helpful books have been written about the rationality of the Christian faith. Those who are serious about their witness will become students of the historical and logical underpinnings of the Christian faith.

Third, Peter says that we should respond to people who "ask us to give a defense" for the hope that is within us. Obviously, we have the responsibility of initiating a discussion of the good news of the gospel. But if we are living for Christ, those who are seeking (namely, the spiritually hungry) will *ask* us why we are different. God provides those opportunities for His people who look for them.

In about 1850 a group of explorers came across a significant amount of gold in a riverbed in Montana. But they were so weary that they decided they would return home, regroup, get better tools, and after a few days return for the gold. They made a pact, promising each other that they would not share the news with anyone so that they could get the gold for themselves.

Yet, incredibly, when they left early one morning to return to the riverbed, fifty of the townspeople followed them. Had someone shared their secret? When they asked for an explanation, they were told, "We knew that you had found gold by the smiles that were on your faces."

Do our colleagues know that we have found gold? If Christ has made us different, others should be attracted to our source of peace and joy. The change within should show without.

Christ has appointed you to represent Him right where you are. You are the best witness many people will ever meet.

God in Your Workplace

Elisabeth Elliot, missionary and author, said that she spent one year working on the details of an obscure language in South America. One day a suitcase with all of the word studies, dictionary, and phonetic structure was stolen. Though many prayed that it would be found, it never was.

Was she bitter because a whole year's work was to no avail? No, anger at God had never occurred to her. "After all," she said, "that year of work was a sacrifice to God, and that could never be lost."

That kind of sacrifice is proof that we actually do believe in God, that we do believe in eternity, and that service to the Almighty will have its rewards in His time.

C. S. Lewis wrote, "The work of a Beethoven and the work of a charwoman become spiritual on precisely the same condition, that of being offered to God, of being done humbly "as to the Lord." This does not, of course, mean that it is for anyone a mere toss-up whether he should sweep rooms or compose symphonies. "A mole must dig to the glory of God and a cock must crow."[5]

How specifically can we begin to take eternity seriously? How can we offer a sacrifice to God that will prove that we can live for heaven here on earth? Though it will take some dedication, we can prove to a skeptical world that God can be believed.

Here are some practical steps to bring God into your workplace:

1. *Surrender yourself and your talents wholly to God.* This transfer of your life should be specific, complete, and repeated every single day.
2. *Begin a program of Scripture reading* (including memorizing verses) that will cause you to focus on God and His promises every morning. The object is to see every one of your responsibilities as coming not from your earthly boss but from Christ Himself. See your duties as an opportunity to "serve Christ from the heart."
3. *Ask God to show you hidden compromises you have made in the workplace.* Ask God for wisdom to begin making the right decisions, no matter the cost. If you are afraid to trust Him, do it anyway in an act of prayerful surrender.
4. *Commit yourself to one other Christian for regular prayer and accountability.* Promise to live in your home and in the workplace as if Christ were returning to earth next week.
5. *Pray daily for every one of your co-workers by name.* Trust God to give you opportunities to witness to the salvation Christ died to give to those who believe.

Only that which passes the test of death is worthy to pass the test of life. When God is central in our work we will be successful in those things that really matter.

Notes

1. Doug Sherman and William Hendricks, *Your Work Matters to God* (Colorado Springs: NavPress, 1988), 131.
2. William Hendricks, "What's Wrong with This Picture?" *Christianity Today,* November 25, 1991, 12.

3. These insights about Christ's vocation as a carpenter are based on Peter Hammond's study. I am indebted to Hammond for this material, presented at The Cove conference center, Asheville, North Carolina, June 29, 1985.

4. Ibid.

5. C. S. Lewis, *The Weight of Glory* (Grand Rapids: Eerdmans, 1947), 48–49.

CHAPTER 2

How Do I Recognize God's Discipline for My Disobedience?

One of the most important responsibilities a father has is to discipline his children. A father who does not take this responsibility seriously is negligent and does not love his children as he ought.

Though God is the Father of all men, He has a special filial relationship to those who have been born into His family through faith in Christ Jesus. Paul the apostle encourages us to develop intimacy with our heavenly Father: "For you have not received a spirit of slavery leading to fear again, but you have received a spirit of adoption as sons by which we cry out, 'Abba! Father!'" (Romans 8:15).

That God disciplines His children is not in doubt, but how He does is not always clear to us. We are especially confused when we try to find a link between a particular transgression and God's disciplinary response.

When a couple, whom I shall call Sally and John, had a deformed baby born to them, they asked a question that we all would likely have asked in their situation: "What did we do to deserve this?"

Eventually, they accepted their bitter disappointment as a judgment from God because they had had premarital sex. The chickens were coming home to roost, they thought.

Yet, when the baby grew up to be a special blessing despite his handicap, they wondered whether they were right in their original assumption about the discipline of God.

William Carey, the famous missionary, spent forty years in India starting churches and doing translation work. Thousands of painstaking hours were invested learning the vocabulary and grammar of strange languages and compiling them into a massive dictionary. But this, along with other of his priceless manuscripts, was destroyed in a warehouse fire in 1812. A lesser man may have never recovered, but Carey accepted this as a judgment from God (perhaps because of his failures as a father) and began the task all over again with even greater zeal.

One Christian woman I know chose to ignore the counsel of the elders in her church and decided to divorce her husband on the grounds of incompatibility. A month later she took sick and nearly died. She interpreted the illness as a direct judgment from God for her rebellion.

We've all entertained the suspicion that one of these days God will get even for our misdeeds. It is natural to interpret our tragedies in light of our past sins and blame ourselves for what has happened. We remind ourselves that the hand of the Lord is against those who do evil.

Though Christians are opposed to the pantheistic doctrine of Karma, we do believe in a general law of cause and effect. Paul wrote, "Do not be deceived, God is not mocked; for whatever a man sows, this he will also reap" (Galatians 6:7). This, we think, gives us the right to interpret the tragedies of life as a judgment for specific sins and failures.

Yet, when we stop to think of how and when God disciplines us, we immediately face some rather puzzling questions.

First, is He not inconsistent? In all three instances given above, we can think of other people who were guilty of the same sins and failures, yet they did not experience God's discipline (or at least they did not have the same tragedies come to them). Some Christians have premarital sex, others fail in raising their children, and still others divorce for no reason, yet these believers live without apparent hardship.

As parents we have been taught to treat all of our children alike; the experts tell us that there must be consistent discipline. But our Heavenly Father seems to disregard this fundamental rule. Document the lives of both His faithful and unfaithful servants and virtually no pattern of discipline is readily discernible.

A second question: How can one be sure of the connection between a particular sin and the discipline? In each of the instances mentioned above, the people involved had other sins or weaknesses in their lives that could have accounted for the discipline. The relationship between sin and its consequences is not always easy to detect.

In this age of grace most of us give little thought to the discipline of the Lord until tragedy strikes. Then we begin to ask whether there is a connection between our sin and the heartaches of life.

To probe this topic we must study God's discipline from a broad perspective and then narrow our focus to try to answer the puzzling questions we have raised.

The Basis of Discipline

The people to whom the book of Hebrews was written were experiencing persecution; indeed, they were on the verge of having to die for their faith. They had joyfully endured the seizure of their property and identified themselves with prisoners of the Lord. This meant increased persecution. But it was becoming wearisome; some wanted to give up their Christian witness.

God speaks to them:

> You have not yet resisted to the point of shedding blood in your striving against sin; and you have forgotten the exhortation which is addressed to you as sons, "My son,

do not regard lightly the discipline of the Lord, nor faint when you are reproved by Him; for those whom the Lord loves He disciplines, and He scourges every son whom He receives." It is for discipline that you endure; God deals with you as with sons; for what son is there whom his father does not discipline? But if you are without discipline of which all have become partakers, then you are illegitimate children and not sons. (Hebrews 12:4–8)

The text could not be clearer: the basis of discipline is sonship. Every one of God's sons is disciplined; indeed, scourging is proof of sonship. We usually think that God should prove His love by delivering us from the hardships of life. Actually, the opposite is the case: these trials prove His love.

We must make a distinction between the way God treats His children as opposed to His relationship to unbelievers. Strictly speaking, God's children never come under His wrath, for they have been shielded from His judicial anger through the redemption of Christ. "There is therefore now no condemnation for those who are in Christ Jesus" (Romans 8:1).

All sin must be paid for. Those who reject the sacrifice of Christ end up bearing the weight of their own sin. And because there is no human suffering that can pay the debt, the condemnation goes on forever.

But those who accept the sacrifice of Christ for themselves are shielded from His wrath. The doctrine of grace teaches that we do not have to get what we deserve.

Thus, although God punishes His enemies, He chastises His children. We must think of this discipline as correction, not condemnation. The Greek word used in the text of Hebrews is *paideia* (from *pais*, child) and refers to instruction. Charles Bridges wrote, "The same hand—but not the same character—gives the stroke to the godly and ungodly. The scourge of the Judge is widely different from the rod of the Father" (*Commentary on Proverbs*, p. 31).

If God didn't discipline His children He would be a negligent Father. He would be displaying cruel disinterest if He were indifferent to whether His children obeyed or not.

In ancient cultures it was unthinkable that a father would not discipline his children. Indeed, the Roman father had total authority over his son, even to the point of being able to execute him if he desired. Such harsh, uncaring discipline is in contrast to that of the heavenly Father, who disciplines us from the standpoint of love and wisdom. His discipline may appear harsh, but it is not based on the misjudgments an earthly father might make.

Our heavenly Father is so consistent in His discipline that not even his beloved Son escaped the scourging that all sons need as they develop toward maturity. "Although He was a Son, He learned obedience from the things which He suffered. And having been made perfect, He became to all those who obey Him the source of eternal salvation" (Hebrews 5:8–9). What this means will be clarified later.

Clearly, there are no exceptions. Every son whom the Father receives is scourged. Far from being inconsistent, our heavenly Father takes great pains not to overlook any of His children.

Two implications follow. First, discipline is a sign of sonship. If we are without discipline, we are illegitimate. We are not born of God the Father but only claim to be.

In practical terms this means that if someone says that he or she is a Christian and lives in sin without any form of discipline, such a person is probably deceived. Since God holds earthly fathers accountable for punishing and admonishing rebellious children, we cannot expect that He would do anything less.

Discipline is not an optional course in God's curriculum; it is required. Just as an oak tree cannot grow without wind, so we cannot become mature without the benefit of scourging.

Second, discipline is a sign of love. We usually think just the opposite, namely, that discipline is a sign of God's anger and displeasure. "Why does God turn against me when I need Him the most?" we ask, as if God's primary motivation is a morbid desire to make life difficult for us and "even the score" at every turn. But God's discipline toward His children is not motivated by revenge, but love.

There is no doubt that God desires to glorify Himself through the lives of His children. But He does not arbitrarily give us difficult circumstances simply to please Himself. We must not lose sight of the fact that discipline is actually for our good.

We've all told our children, "This spanking hurts me more than it does you!" I'm not sure that this is true (at least my children didn't believe me), but the sentiment expressed is that no responsible parent disciplines his children arbitrarily. It is done with the best interest of the child in mind.

One woman, who when told that her tragedies were the result of God's love for her, responded by saying, "I wish He wouldn't love me so much!" But God loves all of us equally in Christ, although some are called upon to suffer more than others. Life is filled with injustices and tragedies that appear to come indiscriminately to the godly as well as the ungodly.

It is better to try to learn the lessons God has in mind for us than to blame our lot in life to a higher degree of love. What is important is to realize that that which comes to believers first passes through God's loving hands.

The basis of discipline is sonship. Our sufferings are appointed for our good and God's glory.

Three Kinds of Discipline

Unfortunately, we usually think of discipline only as God's immediate response to specific sins. But the Bible teaches that our heavenly Father has a more comprehensive curriculum.

EDUCATIVE DISCIPLINE

Frequently, God disciplines us to deepen our relationship with Him. This kind of discipline has no direct relationship to specific sins.

One example is Job, who experienced tragedy, not because he was a great sinner, but because he was righteous. The Lord taunted Satan, "Have you considered My servant Job? For there is no one like him on the earth, a blameless and upright man, fearing God and turning away from evil" (Job 1:8).

Job was put on trial before Satan, angels, and God to see what he would do when faith in God no longer seemed to be beneficial. Satan said that Job was righteous only because of the blessings that were coming to him because of his piety. God had given him a fine family, wealth, and health. But if those were removed, said the devil, Job would curse God to His face.

The rest of the book of Job shows that although Job was considered righteous, he was not perfect. The trial brought needed refinements, along with a new appreciation for God's sovereignty. He was disciplined in order that he might be educated and refined.

Job's three friends made the mistake of thinking that there was always a direct relationship between a man's circumstances and his piety. If Job were righteous, they argued, the tragedies he experienced would not have happened. But they were wrong. Many trials are designed to educate us; they are not the result of specific sins. In other words, we cannot tell the righteous from the wicked by checking the size of their bank accounts or their medical records.

An even clearer example was Christ Himself, who was disciplined not because of sin but because He needed to prove His obedience to the will of the Father. Indeed, Christ was not only sinless, but most theologians believe He was incapable of sin. We might think that since He was the special Son of God it would be beyond His dignity to suffer. Yet we read that He learned obedience by the things that He suffered: "And having been made perfect, He became to all those who obey Him the source of eternal salvation" (Hebrews 5:9).

The discipline was not that His Person might be made perfect but that He might become perfected in His work, the assignment of the cross. Thus He "learned obedience by the things which He suffered." The result was that He became the author of eternal salvation to all who believe.

Usually we think of discipline only as the response of a parent to disobedience. We must broaden our understanding to include the "disciplines" that are needed for all of us to develop in spiritual maturity. James wrote, "And let endurance have its perfect result, that you may be perfect and complete, lacking in nothing" (James 1:4).

When tragedy strikes we cannot always assume that we can trace it to specific sins or failures. That was precisely the error of Job's three friends, who thought that there was a direct correlation between the greatness of one's sin and the greatness of one's personal calamity. But the book of Job ends by proving that God puts some of His most obedient children through the severest trials.

PREVENTATIVE DISCIPLINE

This kind of hardship is brought into our lives to keep us from impending sin. Paul was given a thorn in the flesh, a messenger of Satan. The reason for this trial was that he had been given many special revelations from God and therefore faced the temptation of exalting himself. He writes: "And because of the surpassing greatness of revelations, for this reason, to keep me from exalting myself, there was given me a thorn in the flesh, a messenger of Satan to buffet me—to keep me from exalting myself!" (2 Corinthians 12:7).

If we object to this kind of discipline on the grounds that we are being spanked for something we haven't done yet, we overlook the fact that our heavenly Father knows all things and therefore does not have to wait to see how we will react in a specific situation. An earthly father might not have the right to give us preventative discipline, but our heavenly Father sees us from an omniscient perspective. This kind of discipline fulfills the prayer "Lead us not into temptation, but deliver us from evil." We should ask God to bring roadblocks into our lives that will keep us from sin. The pain of a trial is much better than the wreckage of a ruined life or ministry.

Billy Graham was asked how he remained humble in the face of so much favorable publicity. He replied by enumerating all of the physical ailments he had experienced, from broken ribs to the pain of phlebitis. Like Paul, he was given a thorn in the flesh, a preventative discipline, to keep him from sin.

We will probably never know how many sins we have been kept from because of the preventative discipline of God. Even a lack of funds, the pressure of a busy schedule, and ill health—these and other trials may be used of God to keep us from temptations that would be too hard for us to resist. Our heavenly Father knows what is best for us.

RETRIBUTIVE DISCIPLINE

Sometimes discipline does come as a result of specific sins. Though David confessed his sin of murder and adultery, the Lord said, "Now therefore, the sword shall never depart from your house, because you have despised Me and have taken the wife of Uriah the Hittite to be your wife" (2 Samuel 12:10). Then followed additional judgments: (1) his wives would be publicly humiliated and (2) the child that Bathsheba would bear would die.

All of this, even though David had confessed his sin and was forgiven by God. There are consequences that precede confession and there are others that follow. Here we have a direct cause–effect relationship between sin and punishment.

The Israelites were also forgiven by God, but they were condemned to wander in the desert because of their unbelief at Kadesh-barnea. "Say to them, 'As I live,' says the Lord, 'just as you have spoken in My hearing, so I will surely do to you; your corpses shall fall in this wilderness, even all your numbered men, according to your complete number from twenty years old and upward, who have grumbled against Me'" (Numbers 14:28–29).

Jonah ended up in the belly of a fish because he rebelled against God's instructions. He was given a plant to shade him from the blistering sun; then it was taken away to test his priorities. All of this because of his disobedience.

Identifying the relationship between our sin and the discipline that follows is often difficult, though in some instances it is quite clear. Later I shall give some suggestions as to how we can try to discern the intention of the Almighty.

The Purpose of Discipline

Think back to when you were a child and you received discipline. What was its purpose?

The author of the book of Hebrews continues his discourse by saying, "Furthermore, we had earthly fathers to discipline us, and we respected them; shall we not much rather be subject to the Father of spirits and live? For they disciplined us for a short time as seemed best to them, but He disciplines us for our good, that we may share His holiness" (Hebrews 12:9–10).

Our earthly fathers disciplined us according to their best judgment (there are exceptions, of course), and we responded with respect and obedience. But God disciplines us with unerring discernment and knowledge. He not only has greater wisdom but also a greater purpose.

The specific purpose of the discipline is to motivate us to pursue a deeper relationship with God. There is no doubt that God's hand is often painful, but hurting produces holiness. Indeed, we "share His holiness."

What are the requirements for holiness?

The first is submission. We are to be "subject to the Father of spirits." The phrase "Father of spirits" is an unusual expression found only here in Scripture. Perhaps it means simply, "our spiritual Father." But when we submit to Him, we "live." The implication is that if we don't submit we might die (as we shall see, there is a sin unto death), or perhaps the author means that we enter into a new quality of life here on earth. Either way we benefit.

Every time we were disciplined as children we could either rebel or yield to our father's hand. The discipline either softened us or made us more rebellious. Thus God frequently increases the doses, intending to bring us to a state of complete yieldedness.

Second, discipline requires our loyalty. It is said that when there is a storm at sea sailors either turn to God or to drink. Every person, at some time, comes to the crunch and must choose where he will turn.

I have just spoken to a man who works in a firm where there is not only much bickering but where each of the employees undercuts the others in an attempt to jockey for power and position. This Christian man is trying to learn how to fulfill the admonition of Scripture "Never take your own revenge, beloved, but leave room for the wrath of God, for it is written, 'Vengeance is Mine, I will repay,' says the Lord" (Romans 12:19). The test of his loyalty to God is this: Can he entrust his complaints to God, or must he take matters into his own hand? Virtually every trial of life forces us to choose between loyalty to ourselves or loyalty to God.

When Abraham was asked to offer Isaac as a sacrifice, he successfully faced this supreme test by God. Generations to come would stand in awe of what a man was willing to do for God. No question as to where his loyalty stood.

A third requirement is fear. Yes, that's right, fear. Obedience has its reward, but so does disobedience. The child who has been to God's woodshed and felt the pain of his disobedience is in no mood for a repeat performance. "Before I was afflicted I went astray, but now I keep Thy Word" (Psalm 119:67).

When there has been an offense, discipline always includes restoration. A good father will not only spank his children but will also comfort them once they have yielded to his authority. Though it hurts for a time, later this discipline yields the "peaceable fruit of righteousness" (Hebrews 12:11 KJV).

We've all been able to identify a child because he resembled his father. In fact, if there were no likeness we might be tempted to suppose that the child was illegitimate, conceived by another man. There are Christians whose family pedigree is suspect because they are so unlike our heavenly Father.

When we pray, "Oh, Father, make me godly," we mean, "make me God-like." Christ taught us the reason we should love our enemies: it is so that "your reward will be great, and you will be sons of the Most High; for He Himself is kind to ungrateful and evil men. Be merciful, just as your Father is merciful" (Luke 6:35b–36). The author of Hebrews says that we are to "share His holiness" (Hebrews 12:10).

Discipline should lead us to *a greater degree of family resemblance.* When we were disciplined by our parents the intention (it is hoped) was that we would have the same character traits of honesty and obedience that they had.

We should live up to the family name.

The Methods of Discipline

God deals with His children in a variety of ways, depending on what is needed to bring about repentance and restoration.

All sin has built-in consequences of some kind. Since God has set up the moral system of the universe, it is unthinkable that any sin could be intrinsically free from detrimental effects. To these, God adds His own incentives to bring us to our senses and respond to the prompting of the Holy Spirit.

THE CONTINUING CONSEQUENCE OF SIN

The familiar illustration of nails that leave holes even after being pulled out of a barn door is to the point of our discussion of discipline for sin. The thief, if discovered, must go to prison; the child killed by an alcoholic driver can never be resuscitated; and the man who contracts AIDS through homosexuality cannot be cured.

There are, of course, less obvious ways in which the effects of sin continue. There is regret for a wasted life; there is the unhappiness caused by an unequal marriage (Christian and non-Christian); there is the rebellion of children caused by an adulterous relationship. These consequences continue even after there is repentance and restoration of fellowship with God.

These results of sin teach us that sin can never be profitable. In the end it must always bear bitter fruit. The death of Christ shields us from God's wrath (both now and in the hereafter), but it does not erase all of the natural effects of sin experienced in this life. Those results also teach us that sin is so serious that it can have effects throughout eternity even for Christians (think of the implications of a poor performance at the judgment seat of Christ).

But now we focus on how God works in the life of an individual believer to point out the destructiveness of sin and the value of remaining in fellowship with the Almighty.

THE ANGUISH OF GUILT

When we grieve the Holy Spirit by sinning, we are immediately aware of it. If not, we have grown hard-hearted in our relationship with God. Guilt that awakens the conscience is usually the first indication that we are out of moral agreement with God. That should lead to confession and the claiming of the cleansing of Christ. "If we confess our sins, he is faithful and just to forgive us our sins and to cleanse us from all unrighteousness" (1 John 1:9 KJV).

However, it is crucial to realize that after we have confessed our sin, guilt has done its work. No longer is guilt used by God as a means to discipline; that would call into question the sufficiency of Christ to forgive and restore us.

Many Christians are in spiritual bondage because they are unable to distinguish the prompting of the Holy Spirit from the accusation of the devil. The Holy Spirit convicts us of sins that we have not brought to God in honest confession. Satan brings accusations to us for those sins even after they have been put away by God. Sins that are "under the blood," as the saying goes, no longer need to weigh on our consciences.

Many Christians assume that they must bear the guilt for past sins (though these sins are confessed) as a kind of payment for their misdeeds. They simply do not feel free to enjoy their cleansing, thinking that they do not deserve it.

Of course, we do not deserve it, but that is precisely the meaning of grace! Grace means that we do not get what we deserve. God wipes the slate clean and "remembers our sins no more" (see Hebrews 8:12). For us to remember them, to be controlled by the guilt and power of our memories, is a discredit to the completeness of Christ's work on the cross.

Guilt is God's discipline only until sin is confessed; any continuation of guilt after confession is the work of Satan. Those accusations must be renounced in the name of Christ.

And what if we do not respond to the immediate prompting of the Holy Spirit? Let us consider those disciplines that are brought into our lives if we persist in deliberate sin. God will put us under pressure designed to bring us to repentance.

THE INTENSIFICATION OF SIN'S POWER

As a pastor I have counseled many men who have been slaves to moral impurity, whether pornography, immorality, or some other addiction. The story is always the same: They began to slide into these sins gradually with halting steps that they believed they could control. But they soon became victimized by the vices they tampered with. God taught them that the sin they took lightly was serious business.

There is a principle seen in both the Old and the New Testament, namely, that we will always be ensnared with the sin we tolerate. God warned Israel that if the nation would serve foreign gods, it would come under the subjection of those foreign powers. "For if you ever go back and cling to the rest of these nations, these which remain among you, and intermarry with them, so that you associate with them and they with you, know with certainty that the Lord your God will not continue to drive these nations out from before you; but they shall be a snare and a trap to you, and a whip on your sides and thorns in your eyes, until you perish from off this good land which the Lord your God has given you" (Joshua 23:12–13).

Read the history of the nation Israel and you will find that they were constantly being subjected to the rule of various nations, even being sold as slaves to them, all because they made alliances with those pagan countries. The compromises we make lead to chains of entrapment and servanthood.

Paul wrote, "Do you not know that when you present yourselves to someone as slaves for obedience, you are slaves of the one whom you obey, either of sin resulting in death, or of obedience resulting in righteousness?" (Romans 6:16). The sin to which we give ourselves is the one that eventually ensnares us. Every time we deliberately sin we degrade ourselves to the role of servants and exalt sin as our master.

Many Christians may confess their sin but are unwilling to make a clean break with the cycle of failure. They are too fearful to seek counsel and keep their secrets to themselves. This incomplete repentance results in further spiritual bondage.

One price of disobedience is slavery.

EMOTIONAL TRAUMA

When Moses warned the people that they would be scattered among the nations if they disobeyed the Lord, he added, "And there shall be no resting place for the sole of your foot; but there the Lord will give you a trembling heart, failing of eyes, and despair of soul" (Deuteronomy 28:65).

This "despair of soul" is further defined: "In the morning you shall say, 'Would that it were evening!' And at evening you shall say, 'Would that it were morning!' because of the dread of your heart which you dread, and for the sight of your eyes which you shall see" (v. 67).

Emotional trauma is often God's way of correction; it is His most persistent discipline of His children. We err if we think that His discipline is always external circumstances. Sometimes, perhaps most often, it is an internal despair that makes even the most significant events of life seem futile.

Is there any New Testament evidence that God uses emotional trauma for His discipline even today?

One of the most difficult and controversial passages in the Bible is Hebrews 10:26–31. The author has just invited believers to draw near to God; he has given them encouragement to stay close to the Savior. Then he writes:

> For if we go on sinning willfully after receiving the knowledge of the truth, there no longer remains a sacrifice for sins, but a certain terrifying expectation of judgment and the fury of fire which will consume the adversaries. Anyone who has set aside the Law of Moses

dies without mercy on the testimony of two or three witnesses. How much severer punishment do you think he
will deserve who has trampled under foot the Son of
God, and has regarded as unclean the blood of the covenant by which he was sanctified, and has insulted the
Spirit of grace? For we know Him who said, "Vengeance
is Mine, I will repay." And again, "The Lord will judge
His people." It is a terrifying thing to fall into the hands
of the living God.

Many scholars teach that this is a reference to unbelievers, since we read of the harsh judgment that befalls
the victims who sin willfully. The consequences appear to
be a description of the torments of hell, not the loving rod
of a heavenly Father whose children have erred.

Yet there are two reasons that this must be a reference to believers. First, the author includes himself in the
possibility of falling into willful sin: "If we go on sinning
willfully" (v. 26). Evidently, even he was capable of such a
deviation from the Christian path.

Second, the backslider spoken about was sanctified
by the blood of the covenant. The text says of him that he
is one who "trampled under foot the Son of God, and has
regarded as unclean the blood of the covenant by which
he was sanctified, and has insulted the Spirit of grace" (v.
29). Clearly, no unbeliever has been sanctified by the
blood of the covenant.

The contrast is between the Old Testament, where
someone who spurned the mosaic law was put to death,
and the New Covenant with its greater privileges and responsibilities. If defiance of an inferior covenant could
bring such retribution, what judgment is worthy of the superior covenant? The punishment deserved would obviously be greater.

The people to whom the book of Hebrews was written
were tempted to return to the Old Testament sacrifices
rather than implicitly trust the blood of the New Covenant.
To treat this blood of the covenant as an unholy or com-

mon thing was serious indeed. They were turning their backs on the only sacrifice that could save them. Indeed, they could turn to no other effective sacrifice for sins.

This insult to the Spirit of Grace made the breaches of the Old Covenant seem minor in comparison. The penalty in the Old Testament law was frequently death; this kind of rebellion called for a worse punishment.

And what is this worse punishment? The author of the book of Hebrews describes it as "a certain terrifying expectation of judgment, and the fury of a fire which will consume the adversaries" (v. 27). The reference is to God's method of direct judgment frequently used in the Old Testament. The fire should not be thought of as hell, but the temporal fire that took the lives of the disobedient.

God frequently judged His people in the Old Testament by physical death, but that did not mean that all those who were so judged ended in eternal hell. For example, God pardoned the sin of Israel at Kadesh-barnea, and yet that generation was condemned to die in the desert. Physical and temporal judgment can come to those who will experience ultimate salvation.

Thus, in the context in Hebrews we need not read "hell" when we read of "a fury of fire." This judgment, which is as severe as that of the Old Testament (and logically even greater), is the terrifying expectation of judgment and emotional torment that might make physical death seem more tolerable by comparison.

I have counseled believers involved in the sin of adultery who prayed at night that they would not wake up in the morning. Death was more welcome than the emotional trauma they experienced. And, as we shall see later, such discipline may indeed include physical death itself.

Let us not underestimate the severity of God's judgment toward His children. Our understanding of grace must not include the unworthy notion that God is more tolerant today than He was in the Old Testament. He has not grown mellow with age nor changed His mind about a single sin. Under grace the judgment of unbelievers is postponed that they might be brought to repentance (Acts 17:30), but His children experience the effects of His disciplinary hand in this life. "The Lord will judge His people" (Hebrews 10:30). Severity is consistent with grace if its intention is to bring us back into fellowship, that is, to lead us to repentance.

Naturally the question might be asked whether all emotional trauma can be traced to discipline for disobedience. The answer, of course, is no, for the simple reason that emotional distress may have many causes. Some experience it because they were abused as children; others may be going through a time of physical illness or facing some tragedy even as Job did. A point that will be emphasized later is that it is not necessary for us to know the precise reason from a trial in order to profit from it.

But there are many believers who can pinpoint their distress to specific acts of disobedience. They can recall when they came to a fork in the road, made a sinful decision, and chose to live with it. The emotional turbulence they have subsequently experienced constantly reminds them that disobedience is not worth the cost. God is speaking, or rather shouting, that they might hear His voice once more.

SATANIC HARASSMENT

In keeping with what has been said about the severity of God's judgment, we should not be surprised that God often uses Satan to discipline His children. The evil one is used to inflict the despair of soul, the emotional terror of judgment that is designed to bring God's people back to Him thorough repentance. This is seen both in the Old Testament and the New.

Saul, you will recall, was disobedient to the clear command of God. He was to destroy all of the Amalekites but decided to choose the best of the sheep and oxen and choicest things, along with the king. These he decided to keep for himself and the people. However clever Saul might have appeared to himself, the prophet Samuel was not amused. In fact, the word of the Lord was that God rejected Saul from being king and would give his kingdom to another.

Saul felt trapped by the decree of God. He deeply resented the fact that his kingdom would be taken from him. He was becoming acquainted with a young man named David who was mightily used of God to slay the giant Goliath. What made matters worse is that the women of Israel honored David when he returned from battle by saying, "Saul has slain his thousands, and David his ten thousands" (1 Samuel 18:7).

Saul deeply resented this unfavorable comparison. He expected David to do what Saul himself would have done in a similar situation, namely, to manipulate to establish himself as king. So we read, "And Saul looked at David with suspicion from that day on" (v. 9).

Jealousy was eating the king alive. Since God had said that the kingdom would be taken away from him, he should have bowed to the will of the Almighty. There was little use fighting the inevitable. But he chose to struggle with God, refusing to acknowledge God's right to give the kingdom to whomever he wished.

God viewed Saul's jealousy as one more act of rebellion. To intensify Saul's irrational moods, the Lord sent an evil spirit to add to his woes. "Now it came about on the next day that an evil spirit from God came mightily upon Saul, and he raved in the midst of the house, while David was playing the harp with his hand, as usual; and a spear was in Saul's hand. And Saul hurled the spear for he thought, 'I will pin David to the wall.' But David escaped from his presence twice" (vv. 10–11).

Saul's paranoia was intensified by an evil spirit from the Lord. Far from being surprised by such a statement, we should realize that all evil spirits are under God's direction. The atmosphere is filled with innumerable evil spirits, who are only too happy to add to the emotional trauma of any human being. Thus for God to permit such a spirit to trouble a person means that the Almighty ordained that it be so.

Why? So that jealousy might become Saul's master. Saul had, so to speak, made a league with an enemy called envy, and such alliances always lead to spiritual and moral bondage.

This overwhelming presence of evil should have confronted Saul with the enormity of his sin so that he would be brought to utter desperation. That, if Saul were so inclined, would have led him to repentance.

But Saul did not respond favorably to the discipline. His heart became harder, not softer. Instead of throwing himself upon the mercy of God for pardon and deliverance, he chose the path of anger and manipulation. Evidently, he thought that if he were crafty enough he would be able to thwart the revealed plan of God.

Because Saul spurned God's discipline, his life came to a tragic end. He tried to commit suicide but was only partially successful. He had disobeyed God in not exterminating the Amalekites and now, lying wounded, he asked an Amalekite soldier who was running by to kill him. Thus Saul died at the hand of the enemy he had refused to exterminate! The sin we refuse to put away becomes the sin that eventually destroys us.

To tolerate sin in our lives is like defecting to the enemy in war. This act of treason is welcomed by our adversary the devil and exploited. God supervises, indeed directs, the harassment of Satan as just discipline for persistent sin.

A second illustration comes from the church in Corinth, which was guilty of looking the other way when one of the believers was found to be involved in immoral behavior. Paul admonished the Corinthian believers to excommunicate the offender from the fellowship; indeed Paul himself was prepared to do so though he was not physically present in the fellowship. Here is his exhortation:

> In the name of our Lord Jesus, when you are assembled, and I with you in spirit, with the power of our Lord Jesus, I have decided to deliver such a one to Satan for the destruction of his flesh, that his spirit may be saved in the day of the Lord Jesus. (1 Corinthians 5:4–5)

What does it mean to be "delivered to Satan for the destruction of the flesh"? It meant to be cut off from the spiritual protection of the church. So cut off, this man would be an open target for satanic activity, a pathetic victim of his own sinful choices. That could have eventually led to the destruction of his flesh, that is, physical death. Yet, because he was a believer, his spirit would be saved in the day of Christ.

The man faced a choice as to how he would react. He could harden his heart and continue in immorality, regardless of how seared his conscience became. He could "despise the chastening of the Lord" even to the point of physical destruction.

Or he could do otherwise, namely, seek forgiveness and restoration. He could accept the discipline of the Lord as proper and just, considering the seriousness of the offense. He could choose to put himself under the leadership of the church and follow any procedure they might suggest to heal the wounds his sin had caused. Submission to God's authority would take him out of the realm of Satan's authority.

There is evidence that he chose the latter route. In Paul's second letter, he spoke about an offender's being restored and urged the church to take him back "so that on the contrary you should rather forgive and comfort him, lest somehow such a one overwhelmed by excessive sorrow. Wherefore I urge you to reaffirm your love for him" (2 Corinthians 2:7–8).

If this is the same man referred to (we cannot be sure), then it is a beautiful example of how God's discipline can lead to restoration.

In my counseling I have met Christians who have dabbled in the occult, only to discover that they received a demonic affliction, the harassment of the devil. Try as they might, they could not easily be freed, even with specific counsel. They were puzzled as to why they were not instantly delivered, since believers have authority over the enemy. I believe the reason was because God was teaching them the "exceeding sinfulness of sin." Easy deliverance might give the impression that entering Satan's domain is not too serious. God thinks otherwise and uses the struggle for freedom as His means of discipline. Once the freedom comes, the offender is ready to stay clear of such careless (and rebellious) actions.

"That part of us that we rescue from the cross," wrote Tozer, "becomes the seat of our troubles." The sin that we refuse to yield to God is the one that is exploited by Satan so that we might be bound by our own sinful choices. God knows that some backsliders have to be desperate before they cease their rebellion and return to fellowship with Him.

PHYSICAL DEATH

Old Testament examples of people who died because of specific sins are numerous. Nadab and Abihu, the two sons of Aaron, died because they deliberately disobeyed God (Leviticus 10:1–7); Korah and his family opposed God and died (Numbers 16); and Uzzah touched the Ark, and God killed him (2 Samuel 6).

There are New Testament examples, too. Ananias and Sapphira lied to God about their gift to the church, and both died (Acts 5:1–11). Some believers in Corinth died because they partook of the Lord's supper in a flippant way (1 Corinthians 11:30). And the offender in the Corinthian church referred to earlier would have died if he had not repented.

The apostle John wrote that believers should pray for those whose sin does not lead them to death. But then he also adds: "There is a sin leading to death; I do not say that he should make request for this" (1 John 5:16b). The "sin unto death" is probably not a specific sin but a certain kind of sin that is so severe it merits the physical death of the individual. We have no idea how many people have died prematurely because they did not respond to God's chastening hand.

UNUSUAL BLESSINGS

The idea that God disciplines us through the special gifts of His grace seems inconsistent with all that has been written to this point. But who of us has not been shamed into repentance simply because God blessed us in ways we so clearly did not deserve? One woman said that as a teenager she attended a party where she could have been seduced or even raped. The fact that God protected her from harm (even in the midst of a police raid) led her to such praise to God that she never desired to become involved in such situations again. The hearts of God's people are often won back to Him because of incredible displays of His mercy when they were least expected. Paul taught that the kindness of God is designed to lead unbelievers to repentance; surely this principle applies to believers as well (Romans 2:4).

The bottom line is that God never tolerates sin in the lives of His children. Through the prompting of the Holy Spirit, yes, even through the work of the devil if necessary, He will teach us that sin grieves His heart.

And there are no favorites in His classroom.

Our Response to the Discipline

"My son, do not regard lightly the discipline of the Lord, nor faint when you are reproved by Him" (Hebrews 12:5).

There are three possibilities when we fall under God's disciplinary hand. First, we can take it lightly, that is, disregard it, ignoring the warnings. That, of course, results in great hardness of heart and actually makes further discipline necessary. To regard discipline lightly is to shield ourselves from the lessons God intends to teach us. I have a brother-in-law who was spanked by his father for eating chocolates. Yet even while he was lying across his father's lap receiving his whipping, he reached over and took another one from the box near the couch!

My car has a "Check Engine" light on the control panel. I can ignore it, continue to drive, and get by quite well. But eventually something serious will happen to the motor. If I ignore the warning, I am taking it lightly.

Some people experience great trials and yet never stop to check their spiritual lives to ask, *What is God trying to teach me?* Their sorrows are wasted, or, worse, these people become spiritually insensitive and morally careless.

The second possibility is to faint, that is, simply to give up, unable to integrate the trial into a meaningful spiritual experience. Some backslide, deeply bitter with God because of circumstances they believe are unfair. They decide that the fight is not worthwhile.

The third possibility is, of course, to learn from the trial and let it be the means of drawing us closer to God.

How shall we view the trials or disciplines of life? The following points are a guide.

1. *When we experience the trials or disciplines of life, we should ask God to search our hearts to reveal any sins or failures that might be causing the hardship.* This step seems elementary, but is basic to all our spiritual training. The reason many believers fail to learn from life's disappointments is that they do not give God time to show them what He might be trying to teach them.

The problem of connecting a particular sin with specific discipline is often difficult, sometimes impossible. But we must seek wisdom to know whether God might pinpoint a relationship.

2. *We must not interpret the patience of God as the leniency of God.* If we live with deliberate sin and do not see God's disciplinary hand, we should not deceive ourselves into thinking that He is ignoring our transgressions. He does not take sin lightly. Many a believer has misjudged the severity of God.

A minister who was involved in adultery said he was totally confused when God continued to bless his ministry despite the ongoing affair. He expected the judgment of God to fall on him for his sin, but it didn't, at least not immediately. People continued to be saved, and the church grew despite this secret liaison.

Of course the disciplinary process had already begun, but he did not realize it. The guilt of the adultery, the lies to cover it, and the fear of exposure were already taking their toll on his personal life. God was not ignoring the sin. He was simply disciplining him on His own schedule. The warning light was blinking furiously, but he ignored it.

Eventually his life and ministry came apart, of course. God's hand upon him was severe. He now knew that his heavenly Father had not overlooked the sin despite His long-suffering. Unfortunately, he had interpreted the long-suffering of God as the indifference of God.

One of the most dangerous experiences we can have is to commit deliberate sin and appear to "get by." That will only develop our confidence to repeat the same sin, expecting the same kind of leniency from the Almighty. There are times when God appears to be indifferent to the sins of His children, but He is only waiting for His correct timing.

The woman who commits adultery without getting pregnant or contracting some form of sexually transmitted disease is being chastened by God just as consistently as the person who commits sin and experiences the other consequences listed above. Not a single one of God's children ever gets by with deliberate sin; chastisement of some kind is absolutely inevitable.

3. *Let us remember that we can learn from every trial whether we know the reason for it or not.* It was not necessary for John and Sally to know whether there was a connection between their deformed baby and premarital sex; William Carey might well have been wrong in making a connection between the fire in his library and his personal failure; the woman who got her divorce on a flimsy pretext may have become ill even if she had remained married. There may have been other ways that God was disciplining them for these failures.

We can learn from every trial, even if we are unsure about a connection between personal sin and our hardships. All trials have a broader purpose:

> Blessed be the God and Father of our Lord Jesus Christ, the Father of mercies and God of all comfort; who comforts us in all our affliction so that we may be able to comfort those who are in any affliction with the comfort with which we ourselves are comforted by God. For just as the sufferings of Christ are ours in abundance, so also our comfort is abundant through Christ. (2 Corinthians 1:3–6)

Every trial is designed to draw us closer to God and to teach us the divine comfort of God. The "trial of our faith is more precious than gold that perishes" (see 1 Peter 1:7 KJV).

Blessed is the person who can accept the hardships of life and grow through adversity.

Blessed is the person who can learn from the burdens of life as well as its blessings.

CHAPTER 3

Why Should I Pray When God Doesn't Seem to Answer?

Since God didn't answer all those prayers, I'm not going to bother Him with another request again. What's the use? I don't want to be hurt one more time!" The woman was bitter, and whether justified or not, her attitude was certainly understandable.

Her young pastor had been diagnosed with cancer. His congregation took their responsibility to pray for him seriously. They signed up for round-the-clock prayer so that at least one person was praying for him twenty-four hours a day. Additional prayer meetings were scheduled. The deacons anointed him with oil and prayed. Some fasted and prayed for days on end, beseeching God to heal him.

When he went into the hospital for treatment, some believers came to him with the assurance that he would be healed. God had shown them that this miracle was His will, they said, and He had confirmed it by giving the same assurance to several people independently.

Even when he collapsed into a coma, his wife and small children were assured that this sickness was not unto death. Though God would allow him to come unto the jaws of death, he would be delivered in the end.

But that was not to be.

He died, with his friends and family still full of faith that God would intervene and restore him to health. But unlike Lazarus, there was no earthly resurrection for this man. Perhaps you can understand the disillusionment and even betrayal these church members felt. Over in the nursing home lived older people who had long since lost touch with reality. They no longer recognized their children; they longed for death, but it eluded them. Yet God took a young man with a life of fruitful ministry ahead of him, leaving behind a grieving young family and a sorrowing church.

If God doesn't answer the concerted prayers of His people offered in the name of Christ and for His glory, why bother with prayer? Should we assume that prayer does not affect God?

When such prayers go unanswered, the easy response is to blame it on sin in the lives of the intercessors or on unbelief. Granted, there is no question that sin is a hindrance to prayer. David admitted, "If I regard wickedness in my heart, the Lord will not hear" (Psalm 66:18). But in the case of the pastor described above, that answer is too simplistic. He was a godly man who regularly asked God to search his heart to reveal any sin that needed to be confessed. Doubtless the congregation had its share of carnality, but no overt sin had gone unconfessed or unpunished. Hundreds who prayed for this man were Spirit-filled Christians who sought God for direction in their prayers.

What about unbelief? Christ could do no miracles in Caperneum because of the city's unbelief. Could that be the reason God did not answer the many prayers for that pastor? Perhaps, but it is unlikely. People actually believed—firmly believed—that he would be healed. God had given them this assurance, or so they thought. Far from being filled with unbelief, some of that young pastor's friends actually seemed to believe too much.

James wrote, "You ask and do not receive, because you ask with wrong motives, so that you may spend it on your pleasures" (4:3). Though in some cases self-interest is certainly a hindrance to prayer, those who prayed for this man knew that his healing would contribute to the glory of God. They yearned that the medical doctors be proved wrong in their pessimistic prognosis. What a witness his healing would have been to unbelievers, as well as to skeptical believers!

Where did the will of God fit into this scenario? John wrote, "And this is the confidence which we have before Him, that, if we ask anything according to His will, He hears us. And if we know that He hears us in whatever we ask, we know that we have the requests which we have asked from Him" (1 John 5:14–15). So the question arises, how do we know what the will of God is? In retrospect, it seems obvious that it was God's will for that pastor to die. But how could the congregation have known that? In praying for his restoration were they actually praying contrary to the will of God?

We must tread carefully here, for the phrase "the will of God" is used in two different senses in Scripture. Sometimes it refers to the decree of God, by which God runs everything in His universe. Paul says God "works all things after the counsel of His will" (Ephesians 1:11). In this general sense, virtually everything, even evil, is either directly or indirectly God's will.

The more popular use of the expression "the will of God" refers to the desires God has revealed regarding our conduct and choices in life. For example, Paul wrote, "In everything give thanks; for this is God's will for you in Christ Jesus" (1 Thessalonians 5:18). Or again, "So then do not be foolish, but understand what the will of the Lord is" (Ephesians 5:17).

When we speak of unanswered prayer we wrestle with this second understanding of the will of God. What we want to know is: what was God's plan for that pastor's life? Was it really God's desire for him to die, or was his death the result of spiritual negligence on his part? Was it because of the congregation's unbelief?

In my experience as a pastor I have come to believe that unanswered prayer is one of the most common stumbling blocks to spiritual growth. We've all begged and pleaded about situations that we know God could easily change; we have enlisted the prayer support of others and believed. But many times the heavens have remained silent. So the logical conclusion appears to be that God does not care.

God seems to tease us with promises that are too good to be true. And when we act on them, He does not always come through for us exactly as we think a loving, dependable God should. Thus our hopes, which are held aloft by His promises, are dashed to the ground by His apparently cruel indifference.

Philip Yancey quotes Barbara Sanderville, a young paraplegic, who put it vividly:

> Knowing that God had the power to heal me but wouldn't . . . made me very bitter. I would read Isaiah 53, and 1 Peter 2:24, and accuse God of holding the promise of healing before me like a piece of meat before a starving dog. He tempted me by showing me the potential but never quite allowing me to reach it.[1]

Who can calculate the hurt that overwhelms those who have prayed for a wayward child, only to learn that he has died in a tragic accident or by drug overdose? Who can measure the pain of those who have besought God for healing or the companionship of a marriage partner or harmony in their home? Yet these and a thousand other requests so often go unanswered.

Some Christians are so disappointed with God that they don't even want to get close to Him anymore. They stay at a safe distance, fearing that their confidence will be shattered again.

I'm convinced that the presence of unconfessed sin in our lives, unbelief, and selfish motives all hinder prayer. But the absence of these factors does not guarantee that prayer will be answered. You and I have seen godly people pray with the purest of motives, yet their requests lay like unopened envelopes upon a celestial table.

I've heard it said that God answers all prayers—He just answers some by saying no. That's not exactly comforting. A child would not likely say to his friends, "My father answers all my requests—he just said no when I asked him for a dollar."

In an attempt to find satisfying answers to these questions, we need to discuss the will of God, the sovereignty of God, and faith. But for now, let us survey some of the unanswered prayers in the Bible to see if we can uncover clues that explain how God responds to His people. Later, we will try to find the hidden purposes that God might have in letting our prayers go unanswered.

There are three kinds of unanswered prayers. In some cases the answer is *delayed*. At other times it is *disguised*, that is, God answers the prayer but in an entirely different way than we had expected. Sometimes the answer is *denied*; the door is shut, and the answer is no. We can learn from each of these responses.

The Answer Delayed

Often God chooses to answer our prayers but does so according to His own schedule. One day Abraham cried out to God in confusion. Twenty-five years earlier, the Lord had promised that he would be the father of a great nation. But, of course, to see that promise fulfilled, he had to have a child.

So Abraham sought the Lord: "O Lord God, what wilt Thou give me, since I am childless, and the heir of my house is Eliezer of Damascus?" (Genesis 15:2). God had already specified that the child would come from Abraham's own body, but Abraham was wondering whether he had heard correctly. Sarah was barren, and he himself was approaching old age. Perhaps his heir would come through his servant.

Abraham did not have to wrestle with the question of whether God wanted him to have posterity. Since he had had direct communication with God, he did not have to rely on subjective assurance, an inner voice, or inexplicable peace. The will of God was perfectly clear.

Yet despite the clarity of the promise, Abraham began to doubt God and actually tried to force an answer to his own prayer. Specifically (at the suggestion of Sarah), he had sexual relations with the Egyptian maid Hagar, and Ishmael was born.

That practice was common in Abraham's day, but it did not excuse the fact that he doubted God and chose to sin in order to get an answer to God's promise. If only he had waited. Eventually, God was going to perform a miracle in Sarah's body and in his own, as well. Isaac was the fulfillment of the promise.

Abraham confused the *delay* of God with the *denial* of God. Sometimes we give up too easily; sometimes we are too quick to consign our lot to fate. But God answers us according to His schedule.

All who walk with God must learn to wait for answers to their prayers, even in instances in which the will of God has been clearly revealed. For example, Paul was given a promise that he would carry the gospel to Rome (Acts 23:11). Yet he was imprisoned in Caesarea for two full years before that came about. During that time he probably wondered why God was being so slow to fulfill His will.

But God uses delays. He knew that Paul needed a rest, and He used that time in Caesarea to renew Paul physically for the trek to Rome. What is more, Paul had the opportunity to put his own advice into practice. He had always taught the value of patience (which is really endurance), and in Caesarea he had a chance to deepen his

own inner life. "Tribulation," he wrote, "brings about per-
severance" (Romans 5:3).

Someone has said that *the work God does within us
while we wait is probably as important as the thing we
are waiting for.*

The delays of unanswered prayer give us two opportunities:

1. *Patience and faith are developed.* Those virtues
are precious to God.

2. *Worship of God is increased as we come to appreciate His timing.* It has been observed that we get the
chicken by hatching the egg, not by snatching it. Sometimes we must patiently wait as we watch God's schedule
unfold. At times when we say, "God said no," we really
mean that He said, "Not now."

The Answer Disguised

Sometimes God answers our prayers—but not the
way we expect Him to. One day God confided to Abraham
that the cities of Sodom and Gomorrah would be destroyed because of a heavy concentration of wickedness in
the area. Abraham was devastated, for his nephew Lot
lived in Sodom with his wife and children. God's statement
sparked an emotional time of intercession, as Abraham
pleaded with God to spare the city if some righteous people could be found in it. When that time was over, the
agreement was that if as few as ten righteous were found,
God would not destroy the city (Genesis 18:22–33). Abraham left, confident that the city would not be destroyed.

The next day Abraham went out to look at the valley
and saw billows of smoke ascending toward heaven. God
was raining fire and brimstone upon the city. He realized
that he had miscalculated—evidently there were not even
ten righteous in the city after all.

As it turned out, there were only *four* righteous: Lot
and his wife and their daughters. If God had destroyed the
city with them in it, He would not have been breaking faith

with Abraham. And God *did* destroy the city. Yet God also gave Abraham what he wanted. The patriarch was deeply burdened for his nephew Lot and his family. What Abraham did not foresee was that God would take the righteous out before He destroyed the cities.

Notice this divine commentary, "Thus it came about, when God destroyed the cities of the valley, that God remembered Abraham, and sent Lot out of the midst of the overthrow" (Genesis 19:29). God remembered Abraham! In the end, the patriarch got what he wanted but not what he had expected.

David also prayed about a deep desire that God had put into his heart. His dream was to build a temple for God in Jerusalem. Was that a good desire? Yes. The desire would have passed any test we might wish to put to it. For one thing, it was a task that God wanted done. Jerusalem was the city God had chosen to be the spiritual capital for His people. It was God's will to have a temple built there.

Second, David had the time and the ability to do it. It fell within the range of his aptitudes and "giftedness."

Third, his desire was confirmed by a prophet of God, Nathan. David told Nathan about his vision, and Nathan responded, "Do all that is in your heart, for God is with you" (1 Chronicles 17:2).

Fourth, and most important, David had a pure motive. He did not want to build a monument to himself but to God. Indeed, the Lord said he did well that the desire was in his heart (2 Chronicles 6:8).

Yet later, God spoke to the prophet Nathan and told him that the answer to David's desire was no. David would not be the one to build the temple because he was a man of bloodshed.

God said no to David with great tenderness and encouragement. David was given some new promises. His would be a great name. What's more, rather than David's building a house for God, God promised to build a house for David. The Lord would give him posterity (a house) and a throne that will last forever (the details are given in 1 Chronicles 17). Thus David got to build a house after all, but not the kind he had expected. The house he built for God was the family line through which Christ later came.

But there is still more to the story. God promised that the house (temple) that David had prayed about would would be built by David's son Solomon, whose mother was Bathsheba. And David had a part in that project—he gathered materials for the building. David put stonecutters to work, gathered large quantities of iron and brass, and purchased timbers and cedar logs (1 Chronicles 22:1–4).

What lessons can we learn from prayers that have disguised answers—prayers that are answered, but not in the way we expect?

1. *When God says no, He may substitute something else to take the place of your desire.* If your desire to go to the mission field is unfulfilled, He may enable you to send someone else. If you cannot have children, you may be able to adopt a child. If you want a marriage partner, that desire to love someone may have to be funneled into the lives of other people. All of us at some time or another will have to live with unfulfilled desires, but God is able to give us the grace to endure—if we understand that our desires will probably be redirected.

Let me put it this way. Suppose you have two desires. If the stronger of the two is fulfilled, then the unfulfillment of the lesser one becomes tolerable. George Mueller said that the chief duty of every Christian is to "have his soul happy in God." If that desire is met in our intimacy with the Almighty, then the other struggles of life become manageable.

2. *We must have the grace to see that God's substitute answer is better than our original request.* David worshiped God after He said no to the desire of David's heart. He was able to recognize the goodness and kindness of God, in spite of his disappointment. First, the temple would be built. And, incredibly, it would be built by Da-

vid's son who had been born to Bathsheba, the woman whom David had wronged—the woman whose husband David had killed. Out of the mess that David had made, God promised to do something beautiful and lasting. Second, David was permitted to have a part in the building of the temple. Through gathering materials and giving advice, David played a vital role in the project. His dream was realized through someone else, but *it did come to pass.*

Finally, David built a house, a lineage that would produce the Christ and the eventual establishment of His kingdom forever. David's prayer was not answered according to his specifications, but I believe his desire was fulfilled.

Sometimes when God says no, He may be pointing us in a different direction. In such cases we may get nothing that we asked for, yet all that we hoped for.

> I asked for strength that I might do great things;
> He gave me infirmity that I might do better things.
> I asked for riches that I might be happy;
> He gave me poverty that I might be wise.
> I asked for power that I might sway men;
> He gave me weakness that I might learn God's grace.
> I asked for companionship that I might be fulfilled;
> He gave me loneliness that I might feel my need of God.
> I received nothing I asked for but all that I hoped for.

God's no is often an invitation to a yes we had not thought of before. Look for the answer in unexpected places. It may simply be disguised.

The Answer Denied

The apostle Paul was given many special revelations and was even caught up to the third heaven, that is, to the abode of God, to hear and see things he was not permitted to tell others.

To keep him humble, he was given a "thorn in the flesh" that was a constant reminder of his weakness (2 Corinthians 12:7–10). What was the thorn? The Greek word is *skolops,* which means "a stake," such as was used when prisoners were impaled (the ancient practice was to inflict as much pain as possible). Perhaps Paul suffered from malaria, which one commentator says was as painful as "a red-hot bar thrust through the forehead." Whatever the thorn, it was persistent and painful.

Where did the thorn come from? The *immediate* cause was "a messenger of Satan" (v. 7). The devil was the one who caused Paul's thorn, for he has always delighted in inflicting suffering.

But God was the *ultimate* cause of the trial. "There was given me a thorn in the flesh" (v. 7). And when he asked that it be taken away, Paul did not appeal to Satan but to God. "I entreated the Lord three times" (v. 8). The thorn was from God, but Satan's messenger was permitted to work under God's watchful supervision.

Paul's cry was specific. He wanted the obstruction taken out of the way. It was also persistent. He besought the Lord three times, undeterred by God's apparent reluctance. He met the requirement of prevailing, believing prayer.

The first two times, God didn't say anything. But after the third prayer, God spoke to shed light on Paul's dilemma. The reply: *request not granted.* Paul's prayer did not budge the thorn; God decreed that it would stay put.

However, that was not the end of the story. God did not stand idly by, watching Paul struggle. God gave him something he hadn't asked for —something that enabled him to accept the negative answer.

Paul received two gifts:

The first was grace. He received heavenly strength for the need of the moment. A river flowed from the heart of God and flooded Paul's soul. We usually think of grace as God's unmerited favor bestowed at the time of salvation, and that is true. But grace is also a gift given at the time of special need: "He giveth more grace."

Second, he received strength in the midst of his weakness. The infirmity remained, but there was divine enablement. He was given the power needed to counteract the pain.

How did Paul view being turned down by the Almighty? Suddenly he regarded the pain differently. Rather than seeing it as a hindrance to his ministry, he began to see it as a plus. "Therefore, I will rather boast about my weaknesses," he said.

Pain was no longer his enemy, and now he could say, "My enemy is working for my good." The thorn became a blessing. "Most gladly, therefore, I will rather boast about my weaknesses, that the power of Christ may dwell in me" (v. 9).

From that unanswered prayer, strength emerged. Paul became a better man, a more effective witness. The thorn grew into a rose; the pain became power. Satan could not stop Paul; the apostle was strengthened instead.

Here are some lessons to learn when our request is denied.

1. *God does not lay a burden upon us that is too heavy for us to bear.* If you were carrying a bag of cement, there would be two ways to make it lighter: either someone could help you lift it, or you could be given stronger arms and legs to carry it. Sometimes God chooses the first response, sometimes the second. Either way the burden is made bearable. Paul learned that it didn't matter how heavy his burden was as long as God gave him the ability to bear it.

2. *The thorns of life are specially chosen for those to whom they are given.* Paul said, "There was given to me a thorn in the flesh."

When I buy a suit, it is generally from the rack in the store. Only once, when I was in Hong Kong, did I have a suit tailor-made. I was measured and remeasured to make sure that the measurements were accurate. It fit perfectly.

All of God's trials are made to order; none are given indiscriminately. To ask why He gives a specific trial to one and no trial to another is meaningless. God always has a purpose in trials. The thorns that won't budge are for our good.

It is pointless to suggest, as some have, that if the apostle Paul had confessed the pride in his life, the thorn would have been removed. It is interesting that he does not say he had actually become proud. Rather, the thorn was preventative, that is, its purpose was to keep him from self-exaltation in the future. If we think that means that God spanks us for something we haven't done yet, we miss the fact that God, who knows all things, has a right to discipline us, either because we have already sinned or because we are about to sin. All that we can expect is grace to bear the trial.

When paraplegic Joni Eareckson Tada was asked how how she can bear her handicap, she replied:

> I feel that he will never give us a burden we cannot bear. You know, I look at some of my friends who are more disabled than I, and say, *I couldn't handle it.* I have a friend, Vicki, who at best can only move her head from side to side. I at least can flail my arms and shrug my shoulders. She's far more disabled than I. I've said to her, "Vicki, I don't know how you do it," and she says, "Well, with God's grace I can." When Vicki looks at some of her friends who are hooked up to breathing machines, she doesn't know how they do it. All of us are placed somewhere on this scale of suffering. Some of us suffer more than others, but wherever God places you and me on the scale, he gives us accompanying grace to handle it.[2]

God weighs out our thorns with the same care that a pharmacist weighs out prescription medicine. His grace is sufficient to those who submit to His Word.

3. *Satanic conflict serves to strengthen us, not hinder us.* If we followed the popular teaching of today, we would assume that Paul should have been able to simply rebuke the influence of Satan in his life and be freed from his infirmity. However, that would not have worked for the simple reason that *God wanted Paul to endure the thorn.*

Please do not assume that we should stoically accept the activity of Satan in the life of a believer. I strongly believe that Christians tolerate far too much harassment from the powers of darkness. God wants us to route the enemy and subdue him. Whenever Satan comes to tempt us or to disrupt our emotional lives, we must insist that he flee. Paul's situation was unique in that it involved only a physical infirmity, a trial of the body, not the defeat of the soul. Also, he had specific revelation from God as to its purpose.

Yet from Paul we learn that when the request is denied, God gives us grace to accept the answer. We have the assurance that God can use our disappointment for His glory and honor.

Some Hard Questions

All of this is of some help in understanding the mystery of unanswered prayer, but some tough questions remain.

To us, God often seems to be hard-hearted or indifferent to the plight of His children. A mother nervously attends her sick child, but he eventually dies an excruciating death from leukemia. Worse, children cry to God for deliverance from abuse, yet God does not answer their prayers. We wonder, does He listen? Does He care?

Dorie Van Stone, in her book *No Place to Cry* (Moody, 1990), tells how she was sexually abused in foster homes when she was growing up. She became a Christian at the age of thirteen and knew God's presence. But during those dark days of physical and sexual abuse, her prayers for protection often went unanswered. Why didn't God deliver her from her tormentors? Such stories cause us to wonder whether God really cares or not. To the casual observer, He appears to be cruel.

Contrast that image with that of an earthly father who loves his child. He would never allow him to die a painful, untimely death from cancer if it were in his power to prevent it. He would never stand by and watch his child being tortured year after year; instead, he would swiftly intervene and actively seek justice. We are told that our heavenly Father loves us more than our earthly father does. Why the difference in their reactions to our needs?

These questions must now be addressed in light of a biblical understanding of the relationship God has with His people.

THE PROMISES OF GOD

Effective prayer means that we "claim the promises." Often we hear people say, "God gave me this promise." Such a claim may be quite true, but strictly speaking the same promises are given to everyone. Since the Bible is for all of God's people, it is misleading to imply that some receive a promise that might be denied to others.

Unfortunately, some promises are misapplied.

Some people teach that the Scriptures tell us it is God's will to heal everyone who is sick. Basing their claims on certain texts, they assure us that physical healing is the explicit will of God for every believer who meets the requirements of holiness and faith.

The best-known promises on this subject are found in Isaiah 53 and are quoted again in the New Testament. In Matthew 8:17 we read that Christ went about healing people "in order that what was spoken through Isaiah the prophet might be fulfilled, saying, 'He Himself took our infirmities, and carried away our diseases.'"

Peter wrote, "He Himself bore our sins in His body on the cross, that we might die to sin and live to righteousness; for by His wounds you were healed" (1 Peter 2:24).

Some theologians who are skeptical of divine healing have labored to prove that the healing spoken of in these passages is spiritual, not physical. But the context in Matthew and the implication in Peter is that Christ did indeed die for our physical bodies. In fact, it is consistent with Scripture to affirm that Christ came to redeem the whole man—body, soul, and spirit.

But does this mean that we can have physical healing whenever we prayerfully meet certain conditions? Clearly, the answer is no. Although Christ died for our bodies as well as for our souls, we will not see the fulfillment of that aspect of redemption until we are resurrected into glory. Christ came to redeem us from sin, yet we still have a sin nature; He came to destroy death, yet we die; He came to redeem our bodies, yet we are subject to accidents, poisons, and the frailty of the flesh.

Many who teach that divine healing is instantly available wear glasses, get arthritis, and have implanted hearing aids. All these infirmities bear eloquent testimony to the fact that in this life we see only the beginning of redemption. Yes, sometimes God does heal (particularly as seen in the ministry of Christ), but even then the healing is merely a postponement of future illness and death. None of the healing Christ did on earth was permanent. Every one of those He restored eventually became sick again and died.

This misunderstanding of the promises of Scripture has been the cause of much grief in the Christian community. People who claim healing, insisting that God is obligated to keep His promises, often end up feeling betrayed. When healing does not occur, they point to these verses of Scripture and say that God cannot be trusted. Or, they try to find some other reason—unbelief, unconfessed sin, and so on—to explain why they were not healed, in a misguided effort to protect God's reputation.

Others point to the promise of James that the sick should call for the elders of the church, and, if the sick one is anointed with oil, "the prayer offered in faith will restore the one who is sick, and the Lord will raise him up, and if he has committed sins, they will be forgiven him" (5:15). That cannot mean that a believer will always be raised up; if it did, logic would require that a person could always escape death. He could call the elders of the church each time he became ill and be healed repeatedly.

The answer to this prayer is actually dependent on "the prayer of faith," which means that in specific instances God may grant the elders the united faith to believe in the restoration of the individual. In other instances they may not have such faith. The "raising up" takes place only when God grants the gift of faith for that particular situation. It is impossible for us to manufacture such faith on our own.

Other promises related to prayer come to mind. Christ said to His disciples, "And whatever you ask in My name, that will I do, that the Father may be glorified in the Son. If you ask Me anything in My name, I will do it" (John 14:13–14). If we interpret that statement to be a carte blanche affirmation that we will always get whatever we want, we will be disappointed. We have already documented enough cases of unanswered prayer to know that we often do not receive what we ask for.

Some have suggested that that promise applied only to the apostles and not to their followers. It is interesting that the apostle Paul, who wrote most of the letters of the New Testament, which are for this church era, does not make any such promise about prayer. Rather, he exhorts us, "Be anxious for nothing, but in everything by prayer and supplication with thanksgiving let your requests be made known to God. And the peace of God, which surpasses all comprehension, shall guard your hearts and your minds in Christ Jesus" (Philippians 4:6–7). He gives no assurance that our requests will be fulfilled—only that we will have the peace of Christ and the ability to accept whatever God gives us.

Of course, even if we claim Christ's promise for ourselves, it has certain limitations to it. First, He says that whatever we ask "in His name" we will receive. That means that the request must be consistent with the character of Christ. As an ambassador speaks in the name of the king, so we must be subject to the will and purposes of Christ. He does not lend His good name to just anyone. Some take it upon themselves, of course, and even do miracles "in His name," yet they are barred from the kingdom of heaven (Matthew 7:22–23).

Second, we are to ask "that the Father might be glorified in the Son." Our prayers must be free of self-interest and must instead seek the glory and approval of God. The main purpose of prayer is not to get us out of bankruptcy or lessen the pain of an inflamed tumor, although the Almighty is concerned with such matters. The primary motive of prayer should be the glory of God and the vindication of His honor.

The example of Christ is instructive here. We know that He lived for the glory of God. He pleased the Father, who was glorified at the Son's expense.

Christ's entire life was bathed in prayer, and He prayed no prayer that was not fully answered. The closest He ever came to using prayer as a means to escape physical and spiritual distress was when He prayed in Gethsemane: "Abba! Father! All things are possible for Thee; remove this cup from Me; yet not what I will, but what Thou wilt" (Mark 14:36).

Christ had every right to ask the Father for anything; why did He not insist that He be exempted from the impending torture of the cross? The answer is that *it was God's will that Christ suffer.* The prayer of Gethsemane was the means that Christ used to receive the grace and power to do the will of God. Prayer enabled Christ to gather strength to go through with His assignment; it was not the means of delivering Him from it.

The bottom line is that promises such as the one in John 14:13–14 must always be subjected to the overriding will of God—a will that may involve pain, injustice, and death, just as it did for our Savior.

This naturally leads us to the question posed at the beginning of this chapter: if the will of God for us involves an untimely death (as in the case of the young pastor), how are we to know this? How can we pray effectively if we don't know what the will of God is in a specific situation?

THE WILL OF GOD

Perhaps the best way for us to understand how to pray according to the will of God is to examine Christ's prayers for His disciples and the apostle Paul's prayers for his fellow believers. What is so surprising in these prayers is the absence of any reference to wealth, health, or personal comforts—the very subjects that occupy so much space on our own personal prayer lists. The fact that Christ and the apostles concentrated primarily on the spiritual welfare of individuals rather than on their health, comfort, or financial needs is evident in Christ's promises to His disciples in the Upper Room and in prayers such as are recorded in Luke 22:31–32 and John 17:1–26.

The apostle Paul stressed the spiritual welfare of believers almost exclusively in his prayers (Ephesians 1:18–23; 3:14–21; Philippians 1:9–11; Colossians 1:9–12). Space forbids a detailed analysis of these prayers, so I encourage you to read them on your own. The themes are: faithfulness, the defeat of Satan, spiritual perception, fruitfulness, and an increased desire to know and serve God. The emphasis is on the need for grace to successfully endure hardship rather than on means to escape it.

In other words, when a person is ill or has financial problems or is treated unjustly, we have no biblical basis to know what the will of God is. A young woman asks, "How do I know it is God's will that I get married?" A parent hovering over the bed of a sick child asks, "How do I know whether it is the will of God that my child be healed?" In these and many other instances we must humbly confess that we do not know what the will of God is, for He has not seen fit to reveal it.

What we do know is that it is the will of God for *Christ to be victorious within us, whether the circumstances change or not.* A Christlike response to the injustices and tragedies of life is always God's will.

Does that mean that we should not pray about those matters about which we are in doubt? Of course not! Christ prayed in Gethsemane, though it did not prevent His going to the cross; Paul prayed that his thorn be removed, though prayer did not remove it. We should pray about everything, letting our requests be made known unto God, and the peace of God will keep our hearts and minds in Christ Jesus (Philippians 4:6–7). As we shall see in a moment, prayer has many benefits, even if the requests go unanswered. We make our requests to God and then commit everything into His hands.

What about those who claim to have special knowledge of the will of God that is not revealed in the Scriptures? Many people affirm that the Lord has shown them His specific will about particular situations. Thus in the absence of a Scriptural promise they appeal to "inner peace," a subjective voice, or a sense of assurance.

But it is often difficult for us to distinguish our desires from the will of God. We so earnestly want to see our prayer answered—after all, it seems so reasonable—that we identify the desire itself with the will of God. It may be His will—but not necessarily.

Second, we think we can confirm our desire by the degree of peace God gives us about the situation. The more peace we have, the more confident we are that God is going to answer according to our desires.

That may explain why so many people in the example above believed that their pastor would be healed. They misread the will of God but not because they lacked holiness, sincerity, or even faith. The reason is that they *mistook the peace of God for the plan of God.* God granted them peace about the situation, and they took that as a sign that God would answer as requested. It is easy for any one of us to make that mistake. We pray about a matter and give it wholly to God. The Lord graciously floods our souls with peace, and we interpret that to mean that our prayer will be answered according to our specifications.

At times it may be possible to ascertain the will of God subjectively. But even those who claim they can do so often admit that their perceptions and impressions have been wrong. *In many matters we simply do not know what the will of God is.* When those matters are left wholly to Him, we can rejoice in peace that His will, though presently unknown to us, will be done.

The closer we walk with God, the more we may be able to discern His will in those unrevealed matters. His desires can more often become ours. He may give us burdens that are in accord with the plan He intends to accomplish. But in the absence of specific biblical promises, we simply cannot confirm the specific will of God in each situation.

THE SOVEREIGN PURPOSE OF GOD

Having come this far, we must now ask, Why is God's will so obscure? Shouldn't the will of God be straightforward and reasonable? What could be plainer than the fact that it is His will to heal a young pastor? If it isn't His will, it should be!

The Bible is filled with examples of God's sovereign dealings that prove without question that His ways are not our ways and that His hidden purposes are not revealed to us. We love to tell the story of how God delivered Daniel from the lions. It's a wonderful story, and, even better, it's true. But what shall we make of the fact that thousands of

Christians were thrown to the lions in Rome and no angel appeared to deliver them?

We remember the three Hebrews thrown into a fire. Behold, one like unto the Son of Man walks with them! Indeed, when the three emerge, there is not even the smell of smoke on them. But where was the Son of Man when John Huss and other martyrs died in the flames?

There are two classes of heroes named in Hebrews 11. The author lists all those who triumphed over their enemies: Gideon, Barak, Samson, David, to name a few. Then we read abruptly, "And others experienced mockings and scourgings, yes, also chains and imprisonment. They were stoned, they were sawn in two, they were tempted, they were put to death" (vv. 36–37). Some were delivered, some were not; but both groups are heroes of faith.

This contrast is seen clearly in Acts 12. Herod kills James the brother of John with the sword. He intends to do the same to Peter, but the church prays for his deliverance, and he is miraculously released. One may try to explain Peter's release, saying that the church prayed for him and not for James. However, they did not even pray in faith for Peter; when the servant girl said that he was at the door, they assumed she was temporarily insane.

The effective, fervent prayer of a righteous man does accomplish much. It is the means God uses to fulfill His specific will. God wanted Daniel, the three Hebrews, and Peter delivered, and prayers offered in harmony with His purposes were answered.

What if God's people had not prayed in these cases? We cannot know whether these men would have been delivered or not. God often carries out His will with or without our intercession. We are sure, however, that these prayers would have been of benefit to those who prayed them, even if they had not been answered. The purpose of prayer is not so much to change God's mind about a particular circumstance as it is to change our hearts so that we accept whatever circumstances He gives us. As someone has said, it is much more important that we lay hold of God than that we lay hold of the answer we seek.

The idea that a prayer is useless unless it is answered is false. Many men and women of God have besought God for matters that did not come to pass, but they received much spiritual benefit, and God was honored. Prayer—even unanswered prayer—enables us to develop intimacy with the Almighty. Getting an affirmative answer is not the only purpose of prayer.

In the final analysis we must submit our prayers to the inscrutable will of God, who has the right to do as He wishes with those who are His own. He has every right to treat each person differently.

THE PRIORITY OF GOD

Yet some questions still remain. Why all this unpredictability? Why this apparent divine disinterest in our plight? Why did the family of James have to suffer, whereas the family of Peter experienced deliverance? Why are children of God not automatically protected from rape, accidents, and painful illnesses? If He wanted to, God could easily be more consistent and helpful.

Much is hidden in the counsels of God, but what God desires from us, despite His apparently haphazard dealings with us, is *faith*.

Think this through: if faith is God's ultimate priority for us, what better way could He test it than by refusing to answer a prayer to which we think He should say yes?

In order to illustrate the demands of faith, Basil Mitchell tells this parable:

> In time of war in an occupied country, a member of the resistance meets with a stranger one night who deeply impresses him. They spend the night together in conversation. The stranger affirms that he also is on the side of the resistance—indeed he is in charge of it. He urges the young partisan to have faith in him —no matter what.

The young man is impressed with the stranger and decides to put his trust in him.

The next day he sees the stranger fight on the side of the resistance and he says to his friends, "The stranger is on our side." His faith is vindicated.

However, the following day the stranger is in the uniform of a policeman handing patriots to the occupying power—to the enemy!

The young man's friends murmur against him, insisting that the stranger could not be on their side. But the young partisan is undeterred, believing in the stranger no matter what.

Sometimes he asks for help from the stranger and receives it; sometimes he does not receive it. At times like this he affirms, "The stranger knows best."

This ambiguous behavior on the part of the stranger causes the young man's friends to ridicule his faith saying, "If that's what you mean by being on our side, the sooner he goes over to the other side the better!" Now the young man faces a dilemma: does he conclude that the stranger is not on his side after all, or does he go on believing no matter what?[3]

God has assured us in His Word that He is for us and that nothing shall separate us from His love. Yet His actions are ambiguous, sometimes seeming as if He is not on our side at all. What do we do? At what point can we say, "He does not care"?

The explanation is that it depends on the extent of our friendship with the Stranger (God). The better we know Him, the more likely it is that we will keep trusting Him, even when it appears that He is no longer on our side. We will not judge His love for us by circumstances but by His promises.

This is "the trial of our faith." God sees how much we are able to endure, while we continue to believe that He knows best. God chooses to do the opposite of what seems sensible to us. What a test of our loyalty!

Let's return to the young preacher from the beginning of this chapter. Suppose God wanted to create a set of circumstances that would stretch people's faith in His goodness and loving concern. How could He best do that, except by making it look as if He is acting in a way that belies those exact attributes? When He appears to be on the side of the enemy, do we still believe that He knows best? The question is, Can we believe Him, *no matter what?*

Now we are back to the question posed earlier: Does our heavenly Father really love us more than an earthly father, who is more immediately responsive to our needs and requests?

The answer is that our heavenly Father does love us more than our earthly father does, but He has a different set of priorities. We value health, and so does our heavenly Father. But He values faith even more. We value food, and so does our heavenly Father. But He values patience even more.

What God seeks to do within us is much more important to Him than what happens outside of us. Our circumstances are important to Him—the very hairs on our head are numbered. But more important, He seeks a devoted heart.

After John the Baptist was thrown into prison, he began to have second thoughts as to whether or not Christ was the Messiah. For one thing, the Old Testament predicted that when the Messiah came, the prisoners would be freed (Isaiah 61:1). John made the same error as those who believe that God is obligated to heal us: he misinterpreted the timing and application of that promise.

As John sat in the dungeon, it seemed that Christ was reneging on that promise in Isaiah. And wasn't it unfair that a man who had played such a vital part in Christ's early ministry should be so summarily set aside for taking a righteous stand against Herod's new marriage? So John sent a delegation to pointedly ask, "Are You the Expected One, or shall we look for someone else?" (see Matthew 11:3).

In response, Jesus reminded John that miracles were being done and then added, "Blessed is he who keeps from stumbling over Me" (v. 6). We could paraphrase those words to say, "Blessed is the person who is not upset with the way I run my business."

Blessed is the person who does not say, "I'm never going to bother God with another request again."

Blessed is the person who understands that the purpose of prayer is not merely to get the things we want but to learn to accept whatever God gives us.

Blessed is the person who lets God be God.

Blessed is the person who believes God, no matter what.

Notes

1. Philip Yancey, *Where Is God When It Hurts* (Grand Rapids: Zondervan, 1977), 151.

2. "Here's Joni!" *Today's Christian Woman,* January/February 1990, 24–25.

3. Basil Mitchell in *New Essays in Philosophical Theology,* eds. Anthony Flew and Alastair McIntyre (New York: Macmillan, 1955), 103–4.

CHAPTER 4

How Do I Recognize Satan's Plan for Me?

God loves you and has a wonderful plan for your life!" That's the good news.

The bad news is that Satan hates you and has a *destructive* plan for your life.

Even secularists are beginning to believe. Newspapers carry stories of demon worship and openly discuss the growing belief that there is a personal devil. We should not be surprised that there is empirical evidence that Satan exists, for we have met him in our own lives and in the experiences of others. More important, we know incredible details about him from the pages of the Bible. Not only does he exist, but he is actively seeking recruits.

In fact, I believe that *he has already made meticulous plans for our downfall.* All that is left for us to do is to step into the carefully laid trap. Unfortunately, the trap is hidden—it blends in with our aptitudes and surroundings and looks as if it is the route to fulfillment. Though it appears harmless, the consequences could be disastrous should we fall into it.

Satan is on the prowl, stalking and setting traps for God's people (and yes, for unbelievers, too). He stays out of view, waiting for an unguarded moment. If we could know the extent of his knowledge of us . . . if we could understand his fiendish delight should we become a discredit to Christ, we would pore over the Scriptures to learn about him and about the weaponry God has given us for the battle. Satan himself is abhorrent to us. Knowing that, he comes using different disguises and different names. His goal is *to get us to do something he wants while making us think that the idea is wholly ours.* Understandably, his chief point of attack is the human mind. He has varying degrees of access (depending on the amount of sin we tolerate) and uses his opportunities to the hilt. Since he is not a gentleman and plays only by his own rules, he influences our thoughts and feelings without formal invitation. He is most pleased when his activity is completely hidden.

To alleviate any suspicion or fear, he gives his ideas familiar names that make us feel comfortable. Even the wolf in Little Red Riding Hood was cunning enough to know that he could not say to the grandmother, "Let me in, for I am the wolf!" Instead he disguised his voice and whispered, "I'm Little Red Riding Hood!"

Satan's full-time occupation is *making sin look good to us.* Whatever the lure he employs, it is a highly intelligent spiritual being who plots our downfall. His intention is to cause us shame and to neutralize our effectiveness for Christ.

Satan also has tens of thousands of lesser spirits under his authority who have varying degrees of intelligence and power. They are highly organized and are forced to become his mercenaries, his servants who do his bidding. If they disobey, they are likely punished by their cruel leader.

Of course there would still be addictions, violence, and wasted lives in the world if Satan and his demons did not exist. We have a sin nature that is capable of every kind of evil. Satan, however, plays a key role in tempting us, and, should we say yes to his promptings, he will tighten the chains to keep us bound.

His Greatest Desire

And now for his plan for our lives.

Hunters study animals to become familiar with their likes and dislikes, their habits and whereabouts. Animals don't usually get caught by accident; they are lured into circumstances that look attractive but conceal a deadly hook. If you are catching a mouse you use cheese; a bear will be drawn to a piece of fresh meat; for fish you use worms. You promise your prey what it wants to have but give it what you want it to have. Let's apply this simple analogy to satanic entrapment.

First, Satan tries to develop a keen understanding of his intended victim. Just as we know that mice prefer cheese to dead worms, so Satan knows our weaknesses and habits. He and his demons are keen observers of human nature, but he needs even more specific knowledge of each victim in order to set a trap that will succeed. It is reasonable to assume that evil spirits (one or more) are actually assigned to us to observe our habits and weaknesses.

Second, just as we must determine whether the mouse lives in the basement or the bedroom, so evil spirits observe where we work and with whom we work. They are particularly interested in our daily habits. Of even greater interest is our secret life—those attitudes and behaviors that we keep from others. That provides them with perhaps the most fruitful area of temptation.

Third, just as it would be foolish for us to think we could catch a mouse without a trap, so Satan knows that he must remain hidden. A mousetrap is important because it can be used in our stead; it can catch our victim while we remain out of view. Furthermore, a trap can hold out the promise of food and fulfillment while keeping the ultimate consequences concealed. Mice see only the cheese and do not understand the wire and the powerful spring. Likewise, Satan wants to keep us ignorant of the intriguing dynamics taking place in the spirit world. He wants our circumstances to appear to be ordinary; his traps do not arouse undue suspicion. Yet *behind the trap is the trapper; behind the lie is the liar.*

Satan has as many lures as there are human weaknesses. To change the analogy, he leads us into a hallway with many different doors. To him it does not matter which of these doors we choose, because any one of them will lead to the same dark room of satanic involvement and control.

Later in this chapter I will list twelve of the most common doors that unsuspecting humans enter. But here I simply point out that Satan exploits our weaknesses; his strategy is for us to fulfill some secret passion, some aspiration of the flesh, some kind of occult practice or rebellion. We are free to choose as we wish. Any one of a hundred doors will do.

Satan's greatest desire is to dethrone God and put himself in charge of the universe. That is impossible, of course, and he knows it. So he must settle for a lesser objective, namely to frustrate the plan of God. This he cannot do. Nevertheless he continues to plunge blindly toward actions that increase his own torment.

His strategy is twofold: (1) make sure that unbelievers are comfortable with their unbelief, blinding the minds of those who do not believe (2 Corinthians 4:3–4), and (2) destroy our effectiveness as Christians by gaining a measure of control in our lives (1 Timothy 4:1–3).

Several levels of control exist, which are not always clearly distinguishable but nevertheless provide a general understanding of the extent of demonization in the lives of people.

STAGE 1

As we have learned, Satan begins by injecting into our minds thoughts that we think are our own. That enables him to remain hidden while luring us into sin. It is brilliant strategy because although sin is attractive to believers, Satan is not. If he were to appear to us, we would be terrified; but because we think these thoughts are wholly ours, we have no fear.

Second, the tactic enables him to work through our existing weaknesses. He takes the sins of the flesh and strengthens their power. By making sin attractive he reinforces the evil that already exists in the human heart. In that way he can capitalize on our weaknesses without arousing suspicion and fear.

If we welcome these thoughts into our minds and if they find a home in our hearts, Satan moves to the second level.

STAGE 2

Satan now takes another step in his quest to control humans. The individual now has given him a stronghold: a deeply rooted tendency to repeat sinful, destructive behavior. Some people are preoccupied with covetousness, moral impurity, rebellion, bitterness, or anger. Although the individual may be freed from these sins for periods of time, he or she will fall back into the same rut when the conditions are right.

Thus Satan disguises himself with the sins of the flesh, magnifying their strength and attractiveness.

STAGE 3

Some people experience obsession, which may be a sign of actual demonic invasion. In these cases the victim is not only preoccupied with these thoughts and behaviors but is controlled by them. The obsessive power of evil occupies his mind at almost every waking moment.

At this level there may be such outward signs as compulsive behavior, uncontrolled passion for various drugs, sexual promiscuity, and eating disorders. In others one may see the desire for revenge, indescribable hostility, or irrational behavior. These people may desire to make progress in the Christian life but find that this barrier is always present. Even when there appears to be some progress, the obsession continues to rear its ugly head from time to time. Again let me stress that many of the symptoms listed above may exist without demonic activity. Satan simply makes the behavioral ruts deeper so that change becomes more difficult.

STAGE 4

At this stage the demonic spirits reinforce their control in the human body. The individual often becomes passive; he is so engulfed by evil that a spirit seems to have complete control over him. In extreme instances he may be overcome by supernatural physical strength and find that his vocal cords are controlled by alien powers. There can be withdrawal, compulsiveness, and self-inflicted torture (see Mark 5).

Christians can usually successfully fight levels 1 and 2 on their own. If they repent of all known sin, obey God's Word, put on the armor of God, and fill their lives with music that praises God, these practices will restrict the enemy's powers.

However, levels 3 and 4 almost always necessitate help from other believers. Jesus taught that some spirits do not go away except by prayer and fasting.

Theologians debate whether demonic spirits can actually inhabit a Christian. Since the New Testament uses the word *demonization* for those who are afflicted by the devil, we can understand that there may be different levels of control and effects. It is not always easy to discern whether a demonic spirit is actually within the person or whether he is doing his work from the outside.

The extent to which a believer can be demonized involves a lengthy discussion beyond the scope of this chapter. Let it simply be said that Christians who have been invaded by demonic spirits prior to their conversion often give evidence that all the spirits do not leave after conversion. Also, those who are involved in perpetual disobedience may find that a spirit attaches itself to their personalities. There is ample evidence that Christians can and do experience stages 1 through 3 as outlined above. For further study I recommend *Demon Possession and the Christian—A New Perspective,* by C. Fred Dickason (Crossway, 1989).

To better understand the reason for Satan's anger and the goals he seeks to accomplish, we must now paint the big picture. What was the motive behind his rebellion against God? On what basis can we know he is defeated? What are those doors that we can unwittingly open that will give him a measure of control in our lives? And finally, what can we do to protect ourselves against him and to help those who are bound by him?

What is this conflict all about?

His Greatest Mistake

Thanks to Milton's *Paradise Lost* most of us were taught to believe that Lucifer (later called Satan) had his original abode in heaven and was cast out because of his rebellion. It is more likely, however, that Lucifer was ruling the world long before his fall.

Two expressions in Ezekiel 28 give us a hint about his duties. "You were the anointed cherub who covers, and I placed you there. You were on the holy mountain of God; you walked in the midst of the stones of fire" (v. 14).

The phrase "anointed cherub" refers to some kind of priesthood exercised before his fall. This is further confirmed by the reference to "sanctuaries" (v. 18). Possibly he was the guardian cherub, the chief of the honor guard.

The second phrase, "the mountain of God," symbolizes the rule that Lucifer was given, most likely over the whole world.

Putting those two phrases together, we may conclude that Lucifer was given the responsibility of ruling the world by making sure that the worship of all other angelic beings honored God. As Barnhouse wrote in *The Invisible War*, "It would appear that he received the worship of the universe beneath him and offered it to the Creator above him" (Zondervan, 1965).

At that time there was but one ruling will in the universe. God's honor prevailed in the actions and thoughts of all of His creation. There was harmony, fulfillment, and holiness.

Then follows one of the most probing passages in all the Bible. "You were blameless in your ways from the day you were created, until unrighteousness was found in you" (v. 15). The text continues, "By the abundance of your trade you were internally filled with violence, and you sinned" (v. 16).

Sin began in the heart of Lucifer; it came about that in his transactions with God ("the abundance of your trade") he became dishonest. *He began to take that which belonged to God and keep it for himself.* Thus his heart was filled with violence and rebellion.

That was the beginning of the conflict of the ages, the conflict between the will of God and the will of His creatures, between good and evil, between light and darkness, between Creator and creature.

Satan could not have foreseen the consequences of his action, since there had been no other example of rebellion in the universe. Unfortunately, he had to learn the devastation of sin by experience. In retrospect he might have regretted what he had done, but it was too late.

Once the battle lines were drawn and Satan was forced to entrench himself against God, he became wholly evil. He was not on a par with the Almighty, so there was little use pressing for a truce. Nor could he retreat, for evil can never be satisfied with a humble admission of defeat. Having chosen his path, Satan was compelled to follow his evil nature to its destructive end. Never again would he return to his original position. Indeed, he could not even if he had willed to do so.

With the stage set for the conflict, several conclusions immediately emerged.

First, Satan's right to rule the world was not revoked as a result of his sin. Satan promised Christ the kingdoms of the world in exchange for worship and then added, "For it has been handed over to me, and I give it to whomever I wish" (Luke 4:6). Because Satan is a deceiver, some Bible scholars have disputed his grandiose claim that he had been handed the kingdoms of the world. But it is unlikely that Satan would lie to Christ in the same way that he lies to us. He originally was given dominion over the earth, and he still retains it today.

Second, in contrast to God, whose nature is based on truth, Satan became the embodiment of deception. His entire kingdom is based on lies. Jesus said to the Pharisees, "You are of your father the devil, and you want to do the desires of your father. He was a murderer from the beginning, and does not stand in the truth, because there is no truth in him. Whenever he speaks a lie, he speaks from his own nature; for he is a liar, and the father of lies" (John 8:44). It has been aptly said that the only time we can believe the devil is when he tells us he is lying!

"There is no truth in him." What a revealing commentary on Satan's strategy! When we see him operating in the world, the watchword is deception. Since he is devoid of moral principles and sympathy, no atrocity can be considered too evil, no suffering too painful, and no treachery too vile. He employs *any* evil deception to achieve his ends.

Third, Satan is angry. His hatred toward God is irrational and intense. Irrational, because his predicament was brought on by his own rebellion; intense, because he knows that his time is short. Regardless of how many years he has left, he must face the awful reality that eventually he will be thrown into hell forever. The fact that he has already been checkmated and forced to admit defeat fuels his anger. His primary target is the people of God, for *he attacks us in a vain attempt to get back at God.*

Fourth, evidence exists that a multitude of angels fell with Satan and now serve him in forced obedience. The devil himself is not omnipresent. Though he can travel quickly, he can only be in one place at a time. Yet, through his mercenaries, who are organized according to rank and responsibility, he can appear to be present everywhere at the same time.

Fifth, Satan will not and cannot be redeemed. His transformation into a thoroughly evil being is so complete that he would never desire reconciliation with God. But even if he did, God could not allow such an act.

Scripture requires that a redeemer take on the nature of the one being redeemed. Thus Christ had to become man in order to redeem mankind. "For assuredly He does not give help to angels, but He gives help to the descendant of Abraham. Therefore, He had to be made like His brethren in all things, that He might become a merciful and faithful high priest in things pertaining to God, to make propitiation [reconciliation] for the sins of the people" (Hebrews 2:16–17). Christ's sacrifice on the cross can be only applied to the human race; it cannot benefit fallen angels.

Satan's rebellion is the greatest mistake any creature has ever made. Knowing that it can never be undone only adds to his misery and anger. His foolish plan of self-exaltation backfired, forcing him to endure an eternity of suffering and defeat.

But fallen angels are not the only ones in rebellion against God. The human race is also involved in the continuing conflict.

His Greatest Deception

God could have exterminated Satan or confined him to another planet. But He chose instead to let him rule the world and to allow evil to take its destructive course. In the end, God's plan will triumph on the earth, but it will be through conflict, not by sovereign fiat.

Thus after the creation of Adam and Eve, Satan appeared in the Garden of Eden to lure our first parents away from obeying God. Please note carefully: by that point Satan was keenly aware that his act of disobedience had transformed him into a wicked being, the moral antithesis of God.

He was irritated by the fellowship that existed between man and God. No doubt it reminded him of the time when he had experienced such a blessed relationship. Not content with his own evil nature or any camaraderie with other fallen angels, he sought to draw mankind into his misery. This appeared to be a master stroke against God.

Let us examine Satan's deceptive ploy at work.

First, he cast doubt on the integrity of God. "Indeed, has God said, 'You shall not eat from any tree of the garden?'" (Genesis 3:1). Whether we accept the translation of the King James Version, *"every* tree of the garden," or that of the *New American Standard Bible, "any* tree of the garden," (italics added), the point is the same: "Do you mean to tell me that God has restricted you—for no good reason?"

The strategy was brilliant. By asking a question, he avoided directly attacking God, which would have aroused suspicion. Yet he had introduced the thought that perhaps God's command was arbitrary and unnecessary. He had opened the door for "rational" dialogue.

Note how his question got Eve to shift her focus: rather than focusing on the hundreds of trees from which she could eat, she began to concentrate on the one tree that was forbidden.

Second, he contradicted God directly. If Eve ate of the forbidden fruit, Satan claimed she would not die but would become "like God, knowing good and evil" (v. 5). That was a direct attack on the motive of God. The command, Satan said, was not for Eve's benefit but to protect God's selfish interests. The Almighty fears rivalry in His kingdom, he insinuated. He is intimidated by all that Eve will become if she eats the fruit. If God really loved Eve He would let her eat, but because of His own selfish interests He makes a restriction. What kind of a God would do that? When Satan saw both Adam and Eve eat the forbidden fruit, he must have had a moment of fiendish delight. The human race had joined his rebellion. He had tricked these two foolish people into defying the Almighty.

And so a drop of Satan's rebellion now falls on every human heart. Not only is every child born under the legal condemnation of Adam's sin, but each has a sin nature that exerts self-will rather than the will of God. Satan assumed that the whole human race would become as wicked and irredeemable as he.

But that was not to be.

His Greatest Surprise

Satan is not omniscient; his knowledge is limited. He can only predict the future based on past observations. Perhaps you have wondered whether or not a fortune-teller (assuming that he or she is under the power of Satan) is able to predict the future. The answer is no. Satan cannot know the future with accuracy. In the Old Testament the mark of a false prophet was that his predictions would sometimes be wide of the mark.

After President Kennedy was shot in 1963, several soothsayers came forward to claim that they had predicted the assassination. How much foreknowledge can Satan have of such events? He can know that a man is planning to shoot the president (indeed he may plant the idea in the assassin's mind), but *he cannot be sure that the assassination will be accomplished as planned.* For all Satan knows, the perpetrator might be arrested for carrying a gun into the Dallas Book Room Depository Building, or the bullet might miss the president, or the gun might jam. In other words, Satan can only know what is being planned; he cannot know for certain whether the plans will fail or succeed. His observation of human nature and his past experience do give him a relatively good idea of what lies ahead, but too many variables exist outside the realm of his control.

If Satan cannot foreknow human events, he obviously could not have foreseen that God would create a plan to redeem fallen humanity. He had to stand by helplessly as God selected some members of the human race to be redeemed and to receive privileges greater than those of angels. They were actually given positions of honor, such as heirs of God and joint-heirs of Christ.

In the Garden of Eden, with the first flush of guilt embedded in Adam and Eve's consciences, God gave them a promise in the form of a judgment on Satan. "And I will put enmity between you and the woman, and between your seed and her seed; He shall bruise you on the head, and you shall bruise him on the heel" (Genesis 3:15).

That was a promise of redemption for our first parents. Though there would be conflict throughout the ages, the seed of the woman would crush the head of the serpent. The serpent would retaliate by bruising the heel of the woman's seed.

What a cruel surprise for Satan! How he hates those human beings whom God so mercifully exalts.

The Greatest Defeat

For several thousand years the conflict progressed. Satan was permitted to score notable victories. The ancient worlds of Babylon, Greece, and Rome were steeped in occult religions, indirectly giving allegiance to the prince of darkness. There was immorality, cruelty, and numerous false religions. More important, knowledge of the true God was scarcely found on the earth.

But centuries before this, God revealed Himself to a pagan named Abraham. This man was challenged to go into the land of Canaan to become a servant of the Most

High God. He obeyed and became known as "a friend of God."

His descendants prospered, eventually wresting Canaan from hordes of cruel tribes who had entrenched themselves in the area. The Israelites (as Abraham's descendants were called) lived in the land for a thousand years and were frequently disciplined by God for their attraction to idolatry. Assyria conquered ten regions (or tribes), and later the Babylonians came and conquered the southern part of the land, specifically the city of Jerusalem. They carried off those Israelites to Babylon, but many of them returned to Jerusalem later.

Four hundred years later, Christ was born in Bethlehem, fulfilling the message of judgment God had given to the serpent. And so it was: "But when the fulness of the time came, God sent forth His Son, born of a woman, born under the Law, in order that He might redeem those who were under the Law, that we might receive the adoption as sons" (Galatians 4:4–5).

Christ's primary purpose was to be a sacrifice for sinners, a sacrifice that would be received by God the Father. What that meant was that a part of the human family would not merely alter their allegiance (choosing God rather than Satan), but they would be fully reconciled to God and would receive the coveted status of sons of God.

God defeated Satan's intention to keep all humanity on his side. Of course God could have crushed Satan with raw power, but He chose to do it according to His own laws. He let Satan continue to wield authority over the world, yet He sent Christ to humiliate him by winning a spiritual and moral victory.

Although the death of Christ appeared to be a rather ordinary historical event (indeed, two others were crucified next to Him that very day), it elicited intense, invisible conflict in the spirit world. Satan, though not fully understanding all the implications of what was happening, tried to persuade Christ to avoid the cross and quite possibly sought to kill Him in Gethsemane. But that was just the serpent's attempt to bruise the heel of the woman's seed.

Christ overcame this opposition, of course, and went on to give His blood as a sacrifice for sinners. Satan was crushed. God was reconciling people to Himself, and Satan could do nothing about it. He could only stand by and watch with envy and anger.

This helps us understand Satan's intense desire to see born-again believers offend God by committing sins, thereby coming under the sphere of satanic influence. *Anything* to get back at God.

His Greatest Hoax

Christ's sacrifice does not negate Satan's power, however. As an evil being (former angel) he still has all of his attributes intact. He can travel with incredible swiftness from one part of the world to another. He can fight battles with God's angels and organize legions of his underlings into a fearsome army, causing much spiritual destruction. His strength in the spirit world is so awesome that even Michael the archangel, who disputed with him about the body of Moses, treated him with respect (Jude 9).

Yet for all his power, Satan is personally losing ground every single day. The hoax, if it be called such, is his egotistical theory that he is actually able to thwart the purposes and plans of God.

Satan can gloat over the victories he has won: many believers have been defeated in warfare against him. Homes have been wrecked, Christians have backslidden, and unbelievers remain entrenched in sin, because the evil one has snatched the Word of God from their hearts (Mark 4:15). This litany of victories is surely of some delight to the chief destroyer, who has heaped vengeance upon the Almighty.

But all these victories are only a mirage, for they actually further Satan's own destruction. God uses these "defeats" for His own glory. For example, to the casual observer the death of Christ appeared to be a defeat for the Son of God, yet it was truly a defeat for Satan. God will eventually take all the so-called victories of Satan and turn them upon his own head.

In addition, Satan will be judged for all the evil deeds he commits, and every one of his victories only means his eternal punishment will be that much greater. If he were as wise as he evidently believes he is, he would cease his activity against God immediately!

Don't miss the irony. Satan, whose chief weapon is deception, is evidently himself deceived. Either that, or he, who boasts of his power, lacks even the strength to stop fighting God! He may have physical and spiritual power, but moral power cannot be found in him. Wisdom eludes him.

Nevertheless we must contend with him. He has a plan for us all.

His Greatest Lies

Satan's full-time occupation is to make sin look beneficial to us. He tries to show us the rewards of following our own desires. As already emphasized, he remains hidden, using our natural sinful responses to spring the traps that will keep us bound.

Following are twelve doorways that have this in common: each of them can at some time appear to be an innocent option, yet every one is a deadly trap. They all eventually lead to the same dark room.

REBELLION/SELF-WILL

Because the first sin that was ever committed by Lucifer was rebellion, this sin properly must be listed first. Satan wants us to think that self-will is not abhorrent to God.

Children who rebel against parental authority or adults who refuse to submit to Christ and to church leadership—these and a dozen other kinds of rebellion delight the evil one. The "look out for number one" philosophy did not originate in the human mind but was first embraced by Lucifer when he substituted his will for God's.

Rebellion is like the sin of witchcraft, and insubordination is like idolatry (1 Samuel 15:23). The rebellion of drugs, hard rock music, and violence all play in concert with the devil's tune.

When Paul was listing the qualifications for leadership within the church, he warned that new converts were not ready for such responsibility because of the temptation to pride. He wrote, "and not a new convert, lest he become conceited and fall into the condemnation incurred by the devil" (1 Timothy 3:6).

Our rebellion is as detestable to God as Satan's. To become Satan's servant we need not invite him into our life; we need only to live in rebellion against God and against our properly constituted authorities.

DISHONESTY

One day a couple decided to sell a piece of property and give some of the proceeds to the church. So far, so good. But they also agreed to pretend that they were contributing all of the money from the sale. Like many of us, they wanted to appear to be better Christians than they really were. The apostle Peter rebuked them and asked the husband, "Ananias, why has Satan filled your heart to lie to the Holy Spirit, and to keep back some of the price of the land?" (Acts 5:3).

Dishonesty in speech and actions is not only consistent with Satan's character, but when we act thus, we play into his hands. To lie is to submit to the authority of the father of lies, the devil.

FEAR

The fear of witnessing for Christ, which all of us tend to experience, seems so natural that we seldom think Satan has anything to do with it. Yet, interestingly, before Peter denied that he knew his Savior, Christ explained, "Simon, Simon, behold, Satan has demanded permission to sift you like wheat; but I have prayed for you, that your faith may not fail; and you, when once you have turned again, strengthen your brothers" (Luke 22:31–32).

Fear is one of Satan's most popular weapons. People are afraid of crowds, afraid of the future, afraid of what people will think of them, afraid to witness, afraid to live. John wrote, "Fear involves punishment, and the one who fears is not perfected in love" (1 John 4:18).

To serve fear is to serve Satan (Hebrews 2:14–15).

MORAL IMPURITY/ADDICTIONS

There are several reasons sexual temptations and perversions are often exploited by demonic powers. One is because of the powerful nature of sexual attraction and of the desire for fulfillment. Satan always strikes where we are weakest. Another reason is that the basic unit of society is the family, and sexual sin destroys those relationships.

When Paul was warning the married couples in Corinth about the dangers of prolonged sexual abstinence, he encouraged them to "come together again lest Satan tempt you because of your lack of self-control" (1 Corinthians 7:5).

A member of Wycliffe Bible Translators said that one day while riding on a plane she noticed that the couple next to her refused the meal, explaining that they were fasting. She thought that they might be Christians, but they said that they were worshipers of Satan. They were fasting and praying to him that (1) the Billy Graham crusade about to begin in Vancouver would be a failure and (2) Christian ministers would commit adultery so that their witness for Christ would be destroyed.

Satan wants the desires of the flesh to become addictions. People may become governed by alcoholism, drugs, gluttony, or sexual addictions of various kinds. Satan inflames these desires so that they take over a victim's life.

It is not necessary to attend a seance to serve Satan. All you need to do is pursue your particular lustful desires with abandon, letting them take you wherever they may lead. Those who serve lust serve the devil.

COVETOUSNESS

Coveting the wealth of others may seem to be a harmless occupation. Indeed, our society glories in its unabashed quest for wealth. Some who are millionaires many times over are excruciatingly stingy, hoarding every dime for themselves. According to *Time* magazine, one tycoon whose wealth exceeded $400 million was not known to have given as much as a pair of cuff links to charity.

Why this irrational fascination with more wealth than one could ever use? Paul warned, "For this you know with certainty, that no immoral or impure person or covetous man, who is an idolater, has an inheritance in the kingdom of Christ and God" (Ephesians 5:5).

Covetousness is idolatry, and behind every idol are demonic spirits (1 Corinthians 10:19–20). Satan does not mind which idol we choose, as long as it distracts us from the worship of the true God. Many people who know nothing about Satan have become his most loyal worshipers by becoming consumed with a covetous spirit.

GUILT

The name Adversary means "Accuser."

The prophet Zechariah in one of his visions saw the high priest Joshua (not to be confused with the successor to Moses) standing before the Lord, clothed in filthy garments, which symbolized the sins of the nation. Satan was present too, standing at his right hand to accuse him. But God took the filthy garments from Joshua and clothed him with festal robes (Zechariah 3:1–7).

Whereas the Holy Spirit uses guilt to drive us to Christ for forgiveness, Satan uses guilt to drive a wedge between God and us. He accomplishes this by (1) making us believe that our sins are too great for God to forgive, or (2) making us feel guilty for sins that have already been forgiven. Satan lies not only with words but with emotions. He attempts to create feelings that alienate us from God, from others, and even from ourselves. He finds it most helpful if we brood in isolation and believe our most painful depressions.

Don't let the irony escape you. Satan incites us to sin, and then if we follow his suggestions, he is the first to heap condemnation upon our consciences. He condemns us for the same sins he entices us to commit!

Thankfully, Satan's work of accusation will finally come to an end: "Now the salvation, and the power, and the kingdom of our God and the authority of His Christ have come, for the accuser of our brethren has been thrown down, who accuses them before our God day and night" (Revelation 12:10).

MURDER/HATRED

We might think that when Cain killed Abel in a fit of jealousy and anger, it was a purely human (though criminal) response to a family feud. But Christ taught that Satan was a murderer from the beginning (John 8:44); therefore we should not think it strange that John wrote that Cain killed his brother because he "was of the evil one" (1 John 3:12).

John affirms that one who does not love his brother is acting like a child of the devil. In contrast, the children of God love one another. And then John adds this startling comment: "Everyone who hates his brother is a murderer; and you know that no murderer has eternal life abiding in him" (1 John 3:15). That explains why some who are controlled by an evil spirit have a persistent desire to commit suicide. Such destruction gives Satan great momentary delight.

He is a murderer and a hater. And those who practice these sins come under his authority.

DOCTRINAL DIVISION

Satan inspires people to veer off into false cults that dethrone Christ. He leads people into strange and preferably occultic doctrines.

"But the Spirit explicitly says that in later times some will fall away from the faith, paying attention to deceitful spirits and doctrines of demons" (1 Timothy 4:1). These doctrines may range from asceticism to doctrines that incite hypocritical rationalizations that lead to a hard heart. (Both are mentioned in this context.)

False cults are too numerous to mention in this chapter. Suffice it to say that many teach that Christ is not fully God or that He is not unique because all of us are gods just as He was. Both heresies mislead multitudes.

There is no need to visit a fortune-teller in order to give your soul to satanic powers. Simply accept false doctrine that obscures the true message of the gospel.

ANGER

One sign of demonic activity is irrational, uncontrollable anger. Fits of temper often erupt with little or no provocation. Paul wrote, "Be angry, and yet do not sin; do not let the sun go down on your anger, and do not give the devil an opportunity" (Ephesians 4:26–27).

The Greek word for "opportunity" is *topos*, which means "a foothold." Anger, like other sins, allows an evil spirit to gain at least partial entry into one's life. That wedge in the door can become the basis for further anger and demonic exploitation.

THE OCCULT/NEW AGE TECHNIQUES/DRUGS

This is not the place to discuss all of the various bridges that are available to enter the world of the occult. Astrology, Ouija boards, channeling, fortune-telling, Transcendental Meditation, games such as Dungeons and Dragons®—these and dozens of other techniques are practiced today by many who do not know that all such activities belong to the demonic world. Modern notions about exploring the power of the mind and experiencing "the god within us" are based on pagan theologies. The New Age movement is occultism with a friendly American face.

We are also told that the shortcut to a new perception of reality is psychedelic drugs, which bring about a new state of consciousness. These experiences are an open invitation to the demonic world. To seek such mind-expanding techniques is to enter into Satan's kingdom.

MIRACLES

Some individuals experience apparitions or health cures that are actually accomplished through satanic power. We should not be surprised, for the Antichrist will deceive the world with "power and signs and false wonders" (2 Thessalonians 2:9). The infiltration of Eastern mysticism into America has created so-called miraculous cures, visions, and powers, many of which are demonic in nature.

CHILDHOOD TRAUMA

Satan will exploit any negative feelings you may have developed in your past. A child who felt rejected by his parents may actually discover that he is under the influence of a spirit of rejection. There are spirits of anger, bitterness, and revenge. Many people who confront their past suddenly discover that they are controlled (in varying degrees) by spirits that seek to keep them in emotional and spiritual bondage.

Sometimes ancestral spirits remain within the family lineage. One day Christ was asked to cast out a demon from a child who was being thrown to the ground by a wicked spirit and then ground his teeth and stiffened out (Mark 9:18). Christ asked the father how long it had been happening, and he answered, "From childhood" (v. 21). Clearly, that child had committed no sin to invite the spirit. It seems most probable that relatives had been involved in occultic or immoral practices that resulted in a transference of spirits.

These are just some of the doorways Satan uses to gain a degree of control over us. He invites us into his territory by clever deception. We think we are just serving ourselves and do not realize that we are serving him.

His Greatest Fear

Satan's greatest fear is that Christians will understand that he is defeated and that God has made it possible for us to send him from us. He fears detection and bold confrontation.

One principle that is absolutely essential to realize in our struggle against Satan is that *it is much easier to defend territory that is ours than to reclaim territory that is in the control of the enemy.* A few combat troops can easily defend a hill though they are outnumbered. Once they have entrenched themselves, built reinforcements, and hoarded food and ammunition, they become almost invincible. But once the hill is lost it takes a mighty army to win it back.

Satan's strategy is to get us to surrender some area of our lives to him. His intentions are to (1) make it almost impossible for us to take the territory away from him and to (2) use this stronghold as a launching pad for future conquests.

Have you ever noticed that those who have committed immorality in their past are more easily tempted to fall into the same sin? The same can be said of alcoholism, drug addiction, and gambling. How much better never to have experienced the exhilaration of these sins than to have to root them out once they have become firmly implanted in our lives.

We must learn to recognize Satan's attempts to destroy our witness for Christ by enticing us to submit to his authority.

How do we defend ourselves against satanic attack? And how do we help those who are already bound by him?

THE DEFENSE

1. *We must see all sin as our enemy, never as our friend.* When faced with a moral or spiritual choice, we often think that we can sin without any serious consequences. Sin appears to be our friend. We must remember that if we embrace sin, we embrace the devil. Sin is his playground; it is his trap.

2. *Realize that sometimes the trap does not appear to involve a clear choice between good and evil.* I'm talking about those rationalizations we use when the revealed will of God conflicts with our own emotions or with what seems to be best in our eyes. A woman may be tempted to marry a divorced man whose divorce had no biblical basis. Worse, a man may marry another woman after divorcing his wife simply on the grounds that his first marriage was not fulfilling. He fails to see the evil in his action because he feels love in his heart for his new partner. The rationalizations are legion.

3. *Realize that you can be trapped by Satan in one single act.* The mouse does not have to have a series of experiences with traps in order to be caught. Just one bite of cheese is sufficient.

Some people resist temptation for many years and yet in one act of weakness make a choice that leads them to ruin. One act of immorality or one foolish choice of a marriage partner—these and other sins have led committed believers into lives of spiritual stagnation and deterioration. Of course God is able to make the best of these situations after repentance and surrender to His will. But He cannot reverse the damage. Just ask King David.

4. *Reject sinful suggestions the moment you become aware of them.* Jesus met Satan saying, "Begone, for it is written . . ." Notice that using Scripture did not cause Satan to flee immediately. He returned with another temptation and then another. Luke writes that Satan finally left, "waiting for a more opportune time." Often we must resist Satan just as Christ did by saying, "Begone, Satan, for it is written . . ." Then we quote those promises that assure us of our victory in Christ.

I've observed that Christians who do this sometimes give up too easily. They quote a verse or two, and if they do not experience immediate results, they doubt whether God's Word is effective. But when breaking a stronghold, we must resist Satan repeatedly, perhaps for a long period of time, for he backs off only reluctantly and with the intent to strike again. For example, a man who wishes to overcome addiction to pornography should memorize perhaps twenty verses that can be used at the very point of temptation.

Be encouraged. *The more often you successfully resist Satan, the weaker his temptations will become.* Eventually, he will simply have to back off.

5. *Understand that the best defense is the armor of God.* Space forbids a detailed explanation of the armor of God that is available to every Christian. However, this equipment can be put on every day through prayer. Just read through the passage in Ephesians that lists each piece, affirming that you will receive God's protection for that day (6:13–20).

THE OFFENSE

You may presently be under the influence of a demonic spirit, or perhaps you know someone else who is. I have met people who hear voices that tell them to commit suicide or to kill someone. Sometimes the voices actually speak words of comfort and encouragement. Others claim to have supernatural experiences or psychic powers. Then there are the addicts—alcoholism, drugs, pornography, and immorality. Some are overcome by strange fears or the desire to blaspheme, tear up the Bible, or break glass in irrational anger. Add to the list those who are chronically depressed.

Where do we begin?

1. *We must understand the gospel.* Christ's death on the cross was a sacrifice for those who believe in Him. His resurrection and ascension completed the work of redemption. Trust in Christ must be personal and singular. Not Christ *and* baptism, or Christ *and* the ordinances. It is never Christ *and*—faith in Christ alone saves.

Without the transforming power of the gospel, no one can be set free from the dominion of darkness and transferred into the kingdom of God's dear Son (Colossians 1:13).

2. *We must understand the complete triumph of Christ over the demonic world.* "When He had disarmed the rulers and authorities, He made a public display of them, having triumphed over them through Him" (Colossians 2:15). We do not fight from the standpoint of weakness or doubt but from the solid rock of victory and faith. Unquestionably, Satan has been crushed. *Now it is our responsibility to exert authority over him.*

3. *We must understand repentance and submission.* To reclaim territory that is occupied by forces of evil, we must confess the sin that Satan is using as a cover. This should involve confession of all occult involvement, specific acts of disobedience, rebellion, and sinful habits and attitudes. If we even anticipate committing the same sins again, Satan may still claim some authority over us. All bridges to our past sins must be demolished.

"Submit therefore to God. Resist the devil and he will flee from you" (James 4:7). There is great power in the name of Christ but only for those who are submissive to

His authority. One day the sons of a Jewish priest thought that they could cast out demons in the name of Christ, just as Paul had done. But one evil spirit answered and said to them, "I recognize Jesus, and I know about Paul, but who are you?" (Acts 19:15). Then the man with the evil spirit leaped upon the two sons and tore off their clothes and sent them away in shame. The name of Christ has tremendous authority but only for those who are under His authority. Submission must precede resistance.

4. *We must understand the power of the Body of Christ.* Not one of us can live the Christian life alone. We are especially vulnerable when we are cut off from the fellowship and prayers of other believers. Some cannot be delivered from satanic bondage without the prayerful guidance and counsel of knowledgeable Christians.

Let me recommend the book *The Adversary*, by Mark Bubeck (Moody, 1975), which gives detailed instructions on how to pray effectively against Satan and how to win victories in our lives and the lives of others.

Let us boldly overcome Satan, whom the saints overcame by the blood of the Lamb and the word of their testimony (Revelation 12:11).

Yes, Satan hates us and has a destructive plan for our lives, but we can make sure it is not fulfilled. We can make sure that it will exist only as a dream in his darkened mind. We have the promise, "Greater is He who is in you than he who is in the world" (1 John 4:4).

And again, "But the Lord is faithful, and He will strengthen and protect you from the evil one" (2 Thessalonians 3:3).

You and I can take steps to make sure that Satan's evil plans are shattered. We can know that God loves us, and we can choose *His* plan for our lives.

PART TWO:

Confronting
Questions of Sexuality

CHAPTER 5

How Can a Sexual Past Be Healed?

I hate him for what he did to me, but I'd marry him today if he asked me to!"

This eighteen-year-old girl had every right to loathe her pseudolover, a married man who awakened her sexuality by his advances and seductions. He promised she would be his sweetheart forever, so she felt secure with his affection. But when the affair was discovered he blamed everything on her, falsely accusing her of initiating this sexual liaison. She was betrayed and humiliated and asked to leave the church where they both attended.

Yet, incredibly, she was willing to risk everything and marry him, if only he would ask! Though he was married and the father of three children, this young Christian woman was willing to break up a marriage to have the affection of this man, the first with whom she had had a sexual relationship.

This experience was so indelibly stamped on her soul that even the man's betrayal could not chisel him out of her heart. When she realized that he would not leave his wife and children for her, she sought fulfillment with other lovers, going from one man to another to satisfy her awakened longings for intimacy. Even if she didn't particularly enjoy these liaisons, she felt, in her words, "this is the price I have to pay to mean something to somebody."

Why can one immoral relationship begin a search for other sexual partners in a vain attempt to find fulfillment? This chapter is written to answer that question and others. It will explain:

- The power of sexual sin
- The development of sexual addictions
- The doorway to sexual forgiveness and healing

Our sexuality is the most sensitive aspect of our personality. We are fundamentally sexual beings with deep inner needs that we are tempted to meet even at great risk. If we do not channel those desires correctly, we can embark on a destructive path filled with broken promises that will eventually lead us to a painful dead end.

Pornography is not the only doorway to the world of sexual brokenness, but it is one of the most popular. Young people who watch movies replete with various forms of sexuality often find their passions so stimulated that they want to act out everything they have seen. At least one-half of high school students are sexually active before graduation. Any thought that AIDS might frighten them into maintaining their virginity till marriage seems ill-founded. Yet those who have sex before marriage jeopardize their chances for a happy relationship. (The reasons will be explained later.) This does much to explain why we have so many sexual problems in marriages.

Then there are those who commit adultery or drift into the world of sexual aberrations. Acts of sadomasochism, transvestism, and homosexuality continue to increase, as those driven by sexual desires join the frantic quest for fulfillment with the right partner. Some are victims, suffering from the sexual aggression of others. Incredibly, one in four baby girls born this year will be sexually molested by a relative, neighbor, or trusted friend.[1]

Early in my ministry I would speak about the fulfillment and joy of sex. Now, after a few more years of listening to marriage problems, I realize that for many people sex is not a positive experience. Some women who were molested as children find sex to be a difficult, if not a revolting, experience. At least a few have been raped, others talked into early sexual encounters that have had a devastating effect on their future relationships. And many people, driven by their sexual appetite, are sex addicts.

Sex can become the source of maximum fulfillment or maximum grief. A biblical understanding of sexuality will help us grasp the power of our sexuality. More important, the Bible can show us how to break the power of a destructive sexual past. Only God and His Holy Scriptures can help people move from sexual slavery to sexual sanity.

Please commit yourself to reading this chapter to the end. Only when we understand the whys and wherefores of sexuality will we be able to appreciate the healing that Christ offers to all who come to Him in honest confession.

Christ can forgive and deliver those who are slaves to a sexual past. If He cannot, He has deceived us.

Sexuality and Creation

Think of it: Although Adam had the awesome privilege of walking with God in the Garden of Eden, the Lord still said that something important was missing! "It is not good for the man to be alone; I will make him a helper suitable for him" (Genesis 2:18). God clearly affirms that man is a social creature and needs companionship that is "suitable" for him.

When God created Adam, He chose to use the dust of the ground for the raw material. "Then the Lord God formed man of the dust from the ground, and breathed into his nostrils the breath of life; and man became a living being" (Genesis 2:7).

We might expect that God would make a similar form of dust when He created Eve. But we read, "So the Lord God caused a deep sleep to fall upon the man, and he slept; then He took one of his ribs, and closed up the flesh at that place. And the Lord God fashioned into a woman the rib which He had taken from the man, and brought her to the man" (Genesis 2:21–22).

When God created Eve out of Adam's flesh, He made a powerful statement about our sexuality. God separated femininity out of masculinity, forming two separate people created in the image of God. With this separation came a powerful implanted desire in the male and the female to be reunited in an intimate oneness.

God gave Adam and Eve different characteristics. Men tend to be aggressive and depend upon a rational analysis of life's problems. Women have a strong sense of intuition, basic trust, and sensitivity. Obviously, these are generalizations and there is overlapping. The point is simply that both genders mirror different aspects of God on earth. Both sexes have the image of God, though they reflect God in a different way.

In marriage these characteristics are united in a harmony that should enhance man's representation of God. Paul taught that marriage should give a concrete display of the relationship between Christ and the church.

Here in the creation account are the roots of our sexual natures, proof that sex was created by God as an expression of unity and love between a man and a woman. We cannot ignore or misuse our sexual identity without serious consequences.

Two implications follow: (1) we must accept our sexual desires as from God, and (2) we should positively affirm our sexuality.

SEXUAL DESIRES ARE FROM GOD

All human beings have the desire for sexual intimacy. It is a yearning for completeness. The magnetic attraction between a man and a woman is innate, powerful, and unyielding.

God's entire plan for the human race was dependent on the sex drive inherent within every human being. If

Adam had not been sexually attracted to Eve, the human race would have ended with the death of our two parents. But God made the desire for physical intimacy so strong that there was no chance that Adam would look at Eve and walk away!

The presence of an attractive member of the opposite sex, the fantasies of love that play in our mind, or just the activity of our sex glands without any external stimulation—any one of these can trigger desires for intimacy and sexual expression.

Of course, we are responsible for what we do with those involuntary sexual feelings. Both the Old Testament and the New give specific instruction on what sexual activity is permissible and what is not. Christ taught that when a man lusts (that is, sexually covets) a woman who is not his, he has already committed adultery in his heart. We are created with powerful natural forces of attraction that must be controlled.

That doesn't mean God wants everyone to marry. Some may desire marriage but have not found a suitable partner. Others may have the gift of celibacy, as evidently Paul had (1 Corinthians 7:7). Though the sex drive is powerful, no person need think that sex is necessary for either happiness or fulfillment. Many who are single testify to the contentment of their lifestyle. Others who are married may not be able to have sex because of physical disabilities or other mitigating factors.

It is not necessary to have sexual intercourse in order to accept our sexuality. Masculinity and femininity have their individual characteristics, drives, and aspirations. These must be accepted, whether one is married or single.

SEXUALITY SHOULD BE AFFIRMED

Most of us were raised with some necessary warnings about illicit sexual expression. But if this is all that we know about what God says on the subject, we will live with a sense of shame or at least embarrassment. The prohibitions of Scripture (such as "Thou shalt not commit adultery") are only one side of the coin; we also must understand God's intention in giving us these desires. We must strive to handle our sexuality in such a way that these desires will fulfill us and not destroy us.

Many Christian teenagers, wanting to live a pure moral life, think all sexual desires are shameful. They forget that to feel a powerful attraction to some member of the opposite sex is precisely what God intended. The very act of thanking God for such desires reminds us that our feelings are not a cause for shame but for joy. Our battle against lust actually increases when sexuality is viewed as "dirty." When we accept these desires in themselves as good, as God views them, we can be free to rejoice and to use them rightly, according to God's specifications.

To the ancient Jews, sex within marriage was properly considered a holy act. On his wedding night it was believed that a man actually went into the Holy of Holies when he made love to his wife. Let us not call unclean what God has called holy.

Let us celebrate our sexuality, rejoicing in God's creation. This will help us view our masculinity and femininity from God's perspective.

Sexuality and Marriage

What is marriage? In marriage, a man and a woman are joined by two bonds. The first is a covenant, an agreement that they will live together until "death does them part." The sex act creates the second bond that joins them in body, soul, and spirit.

Some Bible scholars teach that since sex bonds two people together, couples who have shared a bed are already married. According to this view, premarital sex does not exist, for sex equals marriage. This teaching has caused young people to get married, even to partners they neither loved nor respected. Their reasoning is clear: If they are already married in the sight of God, they should complete the union by having a formal wedding ceremony. However, sexual intercourse of itself does not constitute marriage. A man and woman are made husband and wife by a covenant taken in the presence of God and witnesses. The Lord rebuked Israelite men for mistreating their wives and said to each one, "She is your companion and your wife by covenant" (Malachi 2:14). The covenant justifies the sexual relationship; the sexual relationship does not justify the covenant.

It is true the Bible does not mention the wedding ceremony (as we know it). But the bride and groom did enter into an agreement even if it was not ratified in the same way as we do today. Even in the case of Isaac and Rebekah, a covenant was made between Abraham (Isaac's father) and Laban (Rebekah's father). This agreement was spoken by Abraham's servant (Genesis 24:48–49). Gifts were given to signify the betrothal.

As cultures change, so do the customs accompanying the wedding ceremony. But one thing is certain: A couple should not live together without the benefit of a solemn covenantal agreement. Sex binds two people together emotionally and spiritually, but the covenant comes first, establishing the permanent bond.

Today millions of couples are living together without the benefit of a marriage covenant. In most instances this arrangement serves as a back door of escape, just in case the relationship does not work out. But this arrangement communicates a confusing dual message. On the one hand the partners are saying to each other, "I love you so much I want to be sexually intimate with you." On the other hand the second message is, "I don't want to get too close to you so that I have the option of escaping in case you don't meet all my needs." According to P. Roger Hillerstrom, "The result of this double message is an inbred lack of confidence in the relationship."[2] Understandably, these seeds of doubt bear bitter fruit later on.

Some ask, "What difference does a piece of paper make?" We answer with another question: "Would you purchase a house without a formal agreement?" Of course not. One reason for signing a piece of paper is to prevent one of the parties from backing out when a better deal comes along. Marriage, of course, is much more important than purchasing a house. There can be no security in the relationship without a formal covenant to seal the commitment.

To carry the analogy of purchasing a house one step further: After the papers are signed, you have the right to move into the new premises and enjoy them. After the marriage covenant, the couple now has the right to enjoy one another in the sexual relationship.

After the covenant comes the sexual bonding. Some think of this only as a physical bond, but if it were, sex would be only a biological experience (as the humanists affirm). But sex is much more than a physical experience; it actually bonds two persons—body, soul, and spirit. One person who bears the image of God stamps his personality upon the partner, who also bears the image of God.

Marriage reflects the plurality and unity of the Godhead. Though God exists in three persons, we read, "Hear, O Israel! The Lord is our God, the Lord is One!" (Deuteronomy 6:4). The same Hebrew word for one (*ehād*) is used for the marriage union, "and they shall become one flesh" (Genesis 2:24). Just as it is unthinkable that members of the Trinity would operate as separate entities, so a husband and wife should operate together with diversity within unity. The bond that has been formed involves the total personality of each partner; it is a unity with plurality.

Sex creates a "soul tie" between two people, forming the most intimate of all human relationships. When the Bible says, "Adam knew his wife" (King James Version) the word *know* is not simply a euphemism for the sex act. Sexual intercourse actually consummates the highest form of human interpersonal communication and knowledge. Indeed this exclusive familiarity cannot be easily erased.

Once a man and a woman have had sex together, nothing can ever be quite the same between them again. There simply is no such thing as a brand-new beginning.

God intended that the first sexual experience be enjoyed by a man and a woman who are wholly committed to each other with the protection of a covenant. That was to assure the acceptance and unconditional love that guard the most intimate of all human relationships.

Once that bond has been established, it must be nurtured, strengthened, and kept pure. That takes place through mutual caring and the development of trust and respect. When the commitment is threatened, the sexual fulfillment (at least on the part of one partner, if not both) is diminished.

Sexuality and Alien Bonds

Unfortunately, our world is filled with people who have experienced alien, or sinful, bonds. Alien bonds occur when a man and woman are united sexually without a covenant of marriage.

Perhaps one of the most surprising passages in the New Testament regarding the nature of sexuality is found in Paul's words to the Corinthian church. "Do you not know that your bodies are members of Christ? Shall I then take away the members of Christ and make them members of a harlot? May it never be! Or do you not know that the one who joins himself to a harlot is one body with her? For he says, 'The two will become one flesh'" (1 Corinthians 6:15–16).

We would all agree that sex with a prostitute is sex without a commitment, sex without any hint of mutual respect or caring. Prostitution is based on raw lust, sex for mutual exploitation. Yet, incredibly, Paul says that God joins the prostitute to her partner and the "two become one flesh." To prove it he quotes from Genesis 2:24, where God joins Adam and Eve into one in Eden. Sex of any kind always bonds people together, body, soul, and spirit.

Sex with a prostitute forms an alien bond, a bond outside the boundaries and nurture of a marriage covenant. This bond is an intruder, a violation of what God intended. Two persons have come together in an intimate union without the security of a covenant based on respect and trust.

A woman whose husband asked her forgiveness for his promiscuity said, "I feel as if all the other women he has had sex with are in bed there with me." In a sense she was right. AIDS researchers tell us that when we have a sexual relationship, we are, in effect, having sex with all the people our partner has had sex with. This is true medically, but it is also true metaphysically. Because sex joins people into one flesh, past bonds are still there.

What are some of the consequences of alien bonds?

THE POWER OF THE FIRST BOND

When the first sexual experience (or subsequent ones) occurs outside the marriage covenant, the sexual bond can be so powerful that it can even determine the direction of the person's sexual orientation. A boy recruited by an older male homosexual may initially hate the experience, but because sex bonds two people together, he may begin to feel a sense of security and fulfillment within this relationship. Soon he seeks out other male partners, not because he was born a homosexual but because his initial experiences were so stamped upon his soul that he now follows the lead of his newly awakened desires.

This also explains why a young woman may marry a man with whom she has slept even though he is abusive. His personality is indelibly imprinted on her mind and heart, and she feels an obligation to become his wife. Because of sex, he also may have incredible power over her. He may mistreat her, but she will always return to him. Even if the relationship ends, she will find it difficult to put him out of her mind.

Given the importance of the first sexual experience, we should not be surprised that some married partners are tempted to revert back to a previous sexual partner, often the first one with whom they had a relationship. Recently I received a letter from a woman who heard a message I gave at a couples' conference. Even though she was happily married to another man, she sought out a former boyfriend, her first sexual lover. The power of the previous relationship was still there.

Young people should take note: One reason to guard your virginity is that after the first bonding experience, something is lost that can never be regained. That special sexual relationship is best enjoyed within the bounds of the security and trust of a covenant.

THE TENDENCY TO PROMISCUITY

Once an alien sexual bond has been formed, there will be a desire to maintain that bond or seek other ones to replace it. Therefore, one sexual experience outside marriage can begin a spiral of illicit relationships. Once a person has crossed a forbidden sexual barrier, he or she might have a powerful desire to do so again and again.

A young woman who was a virgin had a sexual relationship with her boyfriend in a moment of passion. After the romantic relationship ended (as they usually do), both of them began independently to seek a whole series of sexual encounters with different partners. When the girl got pregnant, she had no idea who the father of the child might be.

The first bond created a "soul tie" that could not be simply ignored. Thinking that sex was the doorway to love and acceptance, she pursued men with the vain hope that she would find the "right relationship." A search for intimacy had developed that she tried to satisfy.

A man discovered on his wedding night that his wife was not a virgin. He became so angry that he vowed to "even the score." During their honeymoon he took a walk down the street and found a prostitute. Five years later he admitted that that one act had led to an addiction that he secretly nurtured three or four times a week. The power of one alien bond!

Today much is written about sexual addiction, but such slavery has existed from the beginning of time. Those who begin the pattern of alien bonding tend to continue it, seeking a fulfillment that of necessity will elude them. One writer said of sexual addicts, "They use sex like a drug, not to consummate loving relationships but rather to drown the pain of feeling empty inside a dark, shameful well of sexual oblivion."[3]

Individuals seldom have an abiding commitment to alien bonds. And because they have experienced intimacy outside the proper boundaries, they will have a tendency to forgo any process of courtship and almost immediately seek genital intimacy. Now that the principle of a covenant relationship has been violated, the temptation to continue the pattern will be persistent and powerful.

Many people are seeking love and acceptance through the sexual relationship, but of course, they do not find it there. A girl who did not have a warm relationship with her father will be tempted to seek love in the arms of other men. She is convinced that given enough time she will find the ultimate partner. Each time she says, "This will be different," but in the end it turns out to be the same failed relationship. The greater her guilt and emptiness the more she will be tempted to continue her hopeless search. She is looking for true love and acceptance in all the wrong places.

Admittedly, an alien bond won't always lead immediately to promiscuity. Some adulterers have been known to be faithful to their illicit partner. But remember that such a person has already violated his covenant with his spouse. Therefore, to violate his "commitment" to his illicit lover will not be difficult when the right time comes.

That explains why a man who commits immorality may lapse even after he has confessed his sin and turned to others for counsel. Sexual addicts, like alcoholics, tend to repeat their behavior patterns even after the most sincere attempt at reform. As we shall see, this cycle can indeed be broken, but the temptation will always be there. All sexual sins have their binding power. Some are addicted to pornography, voyeurism, homosexuality, or child molesting. Any one of us could become slaves to those sins if we just followed our lusts, wherever they may lead.

Those who know how to repent and come under the authority of one of God's representatives will find strength to form wholesome relationships; such a person can stop the strong impulse to repeat the same sin. Battles must be won a day at a time.

DIFFICULTY IN FORMING
AN EXCLUSIVE BOND

Those who have had illicit bonds may find it difficult to form a meaningful permanent bond even within the security of a marriage covenant. Some will fear an exclusive bond, unsure that they will be able to honor such a commitment. Others find it difficult to focus on one relationship; they cannot cope with the emptiness that past immorality generated in their lives. For some, past memories are so powerful that no present relationship can ever compare with the titillation they once had.

Those who come to marriage with many past sexual relationships usually will not form a strong new bond until God breaks the power of the previous ones. Time itself does not heal all wounds. The past must be confronted in the presence of God.

GUILT

Many people deny that guilt must accompany illicit sexual relationships, but because of the nature of sexuality, it is always present. God did not create us for alien bonds, and such relationships violate His will. Because sexuality is such a sensitive part of who we are as persons, a residue of guilt will surface in these relationships.

Suppressed guilt can rear its ugly head in many different ways. For some it becomes irritation and anger; for others it can turn into emptiness, frustration, or depression. Though there may be other causes of these negative emotions, repressed guilt is often the culprit. This guilt often plagues the conscience, quickens past memories, and stifles true joy.

Eventually the guilt turns to shame. Whereas guilt tells us we have *done* wrong, shame says we *are* wrong. Those feelings often hold people bound in self-hatred and condemnation. Often the roots of such feelings develop within a dysfunctional family and are magnified through sexual misconduct. Some think they might as well commit suicide.

Young people may say to themselves, "Let's have this sexual relationship; then we will ask God to forgive us and we will start all over again. Everything will be just as it was before. After all, if God can't forgive us for this, what is the blood of Christ for?" Of course, God does forgive, but the power of the past experiences may still be there. But the same Christ who forgives is able to break the power of past behavior.

How can these bonds be broken? And what can be done in the lives of those who even now are plagued with past memories and addictions?

Dealing with a Sexual Past

A Christian man who had a responsible position in a Christian school began an affair with a woman he met at church. Though his wife suspected his unfaithfulness, he denied it, even asserting, "If I am lying let God strike me dead!"

Because God did not take him up on his bold challenge, he felt comfortable in continuing the relationship. When he was unable to deny it any longer, he wept in repentance, asking forgiveness of both his wife and God. And yet despite his sincere attempts at reconciliation, he secretly continued the relationship, eventually leaving his wife for this other woman. To quote his words exactly, "I know I'm doing wrong, but I am helpless to do otherwise. I am driven to be with her no matter the cost."

At first we might conclude the man was not truly repentant. But remember, alien bonds often give partners incredible power over one another. This man simply could not find the strength to break the relationship. This woman could control him almost as she wished. Perhaps he had the same power over her. All rational considerations for his wife and children were tossed to the wind; all that he cared for was being with her. Never mind that after he got a divorce and married his adulterous lover, the new marriage ended in disaster.

In crossing the barrier into the forbidden world of illicit love, he was trapped by a power greater than his own strength. Little wonder the author of Proverbs warns a young man about prostitution and pessimistically predicts, "For her house sinks down to death, and her tracks lead to the dead; none who go to her return again, nor do they reach the paths of life" (Proverbs 2:18–19).

Why didn't this man break his relationship? First, he was dishonest. Though he finally admitted his adulterous liaison, he lied about the length of time the affair had continued. Despite his tears, his repentance was only partial. Second, he was unwilling to become accountable to other members of the body of Christ. Because of his shame, he insisted that he "handle this alone." Third, he did not break the relationship completely, but thought he could continue a "casual relationship" with the other woman.

Perhaps the primary reason this man returned to the same sin was a basic unwillingness to have God change him, finally and completely. The euphoria of his new-found relationship meant more to him than the will and desire of God. Thus Satan maintained a stronghold in his life that led to disaster.

Thankfully, God can help a man or woman come back from a life of immorality. There is hope on almost every page of the Bible.

There was a woman who was guilty of numerous illicit bonds, yet found emotional and spiritual wholeness through Christ's power. Women are sensitive and often feel the pain of immorality more deeply than men. The fact that she found a new identity and inner peace should encourage every person who is haunted by a sexual past.

Her story is recorded in Luke 7:36–50.

Simon was a Pharisee who threw a feast for Christ, wanting to check out this miracle worker for himself. In those days uninvited guests were welcome to attend as long as they sat along the wall of the room and did not expect to be seated at the table. Evidently this feast was well publicized, and perhaps a number of uninvited guests stopped by.

Among these was a woman who is described as "a sinner." Since all people are sinners, it is clear that Luke wants us to understand that this woman was a sinner of a special sort, namely, an immoral woman. Almost certainly she was a prostitute, a woman who was known to have many alien bonds.

How did she fall into such a lifestyle? Perhaps she was brought up in a good home and just decided that she needed to have her fling. One relationship led to another until she decided to sell her body to make some money. Also possible is that she was sexually abused when growing up and this led to an insatiable appetite for love and affection, so she turned to men for attention. Or maybe her husband betrayed her, creating deep anger. Thus she decided to take out her hostility against God and men by turning to prostitution. The men she hated could be used to earn a living, exacting as much payment as the market could bear.

Whatever the scenario, here was a woman with memories awash with the stain of illicit relationships. When she heard that Jesus would be in the house of Simon, she decided to be there at all cost.

The visitors were seated at a low table, perhaps a foot higher than the floor. In those days they would recline at such a table, each person leaning toward his left, propped up by his left arm and free to eat with his right hand. This woman, seeing Christ reclining at the table, went behind Him and took her vial of precious perfume and began to pour its contents on Christ's extended feet. As she did this, tears poured down her cheeks and in a moment Christ's feet were drenched. Then she wiped His feet with her hair. This act of devotion was done repeatedly, unashamedly.

This was too much for Simon. He was embarrassed, even if Christ was not. He said to himself, "If this man were a prophet He would know who and what sort of person this woman is who is touching Him, that she is a sinner" (v. 39).

What an incredible story! Here is this woman in the presence of both Christ and a Pharisee. Yet, here she found emotional wholeness. In the end, the Lord of Glory told her to "go in peace." What more could an immoral woman ask?

Emotional healing takes time. If you break an ankle, it takes several weeks or even months to heal. The healing of a broken heart takes even longer. But this woman moved through the process quickly. She did in a few moments what it takes some people months to do. She was ready for healing.

Let us notice several principles found in this passage that brought this ruined woman to a place of blessing and peace. She was honest, had faith, and confronted her feelings. We also should follow this pattern.

HONESTY

This woman had no time for hypocrisy or pretense. She had the reputation of being a sinner and evidently deserved it. She knew that coming to the house of a self-righteous Pharisee would elicit derision and scorn. That did not matter to her because she overcame her natural inclination to hide in her shame. Her desire to meet Christ was more powerful than her desire to avoid public scorn. The insults that she experienced on the streets were nothing in comparison to the moral derision she would get from the arrogant, bigoted Pharisee and his friends. Nevertheless, she was there.

Many people with a history of illicit sexual experiences find neither power over their past nor strength for their future. One reason is that the power of their shame is stronger than their desire to be honest. As a result, sex addicts or those with a sordid sexual past often develop layers of denial. They virtually insulate themselves from who they really are and what they have done.

The grace of God does not enter closed doors but works only when deception gives way to honest exposure and humble admission of sin. Most people caught in sexual sin deny it, only admitting to what has been uncovered. This desire to hide allows the root of sin to remain intact.

The first step toward breaking the power of an immoral past is, in the words of another, "to die to the natural inclination to live a lie." God will do miracles for those who are so weary of their sinful secrets that they are prepared to "come clean" before God and all those whom they have wronged.

Those who are victims of other people's sins/crimes also must confront their past. Those molested as children, those who have been raped or otherwise abused, must be willing to face their past in the presence of Christ. Usually, the victim will need other qualified believers to be part of the healing process.

Don't even think you must change yourself to make yourself worthy of coming to Christ. Simply come as you are, openly, honestly, expectantly.

STEP 1: Find at least one person (perhaps your pastor, a counselor, a friend, or your mate) and share your past with him/her. Those who have addictions, emotional wounds, or guilt for past experiences need to be willing to share openly in the presence of God and those who can help. "He who conceals his transgressions will not prosper, but he who confesses and forsakes them will find compassion" (Proverbs 28:13).

FAITH

Christ said to the woman, "Your faith has saved you; go in peace" (v. 50). Let me be clear: It was not her tears that saved her, nor the loving act of pouring expensive perfume on Christ's feet. Her good deeds did not bring the salvation of God to her soul. Faith, and faith alone, in Christ's forgiveness and salvation wiped her sins away.

But her kindness was an evidence of her faith. She believed that Christ would accept her even though He knew all about her past. Perhaps it was the kindness in Christ's face, or maybe she had listened to His messages of love and hope. Whatever, her faith blossomed in the presence of Christ. She knew this man would not use and then discard her as so many others had done.

How thankful she was that Christ was not a Pharisee! Imagine what would have happened if He had said to her, "Woman, I don't appreciate being touched by a prostitute. Don't you know that I am the holy Son of God? Go back to the streets where you belong!" If He had spoken those words, her only option would have been suicide. For if she had been rejected by the only One qualified to forgive her, there was no other place in the universe where she might go to be forgiven. If the Son of God should turn His back, there is but eternal despair. But if He should speak a word of forgiveness, there is eternal joy!

A young woman wrote me saying that an older woman in her office convinced her that they should have sex together. Although initially resistant, she gave in, and thus began a five-year struggle with lesbianism (female homosexuality). "Oh, how I stink in the core of my being!" she wrote. "I know God has forgiven me, but I cannot forgive myself. Many times I cannot help but cry . . . at twenty-five I feel so tired and old. God forbid that I should be a Judas, who felt sorry for what he had done, but nevertheless chose to go in the wrong direction! Is there any hope for someone like me?"

Yes! A thousand times yes, there is hope. We will go into this more in the next chapter.

But why does she still feel defiled though she has confessed her sins, perhaps many times? First, she must not only claim God's forgiveness but also His cleansing, which is her right. Her conscience can be wiped clean, and she can live without the voices of condemnation, without the heaviness that comes with a defiled conscience.

Second, she may be making the error of confusing the accusations of the devil with the voice of the Holy Spirit. The responsibility of the Holy Spirit is to convict us of sin so that we might confess it. After that the work of the Spirit ends. But at this point Satan usually takes over and tries to imitate the work of God and convict us of sins that God has already forgiven! Believers who think the accusations of the devil are the convictions of the Spirit are caught in a vicious cycle—they engage in continual confession without the assurance of forgiveness. Or they believe the lie that they must live with guilt as a payment for sin.

Forgiveness and cleansing are available for all sins. "If we confess our sins, He is faithful and righteous to forgive us our sins and to cleanse us from all unrighteousness" (1 John 1:9). When Christ died on the cross, His death was a payment for the sins of immorality committed by His children. Why should anyone think that he/she must pay a second time by wallowing in guilt? If you have confessed your sin, the next time Satan reminds you of your past remind him of his future!

If a prostitute can be cleansed in the presence of Christ 2,000 years ago, a lesbian can be cleansed today. Both can hear the voice of the Savior, "Your faith has saved you; go in peace."

STEP 2: Accept God's Word that Christ's death was a full and complete payment for your sin. Repent, and be willing to accept the forgiveness that God freely offers. "I, even I, am the one who wipes out your transgressions for my own sake; and I will not remember your sins" (Isaiah 43:25).

FACING THE PAIN

This woman wept. She wept profusely. Her tears ran down her cheeks and fell onto Christ's feet. The present tense of the verbs indicates that she *kept on* weeping, *kept on* anointing His feet, *kept on* wiping His feet with her hair. Her tears proved that she was willing to face her pain; she faced the hurts buried in her sordid past.

Why did she weep? We cannot know, but we can surmise the reasons. First, think of the men who had betrayed her! The broken promises, the assurances of protection and love. Then after they used her, she was tossed aside like the peelings of an orange. She was stripped of all sense of value and self-worth.

Second, she may have wept because of the grief of broken relationships. Perhaps she had met a married man whom she dearly loved, yet she knew that this friendship would have to be permanently broken. Those who are in alien bonds must understand that breaking such relationships sometimes involves the same emotional loss as the death of a spouse. Perhaps she was in mourning.

Third, she may have been weeping because she remembered a family that had been broken by her own sin. She may have been thinking of a sexual relationship with a married man whose marriage came apart because of the relationship. She remembered the little children deprived of the security of a happy father and a mother, and she was an accomplice in it all. Weep she might!

She could have taken all of these feelings and stuffed them deep within her soul, unwilling to face the pain of the past. Then she would have become a tough woman, defiant and angry. She could have told herself, "I will handle my pain and manage my life quite well on my own. I will not let my feelings get to me, no matter the cost!"

Or she could have pursued continuous compulsive sex to deaden the pain of an empty life. She could have continued to flit from one relationship to another, unwilling to admit the fruitlessness of her search for love and acceptance.

Almost every person struggling with a history of sexual brokenness has a moment of truth, a time when he/she finally is willing to confront the pain that has been pushed down in the depths of the soul. For every alien bond there is at least one hurting heart.

I do not mean to imply that we cannot be forgiven unless we weep; nor do I want to imply that her tears paid for her misdeeds. But sexual sin almost always involves deep pain that is buried in the bottom of the soul. Because many addictions have their roots in a dysfunctional family, only through a willingness to confront pain does healing take place.

Victims of abuse must especially be willing to weep. It is said that children who have been abused have "no place in the depths of their soul where they may cry their eyes out." Whether you suffer from sins done against you or sins that you have committed, pain lives in the depths of your soul. If you have never confronted it, weep in the presence of Christ. Tears are not only permissible but welcome.

STEP 3: Ask God to reveal any areas of pain that you have ignored because of denial or a basic unwillingness to admit how deeply you have been hurt or have hurt others. Confront the pain in the presence of Christ and a trusted counselor.

ACCEPTING FORGIVENESS

Christ used the occasion to give Simon a lesson in forgiveness. "'A certain moneylender had two debtors: one owed five hundred denarii, and the other fifty. When they were unable to repay, he graciously forgave them both. Which of them therefore will love him the more?' Simon answered and said, 'I suppose the one whom he forgave more.' And He said to him, 'You have judged correctly'" (vv. 41–43).

Then Christ made His point: He reminded Simon, "Do you see this woman? I entered your house; you gave Me no water for My feet, but she has wet My feet with her tears, and wiped them with her hair. You gave Me no kiss; but she, since the time I came in, has not ceased to kiss My feet. You did not anoint My head with oil, but she anointed My feet with perfume. For this reason I say to you, her sins, which are many, have been forgiven, for she loved much; but he who is forgiven little, loves little" (vv. 44–47).

Christ taught that the degree of our love depended on the degree of our forgiveness. Of course this should not be interpreted to mean that Simon could never love Christ deeply because he had but few sins that needed forgiveness. Christ's intent was to teach that those who *think* they need little forgiveness love only little. Those who see their sin with clearer eyes will love much.

To this woman who in humility saw herself for what she was, Christ said, "Your sins have been forgiven" (v. 48). Right in the presence of this self-righteous, judgmental bigot Christ publicly declared this woman forgiven! Perhaps for the first time in years someone actually spoke to her in kindness; someone gave her the dignity of letting those around her know that she was special to God. What blessed words, "You are forgiven"!

I have counseled many people who committed sexual sins who simply could not receive God's forgiveness. Some thought it didn't seem right that they should be cleansed because they were keenly aware that they didn't deserve it. Of course, no one deserves it! Forgiveness is a free gift based upon the merit of Christ. That's why God does not find it more difficult to forgive big sins than He does small ones!

Others find it difficult to accept forgiveness because they confuse a clear conscience with the consequences of sin. In other words, because the consequences of their sins continue (a broken relationship, a pregnancy, a sexually transmitted disease, etc.), they think they are not entitled to a clear conscience. But let me emphasize: *It is God's will that you be totally cleared of the guilt of your sin regardless of the awful consequences it produced.* If David could be forgiven for adultery and killing Uriah (who would never be raised back to life), why cannot others be forgiven of a sexual sin despite its consequences?

Still others cannot forgive themselves. But think about this for a moment: If the Supreme Lawgiver of the universe has pronounced you clean, do you have the right to pronounce yourself dirty? "Who will bring a charge against God's elect? God is the one who justifies; who is the one who condemns? Christ Jesus is He who died, yes, rather who was raised, who is at the right hand of God, who also intercedes for us" (Romans 8:33–34).

Resist the temptation to come to Christ with something in your hand, some promise of reform, some act of kindness you have done either past or present. Accept His forgiveness just as you are.

Christ is not physically present on earth to say to us, "Your sins are forgiven." But through His Word, we can say exactly those words to those who have confessed their sins. Sometimes I personally have given people that assurance on the basis of Scripture.

Must you live with remorse? No, for remorse is simply repentance made out of sight of Christ. Standing before Him, the past is wiped away.

STEP 4: Praise God for His forgiveness regardless of your past! Accept a clear conscience and the cleansing that is your right as a child of God. Rather than repeatedly confessing your sin, affirm the fact that you have been forgiven (Psalm 32:1–2).

BREAKING PAST RELATIONSHIPS

Christ's final words to this woman were "Go in peace" (v. 50).

In another account we read that the Pharisees brought to Christ a woman who was found in adultery. They asked Christ what to do with her, reminding Him that the law commanded that such should be stoned. He agreed that they could go ahead and stone her, but He requested that the person among them who was without sin (that is, the person who is free of the same sin they accused her of) should cast the first stone. Pierced by their own consciences, the men all walked away, leaving only Christ and the woman. Christ's response: "Neither do I condemn you; go your way. From now on sin no more" (John 8:11).

"Go and sin no more!" Break those sinful relationships that keep causing you to sin! Now that you have come to Christ and received His forgiveness, you must take these additional steps to lay your past to rest.

First, if you have been wronged, you must *choose to forgive all who have mistreated you.* That may take time, but it must be done by an act of the will and with the power of God. Resist any tendency to retain your anger because you crave justice. Your desire for justice is legitimate, but you must wholly give your complaint to God. "Never take your own revenge, beloved, but leave room for the wrath of God, for it is written, 'Vengeance is Mine, I will repay,' says the Lord" (Romans 12:19).

Yes, you must repent of any bitterness toward God or others. Despite the sins of your parents or those who have taken advantage of you, you must forgive. Daughters who have been molested by their fathers, young women who have been raped by their boyfriends, men and women whose spouses have been unfaithful—these and others must release the feelings of bitterness to God. Often the chains of past bonds are strengthened by feelings of bitterness and hostility.

Second, *become accountable to someone who will stand with you* in breaking sinful relationships or habits. Christ, when speaking of adultery and lust, said, "And if your right eye makes you stumble, tear it out and throw it from you; for it is better for you that one of the parts of your body perish, than for your whole body to be thrown into hell" (Matthew 5:29). Obviously it would be painful to have your right eye plucked out, but Christ is saying, "Do anything necessary to keep yourself from sliding into the pit of sexual sin." If that means breaking a relationship with a lover, *do it.* Burn the bridges that lead to your weakness, your addiction. Accept the pain such an act requires as your opportunity to prove that you love God supremely.

Third, *believe the Word of God and not your conscience, memory, or emotions.* If you are a believer, you are in Christ seated above all principalities and powers. You are not an adulterer, homosexual, or a rejected child. You are a child of the King, with all rights and privileges pertaining to such honor (1 Corinthians 6:11). Memorize Scripture that speaks of your position in Christ. "You shall know the truth, and the truth shall make you free" (John 8:32).

Fourth, *accept the power of the Holy Spirit*, who is given to believers. Through faith receive His strength, which can bring emotional wholeness to any needy heart. The destructive memories of the past can be replaced by: love, joy, peace, patience, kindness, goodness, faithfulness, gentleness, and self-control (Galatians 5:22–23).

Fifth, *become acquainted with "spiritual warfare."* That is, learn to resist Satan and enlist others who will pray against his power, as discussed in chapter four. Stand on the fact that you have been joined to Christ in His death, resurrection, and ascension (Romans 6:1–18). Expect to be tempted to return to the sin of which you have repented. Remember, we will always be tempted to return to the sin that once was our master.

As we have learned, in one sense, a person who has committed sexual sin cannot begin over again. But spiritually it is possible to have a new beginning. When Hosea's wife drifted from one lover to another, he said that one day he would win her back, and she would sing again, as in the days of her youth (Hosea 2:15). The Lord, speaking to wayward Israel, says, "And I will betroth you to Me forever; Yes, I will betroth you to Me in righteousness and in justice, in lovingkindness and in compassion, and I will betroth you to Me in faithfulness. Then you will know the Lord" (Hosea 2:19–20).

What Hosea did for his wayward wife, God does for His wayward people today.

Charles Wesley understood that many people whose sin has been canceled by God still come under its power. But he assures us:

> He breaks the power of canceled sin,
> He sets the prisoner free;
> His blood can make the foulest clean;
> His blood availed for me.[4]

Once plagued by their sexual pasts, thousands of people are walking in freedom today, thanks to the power of Christ's blood.

What happened in the past can never be changed. But the power of that past can be laid to rest by the power of forgiveness through the Cross. "Where sin increased, grace abounded all the more" (Romans 5:20).

Notes

1. This figure, commonly reported in the news media, may be low. In a recent study, John Powell at Michigan State University reported that 38 percent of women interviewed had been sexually abused by an adult or family member by age eighteen (as reported in Dan Allender, *The Wounded Heart* [Colorado Springs: NavPress, 1990], back cover).
2. P. Roger Hillerstrom, *Intimate Deception* (Portland: Multnomah, 1989), 30.
3. Michael Castleman, "Addicted to Love," *Chicago Tribune*, Style, January 30, 1991, 6.
4. "O for a Thousand Tongues to Sing," verse 3.

CHAPTER 6

How Do I Deal with Homosexuality?

There was a time when the church thought it did not have to address the subject of homosexuality. The mistaken belief was that only few people exhibited sexual desire toward the same sex. Today with homosexuality receiving so much attention, no one can ignore the struggles of many (yes, Christians too) who find themselves driven with desires they do not want to have but cannot seem to change. We must realize that homosexuals are everywhere, including in our churches.

Unfortunately, issues of sexuality have often been ignored by Christians, evidently under the pretext that if we do not mention a problem, it does not exist. But sexuality is so much a part of us that it cannot be ignored without devastating consequences.

The term *homosexual* applies to either men or women who are erotically attracted toward members of their own sex, though often the word *lesbian* is used to designate a female homosexual. Most homosexuals call themselves "gays" in order to convey the impression that the homosexual lifestyle is filled with carefree pleasures (gay, as in happy).

Unfortunately, society has coined other descriptive terms, such as *fag, weird,* or *queer;* these are frequently used in derision of homosexuals. Such language only con-

tributes to deepening the chasm of misunderstanding between homosexuals and heterosexuals (those who are
attracted to the opposite sex).

Who can imagine the pain that is felt by those who
are the object of such uncaring, unchristian remarks? If homosexuals cannot turn to Christ and His people for love
and understanding, where should they go? A judgmental,
uncaring attitude has driven countless people deeper into
homosexual patterns and behavior. Few groups in society
have faced as much condemnation from the church as homosexuals. We all know that Christ came into the world to
save sinners, but often the impression is given that homosexuals are excluded from His love and grace. Such a gospel is unworthy of the name.

Why this prejudice against homosexuals? One reason
is a lack of perspective. Many people thoughtlessly associate all homosexuals with the radical gay rights activists,
who are determined to force homosexual values on society by intimidation and political activism. But those groups
do not represent all homosexuals, indeed perhaps they
speak for only a fraction of the homosexual population.
Most suffer silently, searching for sexual wholeness. More
of that later.

Second, heterosexuals who consider homosexuality
abhorrent underestimate the depths of confusion and pain
connected with homosexuality. Superficial comments
such as "Why doesn't he get married?" reveal deep insensitivity toward the needs, thoughts, and feelings of the homosexual. If we would take the time to understand the
pain and sense of rejection that they endure, we would be
sympathetic. They have the same need for love and understanding as all people do, perhaps more so. Many of them
attempt to meet these legitimate needs through homosexual relationships.

Put yourself in the shoes of a homosexual: You are a
male eighteen years old. You have powerful erotic attrac-
tions to men. You do not think that you have chosen this

lifestyle. At puberty your desires began to be directed toward the same sex. Your friends are attracted to girls, but you are not interested. The pressure of society and your own feelings remind you that you are abnormal; your peers call you "weird." You try to change but you cannot. You implore God for help, but your passions continue unabated.

What would you do?

Tell your parents? They might not understand. In fact, one organization established to help parents of homosexual children is called the Spatula Club because parents need to be scraped off the ceiling when they hear news of their child's homosexuality!

Tell your pastor? Not if he berates homosexuals from the pulpit. You have no idea what he might say to you. And even if he doesn't say it, you know how he feels.

A common response of homosexuals is to seek out others with whom they can identify. Those who are not Christians may find friends among those who are openly homosexual. Once the homosexual lifestyle is begun, the pattern of behavior generally continues.

Understandably, many homosexuals are bitter because they do not think the church understands them. Many of them have written Christianity off, thinking the church can provide only condemnation. Most are angry with God too, believing that He is to blame for their sexual identity. They think this is the card they have been dealt.

No one should speak about homosexuality without a caring heart. I doubt whether anyone ever changed his sexual identity simply because he heard a sermon condemning homosexuality. The teaching of Scripture must be accompanied by understanding, patience, and love. David Augsburger has wisely said, "It is so much easier to tell a person what to do with his problem than to stand with him in his pain."

Homosexuals are well aware of the stereotypes and hostility that others may feel toward them. And even if those feelings are not present within a congregation, many homosexuals will think that they exist. Here, as in other relationships, perception is often reality.

As already indicated, it is essential to distinguish between avowed homosexuals and those who struggle with homosexuality, knowing that the lifestyle is sinful, but are unable to change. Although this chapter is written primarily to offer hope to those who wish to be freed from homosexuality and to those who wish to understand homosexuality, this important distinction must be discussed in more detail.

The Quest for Homosexual Rights

Some Christian leaders have been criticized for being publicly opposed to "gay rights." Such opposition, we are told, is contrary to the love of Christ and therefore creates a stumbling block in the homosexual community.

However, we must understand the difference between the two groups, the militant homosexuals who are bent on transforming society and the individual who has no intention of using legislation to impose his lifestyle on others.

To summarize: the "Gay Rights Movement" refers to those within the homosexual community who have organized to impose homosexual values on all of society. They are proud to be homosexuals, insisting that they have the right to change society through political action and a sympathetic media.

This movement is so powerful that it has the ability to make demands of psychiatrists, politicians, and health experts and get exactly what it wants.

Consider the gains the movement has made in recent years. (1) In 1974 the Gay Rights Movement persuaded the American Psychiatric Association to drop homosexuality as a sexual deviation. Militant activists disrupted psychiatric meetings, made demands of psychiatrists, and pressured the members to make the change. One prominent psychiatrist said that it was the first time in psychiatric history that a scientific society ignored scientific evidence and yielded to the demands of a militant group (*Psychiatric Annals,* April 1976).

Then (2) homosexuals have lobbied to pass ordinances that give special privileges to homosexuals in the schools, apartment complexes, and the workplace. Under the banner of equality, homosexuality must be taught in the schools as a legitimate alternate lifestyle; landlords and employers no longer have the right to decide whether a person's sexual preference might have relevance in renting an apartment or in setting policies for the workplace. Even organizations such as Big Brothers have been forced to accept homosexuals as prospective "brothers" to fatherless youth. When this happens a boy's mother no longer has the right to choose what kind of "brother" her child would have if she wishes to join the organization.

Homosexuals are seeking the right to legitimize their marriages and to adopt children. A part of the plan is that eventually churches will be forced to hire homosexuals to meet the demands of equal employment. One domino after another is falling as the courts give expansive rights to the homosexual cause.

Also (3) the homosexual movement has opposed specialists in the medical field who years ago insisted that those who have AIDS be quarantined to protect society. By opposing such health precautions and tirelessly campaigning for freedom to practice various forms of sexual behavior, these radicals have in effect defended the right to infect others with a deadly disease.

This crusade was conducted under the banner of civil rights, implying that their struggle was essentially the same as the right of blacks to be regarded as equal members of society. Incredibly, many people, though not personally accepting this misrepresentation, have been silenced through fear of being branded "homophobic." (For the details read *Exposing the AIDS Scandal,* by Paul Cameron [Lafayette, La.: Huntington, 1988].)

Then (4) they have successfully used intimidation to control the media and the public health officials of the United States. At a recent AIDS conference, the presence of homosexuals was noisy and persistent. They cheered and applauded speakers who agreed with them and booed and hissed those who said things that were contrary to their cause. Health considerations were to be subservient to the the homosexual agenda.

When a news commentator made an innocuous comment about homosexuality, he was forced to resign and reinstated only when he apologized to the gay community. So powerful is their intimidation of the media that an objective report on homosexuality is virtually impossible.

As already emphasized, such outspoken homosexuals make it difficult for those who struggle with homosexuality to "come out of the closet" for fear that they will be identified with the radicals.

However, *the legitimate opposition we might have toward these militant spokespersons cannot be transferred to the person who is frightened into suffering in silence.* Let it never be said that we have turned our backs on anyone, homosexual or heterosexual, who seeks the love and compassion of Christ.

That does not mean that we should reinterpret the Bible to suit the prevailing cultural mind-set. It does mean that we try to understand those suffering with a homosexual orientation and listen to what they have to say, feel their rejection, and identify with their anger and disappointments.

This chapter is dedicated to those who struggle with homosexuality as Christians, those who know that homosexual behavior is contrary to the Bible but think they are powerless to change. I also write for those who have discarded Christianity in the mistaken belief that Christ has no relevance to their lifestyle.

Levels of Homosexual Struggle

When we speak of homosexuality we must remember that the term encompasses a broad range of feelings and behaviors. It is best to view homosexuality on a continuum, allowing for many different levels of desire or involvement.

First, there is the person who feels confusion about his sexual identity. He might have attraction to the same sex, and he fears that he might be a homosexual. This experience may be just a phase, a natural curiosity and arousal that need not determine his future sexual identity.

As we shall see later, at puberty teenagers can be ambivalent in their sexual feelings. The decisions that are made in adolescence will play a large role in their future sexual focus. These young people must realize that they are not locked into homosexual fantasies and experiences. Knowing that they are not programmed to be homosexuals will free them from the hopelessness that often accompanies those feelings.

Second, there is the person who has bisexual feelings, that is, who feels sexual attraction to both sexes. Such an individual must realize that his sexual bent will be determined by choice and not some prior, inborn disposition. He must know that his sexual identity will develop according to the fantasies and behavior he adopts. Whatever sexual drive is pursued will determine its ultimate expression.

Making the transition from a homosexual focus to a heterosexual one is much easier when fantasies have not given way to sexual acts. Homosexual encounters make an almost indelible impression upon the soul that makes such behavior more difficult to overcome. The reasons for this will be explained later.

Third, there is the person who has had homosexual encounters and has come to enjoy those relationships, however unnatural they may have appeared to be at first. After the line has been crossed, those experiences begin

to occupy his attention, and he accepts homosexual behavior as a lifestyle. Initially he wished he could change,
but now he thinks that there is no way out of his immoral
patterns. But he continues to hope that perhaps someday
he will be able to walk away from it all. The more open he
is to change the better.

Finally, there is the person who wholeheartedly accepts homosexuality and does not desire change. He feels
no guilt and is content with homosexual relationships. He
has convinced himself that homosexuality is morally equi-
valent to heterosexuality, or perhaps even superior. He either does not care what the Bible teaches or he will
reinterpret it to suit his preference.

Many homosexuals would not change their sexual
identity even if they could. They are content with their partners and have a feeling of acceptance and security within
those relationships. The thought of leaving homosexuality
behind is no longer an option.

The Nature of Sexuality

We cannot understand homosexuality without coming to grips with the more general topic of sexuality. You
and I are sexual beings, created with strong desires that
need direction and control. Our sexual identity is at the
very core of who we are as people.

As discussed in the last chapter, sex is not merely a
pleasurable biological experience, but the act actually
binds two people together, body, soul, and spirit. Sex joins
two personalities into one bond that is not easily broken.

Even sex without any commitment, sex with a prostitute, begets a unity that properly belongs to marriage. This
does not mean that sexual intercourse binds two people
together in marriage, for marriage is protected by a covenant. But the bonding that takes place is the same as that
which occurs between a man and his wife.

Any sexual relationship, whether homosexual or heterosexual, binds two people together in an intimate union

that has far-reaching consequences. There is evidence that God created both male and female simply because both sexes are needed to complete the image of God that we all have stamped upon us. In marriage the image of God is therefore clearly to be seen.

Marriage between a man and a woman is designed to protect this union; the intention of God is that no other person should come between the two who have been joined together in holy matrimony. The particular nature of a man and woman is thus preserved, and the most intimate relationship on earth finds its fulfillment.

A homosexual relationship, like an adulterous relationship, creates an alien bond that of necessity has lasting and detrimental consequences. The unity of two people outside of God's prescribed will eventually increases emptiness and confusion.

What are the results of this alien bonding that occurs in relationships outside of a man/woman marriage?

The first consequence is *guilt*. Modern society delights in denying that there is guilt as a result of these relationships; or else the argument is that guilt is a feeling that must simply be unlearned.

Not so. Try as they might, those who have illicit sexual relationships will experience at least some guilt, which is often sublimated and therefore emerges in other negative emotions, such as anger, depression, or a sense of unfulfillment. Alien bonds are often accompanied by alcohol or drug abuse to deaden the pain of this guilt.

A second consequence is *promiscuity*, the tendency to seek other relationships that will only increase the frustration and guilt. People have no strong commitment to maintain faithfulness to an alien bond. Because of the inherent betrayal these alien bonds perpetuate, the person is driven to seek other relationships, looking for the satisfaction that cannot be found. Thus a cycle of immorality begins.

This explains why the first sexual relationship often will determine the direction of a person's sexual future. Young people who are promiscuous before marriage will not only have the temptation to continue that lifestyle after marriage, but they must cope with the frustration of having the image of a number of other people stamped upon their souls. This produces psychological confusion and unfulfillment.

Those who are introduced to homosexuality by an older companion will have that experience stamped so indelibly upon their souls that they may eventually have the temptation to pursue more of the same. Because the bond created was illicit, they will not find permanent fulfillment in the relationship and so will seek a whole series of sexual companions, seeking what is now impossible to find.

Each successive sexual experience superimposes itself upon the previous one, each relationship vying for allegiance. Yet with so many relationships, the human personality is fragmented, unable to cope with the sense of frustration produced by a multitude of encounters. The victim is therefore driven into more sexual relationships, seeking the fulfillment that now must of necessity elude him/her. Often the result is that he gives himself over to lust, pursuing relationships with abandon.

This explains why homosexuals (or heterosexual adulterers, for that matter), think they are locked into their particular kind of sexual behavior. Their desires are heightened by their pursuit of what they of necessity cannot find; they are convinced that they are enjoying life simply because they try to compensate for their emptiness by pursuing the perfect person they long to connect with.

With the spread of AIDS it was discovered that the average male homosexual admitted to having about 550 sexual partners, many having had thousands of relationships. Some homosexuals said that they had as many as ten or fifteen homosexual experiences in a single evening in a bath or gay bar. An average of two or three new partners a week is not excessive.

This explains why the path leading out of homosexuality is fraught with many battles and temptations. The person who has given himself to homosexuality finds it difficult to master the desires he has so often obeyed.

The Causes of Homosexuality

We must resist the tendency to think that every homosexual fits into a neat stereotype, but there is strong evidence that general patterns emerge when we try to identify the cause of homosexuality.

First, there is the family. According to Dr. George Rekers, "The fathers of homosexual sons are most often described as being aloof, hostile, and rejecting. More than four-fifths of adult male homosexuals report that their fathers were physically or psychologically absent from their homes while they were growing up."[1] These young men lacked strong, healthy male role models; consequently their own sexual identity became confused. They simply could not relate meaningfully to the opposite sex. Often a passive or absentee father accompanies an overprotective, dominant mother in the home. The boy thus identifies with his mother and assumes her sexual role. One former homosexual told me, "My mother dressed me in girls' clothes. At school the kids said, 'He must be queer.' I thought they must be right and I began to think about my identity. Soon I pursued relationships with other males."

If a mother hates men and communicates this to her son, she may make the boy vulnerable to homosexual temptations. Particularly in the absence of a man in the home, the boy might begin to shrink from the male role that he should identify with. No one can calculate the amount of damage that hostility between parents contributes to the confusion of sex roles.

Child abuse also contributes to the reversal of sex roles. If a girl was molested by her father, she may develop an aversion toward men that may drive her into lesbian-ism. To quote Rekers again, "Certain kinds of families can leave a child with unresolved emotional conflict or with feelings that tempt him to pursue a shortcut to intimacy by having sexual relations with a person of the same sex" (p. 67).

A second cause is sexual exploitation. Almost all children are at some time sexually stimulated by thinking about, or seeing, someone of the same sex. For most, it is a fleeting experience. But if those feelings are exploited, they may persist and develop into a homosexual orienta-tion. Psychologists tell us that at the age of puberty a child is particularly impressionable, and if he or she begins to focus on the same sex, homosexual desires are intensi-fied. Understandably, homosexual pornography contrib-utes to inflaming those desires and helps to solidify the direction of the victim's sexual preference.

It is difficult to obtain accurate statistics on how many people are now homosexuals because they were recruited. Roger Montgomery, who died of AIDS on November 6, 1989, was a homosexual prostitute who estimates that he had sexual encounters with between 1,000 and 1,500 dif-ferent men. He often asked his partners how they got into the homosexual lifestyle. By far the majority said that they had been recruited by a neighbor, a friend, or a relative. Usually, this was accompanied by the use of pornography. In his case, this happened when he was molested by a neighbor at the age of six.

Sexual exploitation of children and the widespread number of dysfunctional families make up the soil in which homosexuality most easily grows. Teenagers who do not have the benefit of a family that gives them a strong sense of personal identity often withdraw from pursuing normal relationships and gravitate to the same sex, where they do not feel threatened. Because they are so impres-sionable, they can focus on the same sex, and this contin-ues to lead them into homosexuality.

From within all of us comes a deep desire to be loved and understood. Those who are denied that sense of security and intimacy will be tempted to find it among those who appear to accept them. Whether homosexual or heterosexual, the child who grows up feeling unloved will tend to seek sexual intimacy with a partner, or partners, without the benefit of marriage.

Men and women struggling with a homosexual orientation are particularly driven by the need to be loved and accepted. But because they are convinced that they cannot relate to the opposite sex, they pursue same-sex relationships. That is why there can be no true freedom from homosexuality without the love and support of others. The very thing homosexuals so desperately need is what Christians have been most reluctant to give them, namely, love and acceptance (without condoning the lifestyle).

The Bible and Homosexuality

The Bible clearly teaches that homosexuality is sin, but it makes equally clear that deliverance is possible. Both of these truths must be proclaimed to our society.

In the Old Testament a number of offenses were punishable by death. Among them were adultery and homosexuality. Specifically, God says, "If there is a man who lies with a male as those who lie with a woman, both of them have committed a detestable act; they shall surely be put to death. Their bloodguiltiness is upon them (Leviticus 20:13).

In Romans 1:26–27 we read that homosexuality is against nature. "For this reason God gave them over to degrading passions; for their women exchanged the natural function for that which is unnatural, and in the same way also the men abandoned the natural function of the woman and burned in their desire toward one another, men with men committing indecent acts and receiving in their own bodies the due penalty of their error." That statement means that the homosexual is fighting against the nature of his own body. This is confirmed by Paul's use of the words *exchanged* and *abandoned.* The homosexual has abandoned what his body normally craves. Associated with this transformation are guilt and fear, which often drive the person to pursue further homosexual relationships. When Paul says, "God gave them over," he means that God delivers a person over to sin by intensifying the guilt and desire in a person's life. At this point he (or she) either will be brought to complete repentance or will be driven even more intensely by passions. Paul speaks of homosexuals burning toward one another, an apt description of homosexual passion.

Some evangelicals say that homosexuality must be accepted as an alternate sexual preference. They make a distinction between homosexual acts, which result from a conscious choice on the part of the individual, and homosexual orientation. Those who take this view believe some are born with homosexual tendencies and therefore cannot be held accountable for their "preference."

Of course there is a difference between homosexual behavior and homosexual lust, just as there is a difference between heterosexual lust and behavior, but that does not mean that homosexual desires are normal. Rekers writes: "All homosexual lust is abnormal and fights against normal sexual adjustment. Each instance of homosexual lust conditions the nervous system to an even stronger responsiveness to homosexual stimulation" (p. 24).

The Bible is clear that both homosexual acts and homosexual lusts are sinful and a perversion of God's will for men and women. It may be natural for a person to be a kleptomaniac, but that does not mean that those desires should be accepted as moral. Even homosexuals themselves admit that their desires are contrary to nature.

Dr. Armond Nicholai, chief psychiatrist of the Medical School at Harvard University and editor of the *Harvard Guide to Psychiatry*, said: "I have treated hundreds of homosexuals. None of them, deep down, thought he was normal. Simulating eating is not eating. Simulating being female is not being female. Simulating sex is not sex."[2]

Some people think that they were born homosexuals because they are not aware of any conscious step or experience that caused them to become homosexuals. But in such instances decisions were made and behavior pursued that led the individual to abandon his natural desires in favor of homosexual preferences.

But, as we shall see, that does not mean that a person has to continue to follow those desires. Ruth Barnhouse, a Christian psychotherapist, wrote: "The process of psychotherapy entails a very large element of helping the sufferer to understand that he is not a victim of something beyond himself, but that choices made in the past, however unconsciously, can be reviewed and new decisions taken."

Some people do grow up with homosexual desires because of environmental factors, usually coupled with specific experiences that made them vulnerable to the redirection of their sexual passions. But there is no evidence that anyone is born a homosexual.

Given the fact that the family is the key to developing healthy relationships, we must lament the breakdown of this institution in American life. We've heard it said that God will someday judge America because we have sinned against great light. We expect huge earthquakes or famine. But actually, America is already being judged with a punishment much more severe than those natural phenomena. The final judgment on Israel was the scattering of families (Deuteronomy 28:64).

The emotional consequences of divorce on children are much more severe than a natural disaster could ever be. It is little wonder that God's last Old Testament word to mankind regarding the coming of John the Baptist included these words: "And he will restore the hearts of the fathers to their children, and the hearts of the children to their fathers, lest I come and smite the land with a curse" (Malachi 4:6).

With the breakup of our homes and the harsh and unloving attitudes of some parents toward each other and their children, it is not surprising that we have many who feel the pangs of rejection and hurt. Nor is it surprising that some of these individuals are driven by their inner desires to sinful relationships as a shortcut to intimacy. It is no wonder that homosexuality is on the increase.

Those who live with a homosexual orientation are wounded people. They have been so deeply scarred that they are sensitive to the attitudes and feelings of others. They often disassociate themselves from Christians for fear of being rejected. Unfortunately, that also means that they may be quick to take up an offense and harbor bitterness.

For those who admit their need, we must offer support and encouragement. Who among us has never been bound by a sin that was brought on by the failures of those who have influenced us the most? Homosexuality is only one of many consequences of sin in our fallen world.

Is there a way out?

Christ the Healer

Evangelicals are divided on whether or not Christ actually changes homosexuals into heterosexuals. Because many revert to homosexuality after extensive counseling, some believe we should have a less ambitious goal. The most we can expect, they say, is to teach them to resist temptation. Once an alcoholic, always an alcoholic; once a homosexual, always a homosexual in basic orientation, they say. The goal should be to strengthen them so that they will not be involved in homosexual activity even though they still have homosexual desires.

To pursue this argument further: just as single heterosexuals must learn to curb their passions and abstain from sexual relationships, so a homosexual must learn to live in celibacy. Since all of us are required to say no to lust, it really does not matter whether our lust is homosexual or heterosexual. In either case the same biblical teaching applies: "Do not let sin reign in your mortal body that you should obey its lusts" (Romans 6:12).

Freedom from homosexual acts is important as a first step. Some will be content to be celibate in their relationships, without thinking that they need to actually see a change in the direction of their desires.

But I believe God is able to take a person beyond that to an actual redirection of his or her desires. When Paul discussed various kinds of sinners who had put their past behind them, he included homosexuals:

> Or do you not know that the unrighteous shall not inherit the kingdom of God? Do not be deceived; neither fornicators, nor idolaters, nor adulterers, nor effeminate, nor homosexuals, nor thieves, nor the covetous, nor drunkards, nor revilers, nor swindlers, shall inherit the kingdom of God. And such were some of you; but you were washed, but you were sanctified, but you were justified in name of the Lord Jesus Christ, and in the Spirit of our God. (1 Corinthians 6:9–11)

Paul affirmed that God had delivered them from their preconversion lifestyles. In the Corinthian church there were those who had put their homosexuality behind them.

Of course it is not an easy journey. The homosexual who is a believer must rejoice in God's love toward him and realize that he can grow in his faith even while he struggles. I have met those who have displayed the fruit of the Spirit even while they have regarded their condition with sorrow and contrition, unable to change. They are fellow pilgrims enroute to the heavenly city.

With care, I would like to suggest some basic processes, each of which takes time. One step may blend into another or may need to be repeated. But I believe that Christ is able to deliver individuals from both homosexual desires and actions.

1. *Come to Christ as you are.* It is quite natural (but wrong) to think that we have to become worthy in order for God to accept us. This harmful perception keeps people from coming to Christ, for it leads them to believe that He died for some sinners but not others.

Homosexuals and adulterers, along with all of us, must bask in the love of God; we all must be willing to open our lives to His grace, for He sees our deceitful hearts. God does not turn His back on those who believe in His Son.

> Just as I am, without one plea
> But that Thy blood was shed for me,
> And that Thou bidd'st me come to Thee,
> O Lamb of God, I come!
> I come!

Yes, come to God *as you are!*

2. *Be willing to let God change you.* For many the thought of changing their homosexual identity is far from their minds. Even if change came easily they would not accept it because it would disrupt their present lifestyle and relationships. For them, the best they can do is to continue to adjust to the homosexual lifestyle as best they can and enjoy it.

Others wish to change but have believed the cruel lie that change is impossible. This false notion, perpetuated by the radical homosexual movement and so favorably reported by the media, is one of the stumbling blocks for major change. As Edmund Bergler wrote in *Homosexuality: Disease or Way of Life?* "The homosexual's real enemy is . . . his ignorance of the possibility that he can be helped, plus his psychic masochism which leads him to shun treatment."[3]

When Christ asked the man, "Wilt thou be made whole?" it was not an idle question. If Christ were to heal him, he would have to accept responsibility for some radical adjustments in his lifestyle.

Thus to be free from homosexuality, one must ask: Am I willing to let God make the changes He desires?

3. *Repent of any bitterness toward God or others.* Since, as we have learned, homosexuality grows best in the context of broken relationships, it is understandable that homosexuals often have deep-seated bitterness toward others, usually members of their own family. Parents especially are the targets of such resentment because of failures on their part in nurturing their children.

As previously explained, if a father molests his daughter, she grows up with those experiences stamped upon her soul. She probably will hate men and cringe when she is touched. She may then turn to her own gender as an expression of her sexual desires and need for love and affirmation.

A son may resent his mother, hate women, and turn to men for the attention and sexual expression he now craves. Whatever the scenario, most homosexuals can point to failures within their own families that contributed to their chosen lifestyle.

All of this produces bitterness toward others and toward God. This bitterness must be released in an act of repentance and faith: "Let all bitterness and wrath and anger and clamor and slander be put away from you, along with all malice. And be kind to one another, tender-hearted, forgiving each other, just as God in Christ also has forgiven you" (Ephesians 4:31–32).

If you ask why we must be willing to repent of our anger, even though we struggle with desires we adopted because of the failures of others, think of it this way: If you were born into a family that was greatly in debt, the responsibility for payment would be passed on to you. Even though you would thus be influenced by the choices others made, you, as an heir, would be held responsible for payment.

I don't think that any one of us is truly repentant until we realize that we are held responsible for our inability to obey God. God holds us responsible even though we are by nature the children of wrath. Grace is never poured out until we come to the point of full contrition and humility.

David learned that lesson: "The sacrifices of God are a broken spirit; a broken and a contrite heart, O God, Thou wilt not despise" (Psalm 51:17). There can be no excuses, no appeals to our genes or our environment. Repentance means that we take responsibility for every attitude and every choice. The homosexual must renounce his lifestyle, just as a drunkard or idolater must renounce his.

4. *Break the power of illicit sexual experiences.* I've already emphasized that sex binds two people together, body, soul, and spirit. The person who has had sexual experiences outside of marriage has been united to someone in an alien relationship. The power of those memories must be broken, so that the obligation to repeat the behavior is erased.

That can be done through renunciation; God is able to purify our memories, or at to least break "the power of cancelled sin," to quote the words of Charles Wesley. Past sin need not have dominion over us. That is best done in the presence of a counselor or supportive friend.

5. *Find a support group.* Seldom, if ever, can a person break the power of a homosexual lifestyle without help from others. One girl, struggling with lesbianism, wrote, "Good listening ears were few and far between. I desperately needed people who would listen to me—for hours on end at times. I didn't want pat answers. They were usually much too simplistic or naive to be helpful. I needed someone who would listen with God's patience and compassion."

Most people who come out of homosexuality say that they had a confidant whom they could trust, a friend who would be there to provide encouragement and hope even in the midst of failure. Sometimes these men and women need to know that they can call on that friend at any time, day or night.

We all need fellow believers with whom we have acceptance.

6. *Understand the fact of temptation.* Many people think that God should give them deliverance in an instant without any further struggle with temptations or desires. But Alcoholics Anonymous teaches its clients to say "I am an alcoholic" even after a person has not touched a drink in ten years. This organization understands a basic principle: *We will always be tempted to repeat behavior that at one time was our master.*

A pastor who for years struggled with a secret life of homosexuality was delivered from the bondage that had ensnared him. But later he said that there were times when there was no battle at all and times when the battle was "horrendous."

He writes:

> One thing I have now is the knowledge that Satan can no longer lie to me and tell me that it is just the way I am and that I have to live with it. There have been times when the thoughts have again sought to invade my mind, but now I have a choice. I can refuse to allow them to remain. A few times I have allowed them to remain and when that happens, just a simple confession has destroyed them and again cleaned up my mind. . . . The stronghold of homosexuality has been broken but I continue to battle the thoughts.

Often believers give up too easily, believing the lie that they must continue to be homosexuals.

7. *Be prepared to believe what God says about you as a Christian.* Every homosexual has experienced some emotional deprivation that has driven him to seek sexual experiences with the same sex. He thinks that the word *homosexual* is a fundamental description of his personal identity, that it represents who he really is.

But the moment a person becomes a Christian, he receives a new identity in Christ. Through understanding the

Word of God he must come to the conclusion that God has changed the core of his identity. Rather than being in Adam as all unbelievers are, the Christian who struggles with homosexuality is now "in Christ," with all rights and privileges that accompany such a change.

The key to overcoming any sin is for us to *disbelieve* what our emotions and thoughts tell us and to *believe* what God has said about us. Only such faith can take the victory of Christ and enforce it in our lives.

Scripture memory, though not a cure-all, is essential in changing these thought patterns.

8. *Be prepared for demonic warfare.* Because Satan is involved in immoral relationships, some Bible teachers have taught that deliverance from homosexuality simply involves exorcism, namely, the casting out of a demon of homosexuality.

However, I believe that homosexuality would exist even if God would confine the devil to another planet. Our fallen nature has within itself the capacity for all kinds of sins, of which homosexuality is but one.

Of course, demonic spirits do exploit all illicit sexual experiences, hoping to hold their victim bound by repeated sinful behavior. *That is why it is impossible to be delivered from homosexuality without encountering battles with demonic forces.* I encourage you to read *The Adversary,* by Mark Bubeck.[4]

My point is simply that Satan must be confronted *along with* the inner healing of the soul that comes through the power of the Holy Spirit and the people of God.

The Walk to Freedom

Roger Montgomery, the male prostitute referred to earlier, discovered that there is is a way out of homosexuality. After his conversion he struggled with homosexuality for two years before he felt totally free, and eventually he married a woman with whom he had two children.

Unfortunately, his transformation took place after the AIDS virus had already infected his body. But before his death on November 6, 1989, he recorded a message, "The Walk To Freedom." Before I give a synopsis of the truths that helped him draw on God's resources to overcome his homosexuality, let me briefly recount his story.

Roger's struggle with homosexuality began when he was molested by an older homosexual neighbor. Though the experience was initially painful, soon he began to enjoy the encounters. His homosexual identity was strengthened by the male pornography his mother had in the home.

He thought that if he attended a Bible college, he would be able to overcome homosexuality. But he was dismissed because he continued this behavior. He began to hate and distrust God. He would actually curse God, and even told Him to get out of his life. He gave himself to Satan.

He was without a job and a home, so he turned to prostitution to support himself. This was coupled with cocaine and alcohol abuse. When his fear that he had AIDS was confirmed, he begged God to die.

In a moment of despair he heard the voice of Christ (not audibly), who offered him life instead of death. For the first time he realized that he could come to Christ just as he was, without having to change. There was no new leaf he had to turn over; he would simply come to God as he was. God did not merely offer him change, but a brand new life. At last he was converted.

Soon he had a job and a place to live. Though his struggle with homosexuality continued, the process of change began. He found a pastor and a support group that helped him through the healing process. "By then I realized," he says, "that God had taken me out of homosexuality but had not yet taken the homosexuality out of me."

The deliverance began to happen. Though he experienced much temptation, he eventually discovered that his aversion to women began to change and he became attracted to them. A few years later, he married.

"Homosexuals err when they think that homosexuality is the only sin they have in their lives," says Roger. "But homosexuality is the fruit of sin, not the root of it. There are other sins and attitudes that God has to deal with in order to be free. After I became a Christian, I would ask God when he would work on my sexual desires. But God kept working on my pride and coveteousness. But this was the root that had to be confronted before I was ready to yield to God regarding my homosexuality."

What made the transformation complete? Here are the facts of Scripture that pointed the way to his freedom. The central truth is that God has united us with Christ.

> Therefore we have been buried with Him through baptism into death, in order that as Christ was raised from the dead through the glory of the Father, so we too might walk in newness of life. For if we have become united with Him in the likeness of His death, certainly we shall be also in the likeness of His resurrection, knowing this, that our old self was crucified with Him, that our body of sin might be done away with, that we should no longer be slaves to sin. (Romans 6:4–6)

Our union with Christ is so complete that when Christ died, we died to sin. That means that God miraculously put us into Christ so that we participate in His death and resurrection. Christ died not only that we might be forgiven but that we might be free. The power of sin has been broken in our lives. Now sin need not have dominion over us.

When homosexuality reigns in a person's life, he cannot break its power. But Christ broke sin's power. Heterosexuality is not something to be worked for; it is to be received through Christ. Christ does not expect homosexuals to change themselves. He only expects them to believe the Word of God. If we think God cannot change us, we make Him a liar.

When we are saved, God does something new in our lives. We become a new person. But now we need to learn how to walk in a power that has already been given to us. Sin is no longer our master; it has been nullified. Now that sin's power has been broken, we must choose our master. Will we obey God, or will we continue to pursue our homosexual lifestyle? The choice is ours.

In faith we should consider ourselves dead to sin; and then we must present our bodies to God (Romans 6:11, 13). This is not positive thinking, but resting on true historical facts that we can depend upon. It enables us to see ourselves from a new perspective. As we consider the old self to be dead, the new man within will grow and enable us to walk in the power of the Holy Spirit.

How shall we handle temptation? We can *find* our *heterosexual selves* almost immediately, but there will be *temptations.* We can become sensitive to the conviction of the Holy Spirit. We will know that we should put that magazine down or turn the television set off. We must obey those promptings.

Once again we must choose to believe what God has said about us. We must also trust the Holy Spirit who indwells us to bring the fruit of righteousness into our lives. This is not the product of self-will. If a farmer wants to see a tree bear fruit, branches must be pruned. God does this in our lives as an act of His love for us. It hurts, but the benefits are worth it. The Holy Spirit then produces the purity we seek. Then we can begin to walk in heterosexual wholeness.

We cannot overcome these things by willpower. When we fall into sin, there is no use trying to beat ourselves, but rather we should agree with God about our sins (1 John 1:9). That means that we can come to God and pour out all of our sins, without excuses or fear of rejection. There is *nothing* that we cannot reveal or talk to Him about. As many times as we fall, we must come to Him to receive forgiveness. If we fall ten times a day, we must come to Him to confess our sin ten times. Failure should never discourage us.

The legal basis on which God can forgive us is the death of Christ. Continual cleansing comes only with continual confession. There is no sin that is too great for God; He can cleanse us from all sins.

How can I get rid of immoral thoughts? Christian activities will not bring cleansing of the mind. The transformation is done by God as we present ourselves to Him. There is a metamorphosis, a change that is supernatural. We must continually see the Lord in the Word of God. We cannot behold Him if we neglect the Scriptures. This looking upon Christ means that the change will take place.

Roger says, "Christ is the only true heterosexual. If the truth were known, all men are sexual deviates. It is just a matter of degree. Christ is the only perfect man."

Christ left the church on earth so that all sinners would have a place of healing. Roger says that homosexuals should let believers help them to overcome homosexuality. They need accountability, someone in whom they can confide.

The God of Roger Montgomery is the God who is well qualified to deliver His people from their sins.

And He is the God of all who believe.

Organizations That Help
Promote Sexual Healing

Homosexual Anonymous
Fellowship Services (H.A.F.S.)
P.O. Box 7881
Reading, PA 19603
  (nationwide referral service for H.A. support groups)

Exodus International
P.O. Box 2121
San Rafael, CA 94912
  (referrals for Exodus agencies *only*)

Overcomers: A Christian Ministry
5445 N. Clark Street
Chicago, IL 60640
  (nationwide ministry; referrals for individuals,
    parents, spouses)

Spatula Ministry
P.O. Box 444
La Habra, CA 90631
  (ministry referrals for parents and family members)

Notes

1. *Growing Up Straight* (Chicago: Moody, 1982), 68.
2. Quoted in "Are Gay Rights Rights? A Report on Homosexuality and the Law," by Roger Magnuson (Minneapolis, Minn.: The Berean League), 21.
3. New York: Collier, 1962, 277.
4. Chicago: Moody, 1975.

CHAPTER 7

How Can Marital Conflict Help Me Grow?

H e's so oppressive sometimes I think I'm in a concentration camp, and yet he expects to have sex with me! It's like a guard at Auschwitz wanting to have sex with a woman prisoner and expecting her to enjoy it!"

With all her might this woman tried to be the good Christian wife she was taught to be. For years she lived with a demanding, hot-tempered husband, trusting God to change him. But her submission seemed to have little effect on his attitude and actions. Her question was one that many married partners ask: When is enough, enough?

Although the male species at times may seem to be the most difficult to live with, many women make impossible demands on their husbands, thereby blocking all possible avenues to harmony and mutual respect. "Everything I do is wrong," a man told me. "I receive no affirmation, she is constantly undermining my authority, and she hates sex. Some day I would like to catch her in a good mood!"

No one plans to have an unhappy marriage. Yet marital conflict exists everywhere. Even those who appear to have a fulfilling marriage often live with anger, mistrust, and disharmony. Many wives say they have no one to talk to, they are neglected, and they despair of finding help even after years of struggle. Husbands in turn complain that they are weary of being nagged, weary of being compared to Robert Redford, and exasperated when their wives accuse them of being sexual animals. We would be startled if we knew the amount of verbal and even physical abuse that goes on in homes. Yes, even Christian homes. When the curtains are drawn, only God knows what happens behind the closed doors. And for the most part, it's not a pretty picture. If marriage is to mirror the relationship between Christ and the Church then many (most?) marriages are a tragic failure. Surely God intended something better.

Marital conflict is as old as the human race. But our "fallenness" is having a greater impact on this generation. Look no farther than your daily newspaper and you will see the symptoms of marital discord.

Causes of Conflict

Why all this conflict? Five factors contribute to discord in marriage: the fractured family, unrealistic expectations, sexual immorality, an inadequate understanding of conflict, and the belief that change is impossible.

THE FRACTURED FAMILY

Ever since Cain killed Abel, broken homes have existed, with abuse and hatred spilling into the lives of the children. But thirty years ago here in the United States, this breakdown began to permeate all areas of society—rich and poor, black and white, educated and uneducated. Divorce, which always carried the stigma of failure, now is a popular and sophisticated escape from an unhappy marriage. The social restraints that encouraged people to work out their problems have disappeared.

Children caught in the midst of rejection and power plays have grown up without the warm and secure relationships they crave. They have lacked role models and have been unable to cope with the hostility they have felt toward a father, a mother, or both.

With the proliferation of pornography, sexual moles-
tation and abuse have escalated. We are told that one in
four girls will be sexually abused by a father, a relative, or
a trusted neighbor.[1] Sexual aberrations of various kinds are
common.

Unless these emotional wounds are resolved, rejected
children enter marriage with a huge bundle of emotional
deficiencies and oppressive feelings—feelings bound to
spill over into the most intimate of all relationships. Those
who have their roots in a dysfunctional family often are
unable to give or receive love. Far from curing such deficiencies, marriage actually brings such problems to light.

I'm not suggesting that those who have had a deprived childhood have no chance for marital harmony, but
they may have to work harder to achieve fulfillment in their
marriage relationship. Thankfully, God helps people minimize, if not totally negate, the power of a destructive past.

UNREALISTIC EXPECTATIONS

Incredibly, some people actually expect marriage to
make them happy! Of course, marriage does bring happiness, but only to those who have already found meaning in
their personal relationship with God. In other words, those
who are unhappy single will likely be unhappy married.

Some women think that God created their husbands
for the sole purpose of making them (the wives) happy.
When that doesn't happen, they chip away at their husbands, trying to shape the kind of person who makes them
happy. Unfortunately, their best efforts often backfire, and
the door to progress slams shut.

I've known engaged couples who were clearly mis-
matched but thought that after marriage their problems
would vanish. Too late they discovered that their differences were increased tenfold. Like a magnifying glass,
marriage took manageable irritations and enlarged them.

As a path to happiness marriage is overrated. Two imperfect people cannot come together without mutual dis-

appointments and struggles. If that is so for those who are emotionally well-adjusted, think of the implications for the young man or woman who marries simply to get away from home, or for a couple with only marginal emotional and spiritual stability. "If love is blind," someone observed, "marriage is an eye opener!" Those who think marriage is a shortcut to happiness will wish they had taken the main road.

Marriage cannot do what only God can; that is, bring inner contentment. Marriage is at best two imperfect people, united in body, soul, and spirit in a growing relationship that is to reflect the unity of the Godhead. Every marriage has its stresses, which can be used either to unite the couple or to divide them.

SEXUAL IMMORALITY

Moral impurity sows seeds that eventually can bear bitter fruit. Many couples who do not know how to neutralize the detrimental effects of premarital sex significantly reduce their chances for a happy marriage. Some couples say that they enjoyed sex before marriage, but their relationship went sour immediately after saying "I do." Before marriage they could enjoy sex without resolving deeper issues in their relationship. Real matters of communication and honest differences were buried under artificial intimacy. Marriage forced them to deal with these pressure points. Add to this the mistrust that developed because of their past relationship, and all the ingredients for conflict are present.

Of course there is cleansing and forgiveness for past sexual relationships. But unless the past has been fully faced in the presence of God, a couple that has had premarital relationships will be living with unfinished business.

In chapter five, I discussed the effects of promiscuity and abuse. One must honestly confront his or her sexual past for trust and mutual respect to thrive in marriage. Thankfully, Christ can "break the power of canceled sin," to quote the words of Charles Wesley.

AN INADEQUATE
UNDERSTANDING OF CONFLICT

Many of us were taught to believe that if we "married the right one" we would be free of all marital conflict and would live out our days in uninterrupted harmony and fulfillment.

That is a myth, of course, since God often uses conflict as a means of spiritual growth. How best can God teach us to love except to put us into a relationship where that love is severely tested? How can He teach us patience and the inner resources of joy, except in a marriage where there will be disappointment and misunderstanding? How can He teach us forgiveness except to put us in a relationship where we will have to extend forgiveness as well as receive it?

A Britisher, when told that there were many divorces in America based on incompatibility, replied, "I thought that incompatibility is the purpose of marriage!" After all, when two self-willed people live together in the most intimate of all relationships, what else can we expect except incompatibility?

Obviously I'm not suggesting that an unmarried person should seek an incompatible partner. But once the marriage has taken place, couples should see their conflicts as part of God's training program, teaching them the deeper lessons of God's power even in the midst of their difficulties and failures.

Those who avoid conflict often live with a superficial harmony that never confronts the real issues in the relationship.

THE BELIEF THAT CHANGE IS IMPOSSIBLE

Our disappointments with ourselves and others often leave us with the depressing conclusion that difficulties within a marriage cannot be resolved. Apart from a few cosmetic adjustments, we don't believe that God is able to make a radical change in a mate's attitude and disposition.

But if both the husband and the wife are Christians, they have powerful resources to bring about the love and respect needed for a satisfying relationship. If we say that God cannot bring about such changes, we call His integrity into question. Did He not promise that the Holy Spirit would reproduce the love and power of Christ within us? If the Son shall make us free, are we not "free indeed" (John 8:36)?

God is able to transform those who come from a dysfunctional family, who have committed immorality, or who are filled with anger—He is able to bring about a transformation that is both deep and lasting. There is a price, of course, and that is the willingness to be honest enough to face oneself in the presence of God. More of that later.

As a pastor, I have seen couples struggle through years of conflict; yet they gradually deepened their relationship and love. Against incredible odds, some have persevered to see harmony, respect, and fulfillment.

Unfortunately, I've seen many of the other kind as well. I have watched relationships disintegrate, partners persist in adultery or abuse, and children become scarred by divorce, resentment, and rejection. I've seen marriages, believed to be made in heaven, unravel here on earth.

The difference between success or failure doesn't depend on the depth of the problems, for some of the most hopeless marriages have been turned around for the better. The difference is that one couple opened their lives to the power of Christ and another did not. Some couples faced the pain of their personal failures whereas others would not pay the price that honesty required.

Logic alone does not help us achieve harmony in marriage. A man who believes he can manage his marriage with reason and hard-headed negotiations will probably be judged as a failure by his wife and children. Most issues in marriage are primarily matters of feeling and not of rational considerations. That's why genuine change always involves pain. Happily married couples have learned to respect one another's feelings, even though they cannot understand the whys and the wherefores.

There is hope for unhappy marriages, but it does take the cooperation of both partners. Even those who live with a difficult mate, or a mate who feels that he or she has cooperated and the other partner is at fault, can find hope through scriptural principles. And yes, even when the fight to save the marriage appears hopeless, the Bible gives hope and help.

Principles for Resolving Conflict

Here are seven principles that will help resolve the roots of many conflicts that, from time to time, are found in most marriages. Any desperate couple can apply them for themselves.

SELF-EXAMINATION

Although it takes two to generate strife, blame for marital friction is usually not an equal fifty-fifty. One partner usually bears greater responsibility for the failure of the marriage. But seldom is one partner wholly responsible.

Our tendency to see other peoples' faults more clearly than our own is so deeply rooted in our nature that Jesus used this humorous illustration to get his point across. He said, "And why do you look at the speck that is in your brother's eye, but do not notice the log that is in your own eye? Or how can you say to your brother, 'Let me take the speck out of your eye,' and behold, the log is in your own eye?" (Matthew 7:3–4). The irony is obvious: Visualize a person trying to take out a splinter from his brother's eye when he has a block of wood in his own!

Put a pencil in a glass of water and it will appear crooked. In the same way, our perception of others and especially our perception of ourselves are always skewed. To see ourselves for what we are is so painful that many of us build elaborate defenses for our own insecurities and shortcomings. Anger, pride, and selfishness cause us to see everyone else (particularity our marriage partner) as "bent."

Recall that when King David committed adultery, Nathan the prophet came to him with a story about a rich man who stole a lamb from his poor neighbor. Incredibly, David said that the rich man should be put to death. Not once did he realize that this was a picture of himself taking Bathsheba from another man when he (David) already had many wives. David showed more compassion for a lamb than he did for Uriah, one of his most trusted and mighty soldiers! He could see someone else's faults with 20/20 vision but was blind toward his own.

Ask each partner in a troubled marriage to list the faults of the other and they will do so quickly (often requesting more paper). Ask them to list the strengths of the other and there will be long pauses, as they grudgingly list one or two items.

Denial is the most common barrier to facing ourselves in the presence of God. There are those who simply will not admit that they are abusive, unreasonable, controlling, or angry. Often through years of rationalization, some partners have insulated themselves from seeing themselves as they truly are.

Some men hate women and use the marriage relationship to vent their anger. Such a man may be wholly unconscious of this rage and in counseling will appeal to the biblical command "Wives, submit yourselves to your husbands" to justify his actions. His hostility is proved by the constant need to control his wife. One day she can spend money and he congratulates her; the next day he flies into a rage, throwing her purchases on the floor. This unpredictability is his way of exerting control; he makes sure his wife is always off balance. In his need for control, he will hold his wife to an impossible standard to ensure that she will fail. This then gives him the right to be critical, angry, and even abusive.

Such a man lives in a cocoon called denial. Years of rationalization have clouded his perception. Nothing can change his perspective, for it is necessary for him to always be right. His wife may also have taken flight from reality. She may be deceived by his occasional "nice" behavior. She will think, "After all, he does love me," and so she convinces herself that next time it will be different. Often she will play the role of the martyr, overnurturing, overcaring, believing that she is called to be the one to rescue her wayward husband. Usually, such a woman will take full blame for her husband's ill treatment and think that he will improve if only she does better next time. All the while she does not face up to the deep unresolved needs that prevent him from giving and receiving love.

Of course, many variations exist to the above scenario. The wife may seek to control her husband through manipulation, bad moods, and threats. She may deliberately set up barriers in their relationship so that when her husband becomes angry she can blame all their disputes on him. Because she cannot receive his love she unconsciously makes it impossible for her husband to love her. If she fears intimacy, she will make sure that her marriage is in a constant state of conflict so that she can deny sex to her husband.

In these kinds of marriages, there is a fundamental unwillingness to confront the deep roots of anger, rejection, and insecurity. Let's admit that at some time all of us have been self-deceived. We actually think we are being reasonable when we are not, we believe we are thoughtful when we are manipulative, and we believe we are loving when all that we care about is our own needs.

Some partners have lived with denial for so long that they cannot benefit from any spiritual counsel. All correction is dismissed with hostile rationalizations. Sometimes only a traumatic event will awaken them so that they can see themselves with a degree of objectivity.

A second defense mechanism is *projection,* the tendency to attribute to others the faults that we ourselves have. For example, a person who is angry may accuse his mate of anger; the controlling person may accuse his mate of wanting to exercise control. The very traits we attribute to others may be the ones that dominate our lives.

That is why two people who are alike often have so much friction in marriage. They cannot tolerate what they see in their mates simply because they cannot bear to see themselves. One husband reluctantly came to me after his wife complained that he had verbally and physically abused her. He in turn accused her of being angry and controlling simply because she complained about his abuse! Any kind of resistance was seen as a threat to his authority.

Because we are sinful creatures who love darkness rather than light, we seek to escape the light of the truth. We come to a confrontation armed with our rationalizations, our perceptions, and our most believable lies. Only honesty before God can penetrate the walls that insulate us from needed change.

True marital harmony requires us to evaluate honestly who we really are and how we react to those around us. Often that requires the presence of a counselor, who can help each mate see himself/herself as the other perceives him/her.

But counselors can only go so far. God must break into our souls so that we are able to see ourselves as God sees us apart from Christ. Marital harmony can only begin when we pray with David, "Search me, O God, and know my heart; try me and know my anxious thoughts; and see if there be any hurtful way in me, and lead me in the everlasting way" (Psalm 139:23–24).

One warning, though: Some people who are open and honest about themselves still will exhibit little positive change. They persuade themselves that honesty itself is their ticket to acceptance and the forgiveness of their mate. Honesty becomes a substitute for true repentance and change. "I'm having an affair, but at least I'm honest about it," is an extreme example of the kind of subtle justification that honesty sometimes produces.

Honesty, then, can become a permanent excuse for obstinate behavior. One woman who experienced some childhood abuse used this as an excuse for not having intercourse with her husband. She felt justified in refusing him because of the trauma of her youth. Rather than using her past as an opportunity for growth, it became a convenient peg that held all the excuses she used to not respond in sexual intimacy.

Of course, an honest self-examination is only the first step in resolving marital conflict. Honesty should become a doorway to healing. The open sores of the past should become fading scars, proving that healing has taken place. The purpose of such an examination is not to find a reason why we are in conflict but to discover how we can leave the past behind and become emotionally whole.

What if one partner refuses to allow God to do a thorough spiritual examination? Let that not be an excuse for the other to hold back in such openness toward God. Sometimes when one partner changes the other does also, though there are no guarantees.

One partner can grow spiritually in a marriage even if the other does not. Indeed, some of the most measured growth in our lives happens when we are enclosed with God, unable to depend on any human being for our spiritual nourishment. Our disappointment in our mate often "crowds us to Christ," to borrow a phrase from L. E. Maxwell. To those who think that changes on their part will not bring about changes in their mate, I respond, "Give God a chance . . . and even if there are no observable results, think of how we honor God when we show love to those who do not return it."

Resolving marital conflict begins with honest self-examination so that forgiveness can take place. Through such honesty God wounds us that He might heal us. He breaks us that He might put us back together.

GROWTH ASSIGNMENT:
1. In the presence of God confess your shortcomings and failures: anger, selfishness, moral impurity, a critical spirit.
2. Ask God to give you the appropriate time to confess these failures to your mate.
3. Give your partner to God without any thought of changing him/her through your own efforts.

THE CLARIFICATION OF ROLES

Contemporary society insists that the roles of men and women are interchangeable. Such a move toward equality, it is argued, will minimize the abuse that women have had to endure because of male domination. Some Christians, unduly caught up by the spirit of the age, have actually attempted to interpret the Bible to make it agree with these secular attitudes.

But there are important reasons that God gave men and women different roles in the marriage relationship. To quote Paul, "But as the church is subject to Christ, so also the wives ought to be to their husbands in everything" (Ephesians 5:24). This text, and others like it, are balanced by the responsibilities given to husbands: "Husbands, love your wives, just as Christ also loved the church and gave Himself up for her" (v. 25).

The responsibility of the husband is headship; that is, giving leadership to his wife and children. He should not do this, however, without consulting his wife and serving her and his children. He is responsible for all decisions affecting the direction and care of the home. To exercise leadership does not imply that he must always get his own way. It does mean that he should take the good of the family into account in the decisions that are made.

The role of the wife is submission to her husband's leadership. The Greek word is *hupotasso,* which literally means "to get under the burden of" someone. A wife should get under the burden of her husband, to make choices that affirm her husband as the leader. She understands his goals and aspirations and commits herself to seeing them fulfilled. In a word, *hupotasso* means submission.

Interestingly, nowhere in the New Testament is a man instructed to force his wife to submit to him. The implication seems to be that if the husband treats his wife with love and respect, her submission will grow out of their relationship. Many decisions should be made together, without an appeal to the lines of authority. Just as elders should not "lord it over" those who are to submit to their authority, so the husband should not "lord it over" his wife.

To dilute these biblical roles is to invite more conflict, not less. Recently I heard of one woman who has divorced twice and is now dating another man, looking for "equality in the relationship." Equality, however, will be more likely to destroy a relationship than to build it.

Unless a couple has talked through their understanding of roles in the relationship, disagreements will escalate until the relationship will break under its own weight. Without clarifying expectations, there is little hope of harmony.

What constitutes unwarranted control by a husband in a marriage relationship? Some women do not mind living with a man who has high expectations and gives detailed instructions about virtually everything. Other women resent such intrusion, feeling they are being treated like a child. They insist that they want space and enjoy measured independence. They understand that the husband has the final say in all important decisions in the marriage, but they expect to make the decisions about clothing, food, and the myriad details that pertain to the children. Where that invisible line should be drawn must be decided by every couple.

Is the wife ever justified in choosing to "not submit"? Does there come a point when the demands of her husband are so unreasonable that she should stand her ground? The question of how a wife should respond in such situations will be discussed at the end of this chapter.

What is God's prescription for marital harmony? *The wife must submit to the husband's authority, and the husband should love her with the gentleness of Christ.* Though he bears the ultimate responsibility in the home, he should also submit to her by putting his emotional and spiritual shoulder under her burden and helping her in every way he can.

Think of the harmony that would exist if each partner sincerely tried to lighten the load of his/her spouse. The fight for control would dissipate if each sought the good of the other. Many couples go into marriage without having defined what their expectations are. The man may think that his wife will accept the role that his mother had; the wife may have a perspective based on what she observed in her home, or possibly an ideal drawn from her own imagination.

How often I have seen the wife take the role of the husband because of his own negligence. This appears to work, but in the long run it destroys the marriage by rewarding his weakness.

Blessed is the couple that can discuss openly their expectations of what each is obligated to do within the marriage relationship. Unless these roles are clarified, conflict is bound to exist.

GROWTH ASSIGNMENT:
1. With the help of a commentary, study Ephesians 5:22–33. Honestly discuss the expectations you have of one another.
2. Talk through the different perspectives you have regarding the roles each should play. Talk about your family backgrounds, trying to understand who shaped your views of the marriage relationship.

MEANINGFUL COMMUNICATION

Every couple that lives with marital discord has a problem with communication. That word *communication* refers to the ability to share both verbally and nonverbally so that the message is accepted and understood. Many couples hear only words that trigger various emotional reactions, but they do not understand what is really being said. Wives often complain, "He simply does not listen to what I am saying . . . he doesn't understand the depth of my feelings and hurt." The husband may be shocked when he comes home to discover that she has run away; he didn't realize that she was near the breaking point.

A strong love relationship is not possible without communication. When couples lock one another out of their hearts they communicate only superficially, failing to understand or appreciate what the other is trying to say. They are miles apart in the same house. Soon each wears a "Keep Out" sign over the heart.

Hear the heart cry of one woman: "I feel like a thing. Is my conversation so unintelligible that I am not worth talking to? I could be a post in the ground for all he bothers to communicate with me. All of a sudden I feel like I don't even know my husband. It's as if he has been hiding from me for years."

What makes a person (usually the man) unwilling to reveal who he really is? What makes it nigh impossible to share his innermost struggles and thoughts with his wife?

The first reason is shame, the sense of humiliation that comes when the truth is exposed. After all, none of us likes to have our inmost thoughts revealed. And if some private acts have accompanied those private thoughts, exposure becomes even more dreadful.

Along with shame is fear of rejection. "If my wife really knew me, she could never love me," one man put it simply. But most women would prefer to know the truth from their husbands than to wonder what really goes on beneath that cold, impersonal exterior. It is difficult to love someone whose life is partially hidden, someone who resembles "The Great Stone Face."

A third reason is the realization that changes must take place once the truth is out. A man has a secret romance, or a woman spends more money than her husband knows about—these and a dozen other similar issues must be confronted when communication begins once again.

Some people put all their communication on "autopilot," bypassing their emotions. Talking in depth about their feelings and fears simply is too painful. This is particularly true of those who have suffered abuse years earlier.

Communication, meaningful communication, requires *trust*. Imagine the surprise one wife received when she came home unexpectedly to find her husband dressed in women's clothes, including undergarments! As the truth began to unfold, she discovered that he had been a transvestite for many years without her knowing it. Understandably, it will take a long time before this woman trusts her husband again. No matter how deep their communication, there will be the suspicion that another surprise may be around the corner.

Immorality, a secret life of pornography, and involvement in shady business practices—these and other such revelations damage the trust that is necessary for spiritual unity. Trust can return, but it must be earned through honesty and accountability.

The second requirement for meaningful communication is *respect*. Every time a partner loses his/her temper and uses words to hurt, something in the relationship is lost that will have to be regained. Most marriages have pressure points that are scrupulously avoided because they become the focal point of so much anger that eventually the issues are bypassed and left unresolved. Sex, money, the relatives, children—these matters are simply ignored until they rupture in an outburst of anger and deep hostility.

Unfortunately, many couples attempt to communicate at the wrong time and in the wrong way. Most arguments take place because important issues are discussed under pressure rather than at a time that is calm, free from the immediate context of the disagreement. Couples who do not take time to talk about their differences before they erupt will soon tolerate destructive communication as a part of the daily routine.

Communication can only take place when each mate attempts to honestly look at the issues from the other's point of view. We cannot understand what the other person is feeling unless we are willing to "walk a mile in our mate's sandals."

GROWTH ASSIGNMENT:
1. Prove the power of words by choosing to speak only positive words to your mate for one week.
2. Choose to talk about one of the "untouchables," those issues usually avoided because they spark heated disagreement.
3. Ask your partner to define his/her need. Then seek to meet it.

MUTUAL UNDERSTANDING

Many partners enter marriage totally unaware of the basic differences that exist between a man and a woman. Peter admonished husbands, "Live with your wives in an understanding way, as with a weaker vessel, since she is a woman; and grant her honor as a fellow heir of the grace of life, so that your prayers may not be hindered" (1 Peter 3:7).

What should husbands know about women? They must understand that most women look to their husbands for affirmation, both for their accomplishments and their physical beauty. They desire to know that they are number one in their husband's priorities. Wives want physical affection, not just as a prelude to sex but as a constant affirmation of mutual love and attraction. They want their husbands to understand the burdens they bear and for them to spend time in communication. Usually sensitive, wives often are deeply hurt by half-truths, irresponsibility, and passive leadership.

Similarly, women must try to understand the burdens and aspirations of their husbands. They must also understand the powerful sexual temptations their husbands face. One woman lashed out in judgmental anger when she found a pornographic magazine in her husband's desk. That only drove her husband deeper into the world of pornography, determined to hide his magazines more carefully!

If she had approached him with love, trying to understand the power of this temptation, he might have been willing to express his inner struggles. Such communication might have been an important first step to victory over his secret vice. And if the habit continued, he would have been more open to seeking professional help. Unfortunately, a judgmental, self-righteous rebuke broke the communication.

One day a man called me on the phone, revealing that he had been involved in immorality but could not possibly ask his wife for forgiveness because she had always warned him, "If you ever commit adultery, I will never have you back!" Apparently she thought that her warning would be a deterrent, but actually it only drove the man away from his wife at the very moment he needed her the most.

Peter has some important words for Christian wives who are married to unsaved husbands. After he describes Christ's obedience to the cross, he continues, "In the same way, you wives, be submissive to your own husbands so that even if any of them are disobedient to the word, they may be won without a word by the behavior of their wives, as they observe your chaste and respectful behavior" (1 Peter 3:1–2).

When a woman's husband does not obey the Word, the wife is to exhibit a meek spirit of submission. This may lead him to Christ. (Peter probably is thinking about an unsaved man, though the principle would apply to a carnal Christian husband too.)

Peter understands a basic trait of the male human nature, namely, that men are usually not influenced spiritually by the verbal witness of their wives. Call it male macho, or pride, the fact is men are seldom converted when their wives assume the role of evangelist.

One woman said that when Billy Graham was on television she pushed the portable TV in front of her husband "to give him a good dose of Billy Graham." Another woman's attempt to convert her husband backfired when she painted "REPENT" on the bottom of his beer can. His friends were over to watch a football game, and her husband was hardly impressed when they saw the not so subtle message! He is a believer today and can laugh about it now, but at the time he was not amused.

Peter does not promise that the husband will be saved as a result of the submission of the wife. Certainly, her Christlike spirit will be more likely to bring a change of heart, but it is not guaranteed. Many stories can be told of how wives through their gracious submission have won their husbands to Christ.

Beyond the basic differences between a man and a woman, the two bring distinct personal differences to marriage. Tragically, some of the most minor differences of perspective can cloud a marriage if one or both partners is unwilling to give the other "space," the opportunity to be different even at the personal inconvenience of the other. To live with mutual understanding is to live with the knowledge that marital conflicts are inevitable. Fortunately, these conflicts can be minimized as each partner seeks to understand the other, making allowance for differences of lifestyle and attitude. Partners who seek understanding do not feel the necessity of squeezing their partner into their own mold.

In his book *What Wives Wish Their Husbands Knew About Women,*[2] James Dobson describes many of the differences between males and females. Blessed are those who are continually growing in mutual understanding and acceptance of their mates.

GROWTH ASSIGNMENT:
1. Make a covenant to read 1 Corinthians 13 each day until you can quote it from memory.
2. Trust the Holy Spirit to reproduce those qualities in your life.

FORGIVENESS

All happily married people have learned to forgive. In our fallen world, each of us has been disappointed in our mate. The person who cannot forgive is the person who will not be able to truly love. One measure of the strength of a relationship is the length of time that passes before a couple will reconcile to one another after an argument. I can only pity the married person who cannot utter those simple words, "I'm sorry, will you forgive me?"

When there has been a breach of trust, certain steps must be taken to effect reconciliation. Here are two basic principles to bring emotional unity to a ruptured relationship.

First, *reconciliation can only take place when the offending party asks for forgiveness.* While it is possible for a marriage to survive when one partner "forgives" without being asked, eventually the relationship will become strained. Christ said, "Be on your guard! If your brother sins, rebuke him; and if he repents, forgive him" (Luke 17:3). If the offender is unwilling to humbly admit failure and express a desire to be forgiven, the other mate cannot pretend that life is to continue as if nothing happened. Barriers can only be broken by a spirit of reconciliation.

One woman told me that her husband did not ask her for forgiveness when his adulterous relationship was discovered. He acted as if this infraction was not as serious as his wife made it out to be. By minimizing the affair, he showed an unwillingness to come to terms with his destructive behavior. As a result, it was difficult for his wife to put the incident behind her, pretending that this was but a minor bump along the marital road.

What should a person do whose spouse is unwilling to face the reality of his or her disobedience? There is no one correct answer to this question. Obviously, a qualified pastor or counselor must become involved to bring the offender to accountability. To allow such behavior to continue will only perpetuate, not solve, the problems in the relationship.

Second, *once forgiveness has been granted, it cannot be revoked.* Paul wrote, "And be kind to one another, tender-hearted, forgiving each other, just as God in Christ also has forgiven you" (Ephesians 4:32). How does God forgive us? He takes our sins and throws them into the depths of the sea and remembers them no more (Micah 7:19; Jeremiah 31:34).

One man told me how he humbly confessed his infidelity to his wife. Although she initially said that she would forgive him, she refused to forget. Years later whenever they had a disagreement she would remind him of the past. "For years she rubbed my nose in the dirt," he told me. Though this couple lived together sexually, in their spirits they were never reconciled. That is not forgiveness!

Counselors disagree about whether an adulterous partner should even confess infidelity to the other. Since in some cases the relationship seems irrevocably damaged, the argument is that the offender should simply deal with it on his or her own, or with the help of a counselor. However, I believe it is much better that a partner find out about the relationship directly rather than from a secondary source. Because news of infidelity eventually surfaces, it is generally best that the offender break the news to the other partner. One woman I know was exceedingly angry when she discovered that everyone knew about her husband's affair except she herself! Also, think of the damage done if in withholding this information, one's partner contracts a sexually transmitted disease as a result of the liaison.

"Is the repentance genuine?" Often those partners who are expected to forgive a flagrant moral infraction ask that question. We must remember that those who practice abuse, immorality, or other aberrations may be sincere in their repentance, but that *a change in behavior takes much more than one act of renunciation.* These sins are like alcoholism; they can be sworn off, only to resurface. Many a sincere wife has erred in thinking that her husband will now be different because he tearfully begged for forgiveness. There is a bonding to abuse, immorality, and dishonesty. No matter how sincere the repentance, tomorrow is another day.

Repentance must therefore include several safeguards that are built into the relationship. First, there is accountability. Where there has been a flagrant violation, a third party (a pastor, a counselor, or group) must be brought into the situation to ensure that the future will be different from the past. In many instances a couple simply cannot handle these matters on their own.

Second, steps must be taken to aid in spiritual and emotional growth. There must be evidence that this partner (or both) is willing to actively pursue those things that produce harmony rather than betrayal.

Third, because of the special bonding to sin, the partners must always be on guard lest the same cycle of behavior reappear.

Partners must ask God for wisdom in steering a course between resisting reconciliation and the opposite extreme of naively accepting an intention to do better as a valid reason to believe that the past behavior will never resurface.

Forgiveness and reconciliation must become a part of every marriage and particularly those where trust has been badly damaged. Only when barriers crumble can a marriage be restored.

GROWTH ASSIGNMENT:
1. Ponder the parable of Christ in Matthew 18:21–35.
2. Apply this teaching on forgiveness to your own marriage. How can this teaching change your marriage?

SATANIC CONFLICT

Many marriages will never be harmonious until the couple understands the role of demonic spirits in building barriers to marriage fulfillment.

Of course, there would be conflict even if Satan did not exist, because our sinful nature has the seeds of all the sins that mitigate against harmony and love. But Satan takes those sins and strengthens their power so that the ruts become deeper, the barriers become higher, and the differences appear more hopeless.

One man lived with a woman who would frequently undergo a change in personality, often in a few moments of time. They would be out shopping in relative harmony, then on the way home she would be, in his words, "transformed into a different person." She would erupt suddenly in anger, false accusations, and threats. He quickly realized that she was oppressed by an evil spirit and so began fervent prayer to rebuke this influence. He quietly enlisted the prayer support of many Christian friends, and as a result she has started on the path to emotional stability.

Sometimes when sin enters into a marriage relationship, the effects can bring a whole new set of conflicts. One woman had an affair with a man whom she had known sexually before her marriage. Her husband was crushed when he discovered the relationship, and he began a long battle of spiritual warfare. He became so angry he eventually was oppressed by evil spirits, and he began to abuse his wife. Because she had repented of the relationship, she had authority to address the spirits directly to protect her own life. Without her husband's knowledge she enlisted other believers to pray and experienced significant results. After she had entered a room to pray and rebuke the spirits, she often returned to find her husband subdued, wondering why he had acted as he did.

In answer to prayer, God protected the children from knowing what was happening in the home. In her letter she said, "The battle appears to be over. My husband is one of the most Christlike men I know. We pray together and he is leading our children spiritually."

I do not tell these stories to imply that all women should live with an abusive husband. Nor do I think that with the proper amount and intensity of intercession all abusive husbands will inevitably be transformed into eventempered men of God. And not all abuse derives from the presence of evil spirits. But when spirit-influence exists, *we must remember that evil spirits do all that they can to drive wedges between a man and his wife.* A marriage with deep problems seldom finds resolution without overcoming direct satanic conflict.

Satan is persistent. He wants to wear us down, to bring us to the point of exhaustion so that we will simply give up and walk out of a situation. (For a good primer on spiritual warfare, read *The Adversary* by Mark Bubeck.[3])

GROWTH ASSIGNMENT:
1. Think of as many sins as you can that give Satan a foothold in your marriage.
2. With a commentary, study James 4:1–11 and respond to whatever God shows you through this passage.
3. Pray against Satan's attempt to destroy your marriage.

A TIME FOR SEPARATION

The Bible is silent about what should be done if a husband treats his wife cruelly, either with physical abuse or by asking her to compromise her convictions. Nor does it give specific instructions on how to handle adultery, alcoholism, or child abuse.

The Bible also says that children should obey their parents, and no exceptions are listed. But I must ask: Is a child violating the intention of this command if he tells his teacher that he and his siblings are being abused at home—has he violated Scripture if he was expressly told by his father to keep the abuse of the children a family secret? I think not.

I believe there are times when a person's loyalty to God supersedes one's loyalty to God-ordained social structures. It is unlikely that either Peter or Paul would have expected no exceptions to wives' submission to husbands. If there are times when we do not expect a child to obey his parents (as when asked to remain quite about abuse), there may be times when a wife is no longer expected to obey an oppressive husband. And even if a wife can endure the abuse, what should she do when children are involved? How vividly I recall a woman saying to me, "I could continue to live with him even if he kills me, but I must leave because of what he is doing to my children."

Should a woman who is commanded by her husband to commit adultery (say, for the sake of pleasing a superior) do it in the name of submission? Should she participate in occult rituals just because her husband demands it? Should she keep her husband's abuse of the children a secret just to protect him? Similarly, must a husband live with an adulterous or abusive wife? These are the forces that are tearing marriages apart, leaving little hope for lasting restoration.

In the Bible there are instances where God's people have disobeyed some human authority and have been approved by God for doing so. The midwives of Egypt, Daniel, and the apostles all chose to obey God rather than men. Grudem writes that these passages mean we should "obey except when it would be a sin to obey."[4]

Paul the apostle was realistic enough to know that there are times when couples may have to separate, even if this act does not involve the next step of divorce. "But to the married I give instructions, not I, but the Lord, that the wife should not leave her husband (but if she does leave, let her remain unmarried, or else be reconciled to her husband), and that the husband should not send the wife away" (1 Corinthians 7:10–11).

Each partner should evaluate his/her situation with the help of a godly counselor. There must be a balance, I believe, between the suffering that all of us should be willing to endure for the sake of our partner (and Christ) and the eventual line crossed when the marriage simply is beyond meaningful redemption.

A legal separation differs from a divorce in that the intent is to have legal protection without needing to finally end the marriage. This also allows the possibility of reconciliation (as Paul taught). If it is necessary to take the second step of divorce for the purposes of custody, or a similarly strong reason, the Christian partner should understand that this does not necessarily mean that the marriage bond is broken in the sight of God. Such a divorce may protect both partners' rights, but it does not necessarily give them the right to remarry.

Many of those of us who believe there are "grounds for divorce" admit that the Bible gives evidence for only two, namely, sexual infidelity and desertion. In such cases, remarriage would then be justified. But the Bible gives no other such grounds. Therefore, if a divorce takes place on the grounds of alcoholism or abuse, for example, the believer who has obtained that divorce has no right to remarry. Such a divorce has not broken the original marriage bond. The divorce is simply the means used to take advantage of civil laws.

I know a woman who obtained a divorce because her husband was abusing her children. She realized, however, that this divorce did not break the marriage covenant in the eyes of God. Thus she has chosen to live as a single woman, free only to remarry in the event of her husband's death or his own remarriage (in which case he would break the marriage bond through adultery).

Other pastors/scholars may have different ways to resolve these difficult problems. Each mate must struggle to his/her own conclusion believed to be consistent with the Bible and conscience.

Too many couples look to divorce as a convenient escape. In doing so, they circumvent the suffering that God would use in their lives as a means of spiritual refinement. If separation and divorce become necessary, they always are a *tragic* necessity.

GROWTH ASSIGNMENT:
1. Give yourself and your marriage to God and trust Him to do a miracle so that you will be obedient to His will, and His will alone.
2. Be willing to suffer in your marriage for the sake of Christ to whatever extent God may desire. (Read 1 Peter once each day for one week.)

Keeping the Peace

I conclude with this reminder: *It is possible for one partner to live a godly, dedicated life even if the other is contentious.* Consider the forbearance of the famous English evangelist John Wesley, the founder of the Methodist church. One day he met a young woman, Grace, who appeared to be everything he could ever want in a wife. She was spiritually minded and had a heart for ministry. She even enjoyed horseback riding, and by all accounts she would have made a wonderful companion for John.

However, John's older brother, Charles, objected to the marriage on the grounds that marriage might interfere with the revival movement. Eventually, John accepted his brother's advice and ended the relationship.

Later in life John met a widow named Molly, whom he decided to marry without consulting Charles. But she turned out to be a shrew, an ill-tempered nagger. She was, by all accounts, a miserable woman.

Molly would sell some of John's favorite books when he was on a speaking tour. Sometimes while he was preaching she would shout from the audience, contradicting what he was saying. One day while preaching he said, "I have been accused of every sin in the catalogue except getting drunk." From the back of the auditorium his wife yelled, "Why, John Wesley, you know you were drunk just last week!"

John didn't stop preaching, but he replied, "Thank God, that completes the catalogue!" and went on with his sermon as though nothing had happened.

On one occasion Molly became so angry with him that she grabbed him by the hair and dragged him around the room. (He weighed only 120 pounds, she considerably more.) Wesley reacted calmly, never laying a hand on her to avenge himself. Here was an example of someone in whom the grace of God had done a mighty work!

John learned that conflicts are opportunities for personal growth. Blessed are those who use their conflicts as an opportunity to grow together rather than be torn apart. The rewards for suffering—even marital suffering—are given to those who persevere.

Notes

1. This figure, commonly reported in the news media, may be low. In a recent study, John Powell at Michigan State University reported that 38 percent of women interviewed had been sexually abused by an adult or family member by age eighteen (as reported in Dan Allender, *The Wounded Heart* [Colorado Springs: NavPress, 1990], back cover).

2. Tyndale House, 1977.

3. Chicago: Moody, 1975.

4. William Grudem, *Recovering Biblical Manhood and Womanhood* (Wheaton, Ill.: Crossway, 1991), 195.

PART THREE:

Confronting Eternity

CHAPTER 8

What Can We Know About Death and Dying?

During the last few months of her struggle with cancer, Jacquelyn Helton kept a diary. Her thoughts and feelings would become a legacy for her husband, Tom, and her eighteen-month-old daughter, Jennifer.

In her diary she wonders what death would be like. What clothes should she wear for burial? She thinks of her daughter. *Who will love her? Put her to sleep?* In her writings she tells Jennifer that when it hurts she should remember that her mother would have cared. Then she thinks of her husband and the needs he will have after she is gone.

Finally she cries out, "What is the matter with you, God? My family is not a bunch of Boy Scouts who can figure all these things out for themselves—you're some kind of idiot to pull something like this!"[1]

Denial, anger, fear, depression, and helpless resignation—all of these feelings erupt in the souls of those who face death. No matter that death is common to the human race; each person must face this ultimate humiliation individually. Friends and family can walk only as far as the curtain; the dying one must disappear behind the veil alone.

Tom Howard says that when we face death we are like a hen before a cobra, incapable of doing anything at

210 MATTERS OF LIFE AND DEATH

all in the presence of the very thing that seems to call for the most drastic and decisive action. "There is, in fact, nothing we can do," he writes. "Say what we will, dance how we will, we will soon enough be a heap of ruined feathers and bones, indistinguishable from the rest of the ruins that lie about. It will not appear to matter in the slightest whether we met the enemy with equanimity, shrieks, or a trumped-up gaiety, *there we will be.*"

Yet, some people believe that the almost universal fear of death is unfounded. When actor Michael Landon, of TV's "Little House on the Prairie" and "Bonanza," lay on his deathbed, he confided to friends that he saw a "bright white light" that eased his fears and made him look forward to what awaited him on the other side. He died calmly, anticipating what he called "quite an experience."

Hollywood is obsessed with the theme of death. In 1991 at least a dozen movies dealt with the hereafter. Reincarnation, altered states of consciousness, and glad reunions in a metaphysical place such as heaven are popular themes at the box office. Larry Gordon, chief executive of Largo Entertainment, says, "People are looking for something that makes them feel good. We all want to believe that death isn't so bad."[2]

Hellfire has been supplanted by blissful feelings about a hereafter where everyone ends happily reunited. There is no judgment, no careful review of one's life. Death has mystery but is not to be feared. Given this positive assessment of the Great Beyond we should not be surprised that some people want to hasten their arrival at this destination.

This chapter is written to answer several questions about death and dying:

- Is suicide a reasonable option in the face of prolonged emotional or physical suffering?
- How should we interpret the paranormal experiences that seem to confirm life after death?

- How can a Christian receive comfort in view of his/her impending death?
- What role should grief play in dealing with death?
- What can we learn about how to die from Christ's example?

Above all, this is a chapter of hope, a scriptural discussion of how a Christian can witness the faithfulness of God while facing death.

Before we investigate this message of comfort, however, we must expose some false contemporary ideas about the hereafter.

The Do-It-Yourself Approach

The suffering that often precedes death is so excruciating that many people hope to leapfrog over the process of dying to get to death itself. Books explaining how to commit suicide are selling briskly; a growing number of people want to "control their own destinies" rather than be at the mercy of modern medicine.

The best-selling book *Final Exit,* by Derek Humphry, is a death manual loaded with charts of lethal dosages for eighteen prescription drugs and sleeping tablets. It includes information about asphyxiation and auto exhaust. Practical tips on how to make sure no one will suspect that you are taking your life are also included. The author's intention is to help individuals commit suicide without fear of botching the attempt.

One argument for assisting in death is that medical technology has artificially prolonged life. Modern medicine sometimes *has* gone too far in keeping people alive long after any hope of recovery is past. However, the idea that we all have the right to "die with dignity" is based on a false premise. If taken seriously by society in general, it would lead to disastrous consequences.

Strictly speaking, no one "dies with dignity." Ever since sin entered the world and brought death with it, death has always been the final humiliation, the one unalterable fact that confirms our mortality and reduces our bodies (yes, even beautiful ones) to ashes.

Jesus Himself hung on a cross naked, exposed to the gawkers that walked by outside the walls of Jerusalem. Thankfully, none of us will likely have to endure such shameful public torture, but death is never pretty. Death is the ultimate affirmation that we are but dust and to dust we shall return.

Those who choose suicide (for whatever reason) should remember that physical death is not the end, but a doorway to an eternal existence. Sadly, some who find the pain of dying intolerable will awaken in a realm that is even more terrible, more frightening, more hopeless than the dying experienced on earth. For such, suicide is a self-inflicted wound that leads to irreparable alienation from God.

Others, who have become Christians before their early death, shall see heaven. Nonetheless, their suicide remains an act of rebellion against God's will and purpose; it is the final confession of failure.

Suicide is never a sensible option. Those who contemplate this escape should seek immediate help from a pastor, counselor, or friend.

Evidence for Life After Death

There is a growing belief that a moment after we die we will be conscious, experiencing a new dimension of reality. Many are convinced that the immortality of the soul is now confirmed by paranormal experiences that can have no other explanation but that the soul survives the death of the body. Let's carefully weigh the evidence.

THE OCCULT

Some descriptions of life after death come from the occultic realm. In his book *The Other Side,* Bishop Pike described in detail how he made contact with his son who had committed suicide. Using a spirit medium, the bishop had what he believed to be several extensive conversations with the boy.

"I failed the test, I can't face you, can't face life," Pike's son reportedly said. "I'm confused . . . I am not in purgatory, but something like Hell, here . . . yet nobody blames me here."[3] Jesus, the boy said, was an example but not a Savior.

A surprise was the alleged appearance in spirit of a friend, Paul Tillich, a well known German-American theologian who had died several months before. Pike was caught off guard when he discerned his deceased friend's German accent passing through the lips of the medium.

How should this evidence be interpreted? Liberal theologian that he was, Pike did not realize that demons impersonate the dead to create the illusion that the living can communicate with the dead. These spirits have astonishing knowledge of the dead person's life since they carefully observe individuals while they are living. Through the power of deception they can mimic a deceased person's voice, personality, and even appearance. The King James Version of the Bible actually translates the word *medium* as those who have "familiar spirits" (Leviticus 19:31; 20:6, 27; Deuteronomy 18:11), suggesting the familiarity some demons have with individuals.

Although Samuel was apparently brought back from the dead, a more careful reading of the text shows that this miracle was done by God and not the witch at Endor (1 Samuel 28:3–25). This explains the medium's terror (v. 12).

Be assured that no one has ever talked to your dead uncle, cousin, or grandmother. There are, however, spirits that impersonate the dead. Their trickery is compounded because they may actually talk about love, the value of religion, or make favorable references to Christ.

This ability of demonic spirits to masquerade as the personality of the dead helps us understand haunted houses. While I was staying in a hotel near Calgary, a local newspaper carried a story saying that there were at least two ghosts in the beautiful building. One of the employees showed us a marble staircase where one of these ghosts lived (verified by the testimony of employees). A new bride had stumbled down the stairs years ago and hit her head, resulting in her death. We were told that her spirit now lives on the stairs, appearing with some regularity.

How do we explain this phenomenon? When a person who is inhabited by evil spirits dies, these demons need to relocate. Often they choose to stay in the place where the death took place (this seems particularly true in the case of violent deaths such as murder or suicide). They will take the name and characteristics of the deceased person and make occasional appearances under these pretenses. Such entities are evil spirits who often pose as "friendly ghosts."

To try to contact the dead is to invite fellowship with hosts of darkness pretending to be helpful angels of light. Isaiah the prophet warned the people that to consult a medium was to turn one's back on God (Isaiah 8:19–20).

REINCARNATION

Another form of occultism that purports to give information about life after death is reincarnationism. This doctrine teaches that we just keep being recycled; death is nothing more than a transition from one body to another. Thus Shirley MacLaine claims we can eliminate the fear of death by proclaiming that it does not exist. Through contacts in the spirit world, she has discovered that in a previous existence she was a princess in Atlantis, an Inca in Peru, and even was a child raised by elephants. In some previous existences she was male, in others female.

A woman I met on a plane told me that as a child she had detailed knowledge of a house in Vermont that she had never visited. Later, as an adult, the accuracy of her visions was confirmed; she discovered that she had lived there in the eighteenth century. I pointed out that there is no such thing as a transmigration of souls, but there is a transmigration of demons. She was getting knowledge about an eighteenth century family from evil spirits.

"But," she protested, "I have nothing to do with evil spirits; I communicate only with good ones!"

"How do you tell the difference between good spirits and evil ones?" I asked.

"I communicate only with those spirits that come to me clothed in light."

I reminded her of 2 Corinthians 11:13–14, "For such men are false apostles, deceitful workers, disguising themselves as apostles of Christ. And no wonder, for even Satan disguises himself as an angel of light." Yes, light indeed!

Her experiences and similar ones do not prove reincarnation, but rather confirm that people of all ages can become the victims of demonic influence. There is evidence that even children sometimes inherit the demonically induced traits of their parents or ancestors. This would explain why some children, a few months old, have reportedly babbled blasphemies and obscenities that they could never have learned personally in their short life.

Occultism, of whatever variety, is not a reliable source of information regarding what happens after death. It proves only the existence of a spirit world, a world of deception and dark intelligence. God considers all forms of occultism an abomination (see the strong condemnations in Leviticus 19:31; Deuteronomy 18:9–12; Isaiah 8:19–20; 1 Corinthians 10:14–22).

NEAR-DEATH EXPERIENCES

A second source of information regarding life after death comes from so-called near-death experiences. In *Life After Life* (Mocking Bird), Raymond Moody recorded the interviews of many who were near death but were successfully resuscitated. Their stories, for the most part, had many similar elements: the patient would hear himself being pronounced dead; he would be out of his body, watching the doctors work over his corpse. While in this state, he would meet relatives or friends who had died and then encounter a "being of light." When he knows that he must return to his body, he does so reluctantly because the experience of love and peace has engulfed him.

Melvin Morse, in his book *Closer to the Light*, recounts the stories of children who have had near-death experiences. Their stories are again remarkably similar, and in almost all instances very positive. Typical is the account of a sixteen-year-old boy who was rushed to the hospital with a severe kidney problem. While in the admitting room, he slumped over in his chair. A nurse searched for his pulse but found none. Thankfully, he was eventually resuscitated. Later he told of a supernatural experience:

> I reached a certain point in the tunnel where lights suddenly began flashing all around me. They made me certain that I was in some kind of tunnel, and the way I moved past them, I knew I was going hundreds of miles an hour.
>
> At this point I also noticed that there was somebody with me. He was about seven feet tall and wore a long white gown with a simple belt tied at the waist. His hair was golden, and although he didn't say anything, I wasn't afraid because I could feel him radiating peace and love.
>
> No, he wasn't the Christ, but I knew that he was sent from Christ. It was probably one of his angels or someone else sent to transport me to Heaven.[4]

These near-death experiences are positive and inviting. Other research, however, indicates that many have dark and foreboding experiences. In *The Edge of Death*, by Philip J. Swihart, and *Beyond Death's Door*, by Maurice Rawlings, there are accounts of those who tell terrifying stories of the life beyond. Some have seen a lake of fire or abysmal darkness along with tormented persons, all of whom are awaiting judgment. These reports, the authors contend, are more accurate because they were gained through interviews almost immediately after near-death and resuscitation. These dark experiences apparently are often lost to the memory after a short period of time.

What do these experiences prove? Apparently, they do confirm that at death the soul separates from the body. A few patients not only looked back and saw doctors hover around their body, but could see what was happening in other places in the hospital. This, it seems, is impossible unless the soul had actually left the body and could review earth from a different perspective.

But let us remember that these experiences may or may not reflect the true conditions of life beyond death. For that we need a more reliable guide. Christians believe that near-death experiences must be carefully evaluated to see whether they conform to the biblical picture of the hereafter. Some experiences may provide a glimpse of the other side; others may be misleading.

We have reason to believe that a person may see Christ in the twilight zone between life and death. Before Stephen was stoned God gave him a glimpse into heaven. He said, "Behold I see the heavens opened up and the Son of man standing at the right hand of God" (Acts 7:56). Though Stephen was not physically ill (the stones had not yet begun to fly), he was given this special revelation of the spirit world. Here was positive encouragement that heaven was waiting to receive him.

If Stephen saw our Lord, other believers might also have such a vision. Paul the apostle himself had a vision in which he was caught up to the third heaven (2 Corinthians 12:3–5). But let us remember that Satan would want to give the same positive experience to unbelievers. The Great Deceiver wants people to think a relationship with Jesus Christ cannot affect the beauty and bliss that awaits everyone.

We know that at least some positive near-death experiences are demonic because they sharply contradict the teaching of the Bible. First, some who encounter death say that everyone will have an equally blissful welcome into the life beyond. Second, we are told that there is no judgment, no rigorous examination of a person's life. Several of the people explicitly mention that the "being" they met gives everyone an unconditional welcome.

One woman reported that when she crossed the line between life and death she met Christ, who explained that all the religions of the world were paths to the same destination. There was a Buddhist path, a Hindu path, a Muslim path, and of course a Christian path. But like spokes in a wheel, all of them led to the central hub of heaven. In other words, everyone will be saved. This, as always, has been Satan's most believable lie.

Personally, I am much more concerned about what I will experience *after* death than what I will experience when I am *near* death. It's not the transition but the destination that really counts. Thus, to find out what really lies on the other side, we must go to a more reliable map, a more certain authority than people who go only to the threshold of the life beyond.

We will do much better if we trust someone who actually was dead, not someone who was just near death. Christ was dead, so dead that His body became cold and was put into a tomb. Three days later He was raised from the dead with a glorified body. To John, this risen Christ said, "Do not be afraid; I am the first and the last, and the living One; and I was dead, and behold, I am alive forevermore, and I have the keys of death and Hades" (Revelation 1:17b–18).

The Bible on Life After Death

We now turn from the limitations of human experience to the clear teaching of the Bible. Yes, there is life after death. And no, it is not a pleasant experience for everyone.

Death originated when Adam and Eve rebelled against the direct command of God. Our first parents were free to eat from any tree of the garden, "but from the tree of the knowledge of good and evil you shall not eat, for in the day that you eat from it you shall surely die" (Genesis 2:17).

Death is proof that God judges sin. On that fateful day in Eden, Adam and Eve died *spiritually* in that they were separated from God and tried to hide from Him. They also began to die *physically*, as their bodies began the journey to the grave. And if Adam and Eve had not been redeemed by God, they would have died *eternally*, which is the third form of death. From disobedience in Eden, death in all of its forms began its trek throughout the world.

But a blessing is concealed behind the terror of death. When God provided the clothes of animals for Adam and Eve, He was signaling His intention to redeem at least a part of the human race. The Redeemer would crush the head of the serpent and the apparent advantage Satan had would only be temporary.

SHEOL AND HELL

In the Old Testament the Hebrew word Sheol referred to the place of the dead. The KJV translates it "the grave" thirty-one times, "hell" thirty times, and "the pit" three times.

Scholars disagree about whether it refers to the place of the unbelieving dead or a place where all men went at death. The problem is that both good men (such as Jacob) and bad men (such as Korah and Dathan) go there. This led the early church to believe that there were two compartments in Sheol, one for the righteous and the other for the wicked.

Others believe that Sheol simply means the grave, and thus refers only to the destination of the body. The destiny of the soul is found by appealing to other passages of Scripture that speak of the afterlife. Although in the Old Testament the fate of the wicked and righteous is not always clearly distinguished, some passages do contrast the separate destinies of believers and unbelievers. (See Psalms 49:14–15; 9:17; 16:10; 31:17; 55:15; Job 24:19; Daniel 12:2.)

If the door to the afterlife is open but a crack in the Old Testament, it swings wide open in the New. Here we have detailed descriptions of both the righteous and the wicked after death. The contrast is between everlasting bliss and everlasting damnation.

Jesus told the story of a rich man who died and whose soul was taken to hades; meanwhile a beggar named Lazarus who had lain at the rich man's gate also died and was carried into Abraham's bosom (apparently another term for heaven or paradise). Christ's description of the hereafter is revealing:

> And in Hades he lifted up his eyes, being in torment, and saw Abraham far away, and Lazarus in his bosom. And he cried out and said, "Father Abraham, have mercy on me, and send Lazarus, that he may dip the tip of his finger in water and cool off my tongue; for I am in agony in this flame."
>
> But Abraham said, "Child, remember that during your life you received good things, and likewise Lazarus bad things; but now he is being comforted here, and you are in agony. And besides all this, between us and you there is a great chasm fixed, in order that those who wish to come over from here to you may not be able, and that none may cross over from there to us." (Luke 16:23–26)

Notice that both men were fully conscious immediately after death. Memory, speaking, pain, and bliss—all of these were a part of their experience. Some interpreters teach the doctrine of "soul sleep," that is, that the soul is unconscious at death and "sleeps" until the day of resurrection. But this story, along with other passages of Scripture, contradicts that theory.

Paul was so anxious to see Christ that he preferred death to life. "We are of good courage, I say, and prefer rather to be absent from the body and to be at home with the Lord" (2 Corinthians 5:8). He knew that death meant instant transport of his soul to the presence of God in heaven. Christ assured the thief on the cross that they would meet in paradise that very day (Luke 23:43).

NO EXIT

In addition, the two men's eternal destinies were irrevocably fixed. "Between us and you there is a great chasm fixed, in order that those who wish to come over from here to you may not be able, and that none may cross over from there to us." At death our destination can never be changed.

Christ's account also reveals that godless man faces isolation and final judgment. The rich man was not yet in hell, but hades. Even now as I write this chapter on my computer, this man is still in hades awaiting final judgment in hell. Those who have not come under the protection of Christ's sacrifice must bear the full weight of their sin alone.

Hades is not purgatory. The doctrine of purgatory is not found in the Bible but was accepted as a tradition in medieval times because of a faulty doctrine of salvation. The belief was that nobody (or almost nobody) was righteous enough to enter into heaven at death, thus there must be a place where men and women are purged from their sins to prepare them for heavenly bliss. Purgatory, the theory went, may last for millions of years (depending on the level of righteousness one has attained), but eventually it would come to an end.

Although purgatory does not exist, hades does and it has no exit; eventually it will be thrown into the lake of fire. As Dante wrote, "Abandon all hope ye who enter here!" (The final section of this chapter, "Assurance of Heaven," tells how to avoid this terrible fate.)

Death, then, has two faces: to the unbeliever it is the doorway to eternal damnation. But for those who have made their peace with God, death is a blessing; it is a means of redemption, a doorway into a blissful eternity. Paul included death among the possessions of the Christian, "For all things belong to you, whether Paul or Apollos or Cephas or the world or life or death or things present or things to come; all things belong to you, and you belong to Christ; and Christ belongs to God" (1 Corinthians 3:21–23).

Every human person is in the process of becoming a noble being; noble beyond imagination. Or else, alas, a vile being, evil beyond redemption, writes C. S. Lewis. He exhorts us "to remember that the dullest and most uninteresting person you talk to may one day be a creature which, if you saw it now, you would be strongly tempted to worship, or else a horror and a corruption such as you now meet, if at all, only in a nightmare. There are no *ordinary* people. . . . It is immortals who we joke with, work with, marry, snub and exploit—immortal horrors or everlasting splendors."[5]

Thus the race stands divided between those who die under the protection of Christ and those who will stand before God on the strength of their own flawed performance.

Facing the Final Moments

For the Christian, death is God's servant used to transport His people from earth to heaven. Christ died that He "might deliver those who through fear of death were subject to slavery all of their lives" (Hebrews 2:15).

Little wonder Paul wrote, "O death, where is your victory? O death, where is your sting?" (1 Corinthians 15:55). A bee can sting a man only once. Although the insect can still frighten us when the stinger is gone, if we know the truth we need have no fear. Because Christ removed death's sting, it can only threaten; it cannot make good on its threats.

When facing death, we can find comfort in hope, peace—and even *good* grief. We need only see that final earthly event as God does. The New Testament uses several figures of speech to help us understand what death truly means for those who know God and His Son, Jesus Christ.

DEATH AS DEPARTURE

First, death is a departure. On the Mount of Transfiguration Moses and Elijah appeared with Christ and "were speaking of His departure which He was about to accomplish in Jerusalem" (Luke 9:31). In Greek the word *departure* is *exodus*, the name of the second book of the Old Testament that gives the details regarding the exit of the children of Israel from Egypt.

Just as Moses led his people out of slavery, so now Christ passed through the iron gates of death so that He can safely conduct us from earth to heaven.

There was nothing fearful about taking the journey from Egypt to Canaan; the people simply had to follow Moses the servant of God. Neither is it fearful for us to make our exodus, for we are following our leader who has gone on ahead. When the curtain parts, we shall find Him waiting on the other side.

A little girl was asked whether she feared walking through the cemetery. She replied, "No, I'm not afraid, for my home is on the other side!"

DEATH AS SLEEP

Second, death is likened to sleep. When Christ entered the home of the ruler of the synagogue, He comforted the crowd by saying that the man's daughter was not dead but sleeping (Luke 8:52). Then as Christ began His trip to Bethany He said to the disciples, "Our friend Lazarus has fallen asleep; but I go, that I may awaken him out of sleep" (John 11:11).

Paul used the same figure of speech when he taught that some believers would not see death but would be caught up to meet Christ. "Behold, I tell you a mystery; we shall not all sleep, but we shall all be changed" (1 Corinthians 15:51). Only the body sleeps; the soul does not.

Sleep is used as a figure of death because it is a means of rejuvenation. We look forward to sleep when we feel exhausted and our work is done. Furthermore, we do not fear falling asleep for we have the assurance that we shall awaken in the morning. Yes, we shall awaken and be more alive than we ever have been!

"Blessed are the dead who die in the Lord from now on . . . that they may rest from their labors, for their deeds follow with them" (Revelation 14:13). Rest at last!

A COLLAPSING TENT

Paul spoke of death as the dismantling of a tent. "For we know that if the earthly tent which is our house is torn down, we have a building from God, a house not made with hands, eternal in the heavens" (2 Corinthians 5:1).

Our present body is like a tent where our spirit dwells; it is a temporary structure. Tents deteriorate in the face of changing weather and storms. A tattered tent is a sign that we will soon have to move. Death takes us from the tent to the palace; it is changing our address from earth to heaven.

To the terrified disciples Christ said, "Let not your heart be troubled; believe in God, believe also in Me. In My Father's house are many dwelling places; if it were not so, I would have told you; for I go to prepare a place for you. And if I go and prepare a place for you, I will come again, and receive you to Myself; that where I am, there you may be also" (John 14:1–3).

A tent reminds us that we are only pilgrims here on earth, en route to our final home. Someone has said that we should not drive in our stakes too deeply for we are leaving in the morning!

DEATH AS A SAILING SHIP

Finally, Paul speaks of death as the sailing of a ship. He wrote, "But I am hard-pressed from both directions, having the desire to depart and to be with Christ, for that is very much better" (Philippians 1:23). That word *depart* was used for the loosing of an anchor. A. T. Robertson translates it, "To weigh anchor and put out to sea."

Thanks to Christ, Paul was ready to embark on this special journey that would take him to his heavenly destination. Christ had already successfully navigated to the other side and was waiting with a host of Paul's friends. Of course, he had some friends on this side too; that's why he added, "Yet to remain on in the flesh is more necessary for your sake" (v. 24).

Paul's bags were packed, he was ready to go. But for now the Captain said, "Wait!" A few years later Paul was closer to leaving earth's shore. Again he spoke of death as his departure: "For I am already being poured out as a drink offering, and the time of my departure has come" (2 Timothy 4:6). The signal for him to push off was imminent. He said "good-bye," but only for the time being. He would not return to Timothy, but Timothy would soon cross over and they would meet again.

John Drummond tells the story of a sea captain who was asked to visit a dying man in a hospital. When the captain reached the sick man's room he noticed decorated flags of different colors surrounding his bed. As they talked the captain learned that both of them had actually served on the same ship many years earlier.

"What do these flags mean?" the captain wondered.

"Have you forgotten the symbols?" the dying man asked.

Then he continued, "These flags mean that the ship is ready to sail and is awaiting orders."

Our flags must always be flying for we know neither the day nor the hour of our departure. Some are given more notice than others, but all must go when the Celestial Clock strikes.

But will we have grace to face our exit victoriously? I have not had to face my own imminent death, nor have there been any recent deaths in our immediate family. I can't predict how I might react if I were told that I had a terminal disease.

I, for one, would like to have dying grace long before I need it! But the famous English preacher Charles Haddon Spurgeon says that death is the last enemy to be destroyed and we should leave him to the last. He adds,

> Brother, you do not want dying grace till dying moments. What would be the good of dying grace while you are yet alive? A boat will only be needful when you reach a river. Ask for living grace, and glorify Christ thereby, and then you shall have dying grace when the dying time comes.
>
> Your enemy is going to be destroyed but not today. . . . Leave the final shock of arms till the last adversary advances, and meanwhile hold your place in the conflict. God will in due time help you to overcome your last enemy, but meanwhile see to it that you overcome the world, the flesh and the devil.[6]

Some believers who thought they could not face death discovered they had the strength to die gracefully when their time came. The same God who guides us on earth will escort us all the way to heaven. "With Thy counsel Thou wilt guide me, and afterward receive me to glory" (Psalm 73:24).

GOOD GRIEF

Dying grace does not mean that we will be free from sorrow, whether at our own impending death or the death of someone we love. Some Christians have mistakenly thought that grief demonstrates a lack of faith. Thus they have felt it necessary to maintain strength rather than deal honestly with a painful loss.

Good grief is grief that enables us to make the transition to a new phase of existence. The widow must learn to live alone; the parents must bear the loneliness brought on by the death of a child. Grief that deals honestly with the pain is a part of the healing process. Christ wept at the tomb of Lazarus and agonized with "loud crying and tears" in Gethsemane at His own impending death (Hebrews 5:7).

Some Christians have thought that there should be no sorrow at funerals; only rejoicing should be expected. How contrary this is to the teaching of the Bible! Dozens of passages in the Old and New Testament tell how the saints mourned. When Stephen, the first Christian martyr, was stoned we read, "And some devout men buried Stephen, and made loud lamentation over him" (Acts 8:2).

Let those of us who wish to comfort the sorrowing remember that words can have a hollow ring for those who are overwhelmed with grief. Let us by our presence "weep with those who weep" (Romans 12:15). We must say we care much louder with our actions than with our words.

As Christians we live with the tension between what is already ours and the "not yet" of our experience. Paul said believers should look forward to Christ's return "that you may not grieve, as do the rest who have no hope" (1 Thessalonians 4:13). Grief was expected, but it is different from the grief of the world. There is a difference between tears of hope and tears of hopelessness.

A Lesson in How to Die

What attitude should a Christian have toward death? Cancer, accidents, and a hundred different diseases lurk about waiting for an opportunity to devour us. Death awaits us, as the concrete floor awaits the falling light bulb.

Christ is our best example of how to face the final hour that will come to us all. He died so that we could die triumphantly. Through death Christ "rendered powerless him who had the power of death, that is, the devil; and might deliver those who through fear of death were subject to slavery all their lives" (Hebrews 2:14b–15).

When we understand the reality of the life beyond we will never have to say of a believer "he has departed." Rather, he has arrived! Heaven is the Christian's final destination. Thanks to Christ we can be free from the fear of death. We can understand how to face death as we notice how Jesus faced death.

DYING WITH THE RIGHT ATTITUDE

First, He died with the right attitude. Christ died with a mixture of grief and joy. In Gethsemane He declared, "My soul is deeply grieved to the point of death; remain here and keep watch with Me" (Matthew 26:38). The disciples failed him, so alone He pleaded with His Father, "My Father, if this cannot pass away unless I drink it, Thy will be done" (v. 42).

He agonized as He contemplated becoming identified with the sins of the world. He would soon become legally guilty of adultery, theft, and murder. As the sin bearer, He knew that His personal holiness would come in contact with the defilement of sin. He was sorrowful unto death as He wrestled with the trauma that awaited Him.

But there was hope too. His impending death was a doorway leading back to the Father; it was the path to victory. Moments before He went to Gethsemane, He said, "And now, glorify Thou Me together with Thyself, Father, with the glory which I had with Thee before the world was" (John 17:5). We read elsewhere that He endured the cross "for the joy set before Him . . . despising the shame, and has sat down at the right hand of the throne of God" (Hebrews 12:2). For the short term there was pain; but long term, there was glory and joy.

We should not feel guilty about facing death with apprehension, for Christ Himself experienced emotional agony the night before the horror of the cross. Yet, with the fear came comfort; joy and sorrow existed in the same heart. Death was, after all, the Father's will for Christ, and for us all.

A daughter said of her godly father who died of cancer, "In his closing days, Dad spent more time in heaven than he did on earth." If we can look beyond the immediate heartache to the eventual glory, there is joy. The exit is grievous; the entrance is joyful.

DYING AT THE RIGHT TIME

Second, He died at the right time. The night of His betrayal Christ chose to eat the Passover with His disciples. "Now before the Feast of the Passover, Jesus knowing that His hour had come that He should depart out of this world to the Father, having loved His own who were in the world, He loved them to the end" (John 13:1).

This was the hour into which was compacted the agony of Gethsemane, the betrayal of Judas, and the excruciating death of the cross. Interestingly, three times before this we read that His hour had not come (John 2:4; 7:30; 8:20). Until "the hour" arrived, His enemies were powerless against Him.

What sustained Christ? We read, "Jesus, knowing that the Father had given all things into His hands, and that He had come forth from God, and was going back to God, rose from supper, and laid aside His garments; and taking a towel, He girded Himself about" (John 13:3–4).

He had come to earth at an hour appointed by God, and now He was returning on schedule. There was not the slightest possibility that Christ would die sooner than God planned.

Christ died during Passover, just as God intended, a striking reminder that He was indeed "the lamb of God who takes away the sin of the world" (John 1:29). He was only thirty-three, young by today's standards and those of ancient Middle Eastern culture. Why not fifty-three so that He could have many more years of healing the sick and preaching the love of God to the multitudes?

But though He died young, His work was finished. *You and I don't have to live a long life to do all that God has planned for us to do.* Some of God's best servants have died at an early age—early from our standpoint, on time from God's.

The death of a child seems like mockery since God is taking a life before he/she has the joy of accomplishment. As Jung says, "It is like putting a period before the end of the sentence."

But a child's short life can fulfill the will of God. Though we do not understand it, that little one has also "finished the work God has given him/her to do."

Jim Elliot, who himself was killed at a young age while doing missionary work among the Indians of Ecuador, said, "God is peopling Heaven, why should He limit Himself to old people?"

Why, indeed! If the Almighty wants to reach down and take one of His little lambs, or if He wishes to take a servant in the prime of life, He has that right. We think it cruel only because we cannot see behind the dark curtain.

Our death is just as meticulously planned as the death of Christ. Evil men, disease, or accident cannot come to us as long as God has work for us to do. We die according to God's timetable and not ours.

Christ's own death was brought about by the vicious actions of evildoers. The apostle Peter explains the crime as part of God's good plan: "For truly in this city there were gathered together against Thy holy servant Jesus, whom Thou didst anoint, both Herod and Pontius Pilate, along with the Gentiles and the peoples of Israel, to do whatever Thy hand and Thy purpose predestined to occur" (Acts

4:27–28). They could not act until God's clock struck. The "hour" had to come.

If the violent and unjust death of Christ was part of God's meticulous plan, we can be confident that our own death is equally a part of God's design. No believer who walks with God dies until his work is finished, until his "hour" has come.

DYING THE RIGHT WAY

He died in the right way. There are many ways to die: disease, accidents, murder, to name a few. The circumstances differ for each individual. In God's plan, Christ was to die on a cross, for that was a symbol of humiliation and an unmistakable sign that He was cursed by God. It was death without dignity.

Today many people are able to die under heavy sedation so that their exit is made as peaceful as possible. When Christ was offered wine mingled with myrrh, He refused this ancient sedative so that He could die with all of his senses fully aware of His surroundings. He took all the horror that death could offer.

If Christ, who was brutally murdered by jealous religious leaders, died as planned by God, why should we think that a believer who is gunned down in a robbery is any less under the care of the Almighty? Car accidents, heart attacks, cancer—all of these are the means used to open heaven to the children of God. The immediate cause of our death is neither haphazard or arbitrary. The one who knows the number of hairs on our heads and sees the sparrow fall has the destiny of every one of our days in His loving hands.

Little wonder Christ could say, "And do not fear those who kill the body, but are unable to kill the soul; but rather fear Him who is able to destroy both soul and body in hell" (Matthew 10:28). If we fear God, we need fear nothing else.

DYING FOR THE RIGHT PURPOSE

Death always has a divine purpose. God does not let life simply slip away. His Son, Jesus, did not die in tragedy. Within the will of God, His death accomplished redemption for the people whom God had chosen. When He cried, "It is finished," the work was complete.

Our death also has a divine purpose. Obviously, our death does not accomplish redemption, but it is the means by which we finally experience the redemption Christ accomplished for us. Death is the doorway by which we can leave the limitations and pains of this existence and enter into the heavenly realm.

Although we can be thankful for the wonders of modern medicine, there does come a time when believers must answer the call to "come up higher." So often when a Christian becomes ill, we immediately pray for his or her physical restoration. How can we be so sure that it is not God's time to have the person enter into the inheritance that is reserved for him (I Peter 1:4)?

When a person has lived a long life and has virtually no hope of recovery, we must simply commit him to God rather than use heroic measures to eke out one more day of pitiful existence. The day of our death is the day of our glorification. Death is the grand entrance, the door that swings into eternity. Eventually it will open in God's time and God's way to let another child come home where he/she belongs.

DYING WITH THE RIGHT COMMITMENT

Death can be a time of trust in God's deliverance. Christ's last comment was "Father, into Thy hands I commit My spirit" (Luke 23:46); thus He died entrusting Himself to the Father whom He so passionately loved.

Many Christians believe that Christ descended into hell (or more accurately hades) before He went to the Father. This teaching has been reinforced by the Apostles'

Creed, which says "He descended into hell." But until A.D. 650 no version of the creed included this phrase. The only version before this date that includes it gave the meaning "He descended into the grave." Support for the idea that He did enter hades is found in Acts 2:27, a quotation from Psalm 16:10. But many scholars believe that the Old Testament word *sheol* and the New Testament translation *hades* refer simply to the grave or death. This sense is preferable because the context emphasizes the fact that Christ's body rose from the grave, as opposed to David's body, which remained in the grave.

I believe that Christ's soul went immediately to God. To the thief hanging on His left Christ said, "Today you shall be with Me in Paradise" (Luke 23:43). Together they enjoyed the beauty of heaven on that very day. Three days later Christ was raised from the dead with a glorified body and later ascended into heaven.

To summarize: Although the *immediate* cause of Christ's death was the decision of the religious/political leaders, Christ knew the *ultimate* cause was God. "But the Lord was pleased to crush Him, putting Him to grief" (Isaiah 53:10).

Before his death, John Calvin had the same confidence when he said, "Thou Lord bruiseth me. But I am abundantly satisfied since it is from Thy hand."

Death can steal nothing from a Christian. Health, wealth, and joy—all of these come in greater abundance when the spirit goes to God.

Your Assurance of Heaven

This chapter has emphasized that there are two classes of people: those who have come to trust in the righteousness of Christ and who will someday stand before God on their own record, and those who will stand before the holiness and wrath of God without the protection that Christ affords.

Christ's sacrifice on the cross was so complete that those who trust Him are immediately fitted for heaven. This act of trust on our part must include an admission of our own helplessness; a confession that we are sinners unable to save ourselves, unable to even contribute to our salvation.

Then we must see the completed work of the cross: Christ's payment for sinners was absolutely perfect. These benefits are credited to those who believe. "But as many as received Him, to them He gave the right to become children of God, even to those who believe in His name" (John 1:12).

Here is a prayer you can use to make your trust in Christ personal and final:

Dear God,
I realize that I am a sinner and I can do nothing to save myself. I admit that all of my attempts to earn your favor are futile; forgive me for trusting in rituals and my own attempts at human goodness. I am grateful that Christ died on the cross for sinners like me. Right now I transfer all of my trust to Him for my forgiveness and acceptance before You. On the basis of Your promises I receive Christ as my personal Savior and believe You will receive me into heaven. Thank You for accepting me into Your family. Amen.

Strictly speaking, if you have trusted Christ, you are already in heaven! Paul says believers have been raised with Christ and are "seated with Him in the heavenly places, in Christ Jesus" (Ephesians 2:6). Because we have already established residence in heaven, we need have no fear when we cross the border into our eternal home.

Death is God's will for you and me. It is a dark doorway that leads to eternal light. Thankfully Christ came so that we do not have to walk behind the parted curtain alone.

Notes

1. Jacquelyn Helton died from cancer months after exclaiming her anger. Her story was reported in an edition of the *Chicago Tribune*.

2. Martha Smilgis, "Hollywood Goes to Heaven," *Time*, June 3, 1991, 70.

3. James A. Pike and Diane Kennedy, *The Other Side* (New York: Doubleday, 1968), 115.

4. Melvin Morse, *Closer to the Light* (New York: Ivy, 1990), 33.

5. C. S. Lewis, *The Weight of Glory* (Grand Rapids: Eerdmans, 1947), 15.

6. "Death Be Not Hurried: Charles Spurgeon's Counsel on Dying Grace," *Eternity*, February 1976, 14.

CHAPTER 9

How Can Modern Man Believe in Hell?

Hell disappeared. And no one noticed."

With that terse observation American church historian Martin Marty summarized our attitude toward a vanishing doctrine that received careful attention in previous generations. If you are a churchgoer, ask yourself when you last heard an entire sermon or Sunday school lesson on the topic.

A recent *Newsweek* article says, "Today, hell is theology's H-word, a subject too trite for serious scholarship." Gordon Kaufman of Harvard Divinity School believes we have gone through a transformation of ideas, and he says, "I don't think there can be any future for heaven and hell."

Admittedly, hell is an unpleasant topic. Unbelievers disbelieve in it; most Christians ignore it. Even staunchly biblical diehards are often silent out of embarrassment. Hell, more than any doctrine of the Bible, seems to be out of step with our times.

Reasons to Disbelieve

There are, of course, reasons this doctrine suffers obvious neglect. At the top of the list is the difficulty of reconciling hell with the love of God. That millions of people will be in conscious torment forever is beyond the grasp of the human mind. Bishop Robinson, who gained notoriety with his liberal views in *Honest to God*, writes,

> Christ . . . remains on the Cross as long as one sinner remains in hell. That is not speculation; it is a statement grounded in the very necessity of God's nature. In a universe of love there can be no heaven that tolerates a chamber of horrors; no hell for any which does not at the same time make it hell for God. He cannot endure that, for that would be a final mockery of his nature. And He will not.[1]

The doctrine of hell has driven many people away from Christianity. James Mill expressed what many have felt. "I will call no being good, who is not what I mean by good when I use that word of my fellow creatures; and if there be a Being who can send me to hell for not so calling him, to hell I will go."[2]

One man said that he would not want to be in heaven with a God who sends people to hell. His preference was to be in hell so that he could live in defiance of such a God. "If such a God exists," he complained, "He is the devil."

To put it simply, to us the punishment of hell does not fit the crime. Yes, all men do some evil and a few do great evils, but nothing that anyone has ever done can justify eternal torment. And to think that millions of good people will be in hell simply because they have not heard of Christ (as Christianity affirms) strains credulity. It's like capital punishment for a traffic violation.

Second, serious thinking about hell all but disappeared because of the medieval distortions that have become associated with this place of torment. Dante in *The Inferno* describes his tour through hell with vivid images of demons who tear sinners apart with claws and grappling hooks if they can catch them before they sink beneath the boiling pitch. He depicted the judgment of God in exact symbolic retribution. If a person used music in this world in the service of evil, demons will blow trumpets into his ears so that fire gushes out of his ears, eyes, and nostrils.

Such medieval authors took biblical teaching and combined it with pagan mythology resulting in caricatures that are still with us. We should note in passing that the Bible teaches that Satan and his demons will be the tormented, not the tormentors. The suffering of hell (to be discussed later) will be meted out by God, not inflicted by one sinful being onto another.

A third reason belief in hell has waned is because of the growing acceptance of reincarnation. Twenty-four percent of Americans now profess to believe that they will reappear in a different body. Shirley MacLaine says it is like show business. "You just keep going around until you get it right."

If liberalism allows us to believe in God without an afterlife, reincarnation enables us to believe in an afterlife without God. Thus millions of Westerners believe in some kind of afterlife, but it is one of bliss, not misery. Genuine fear of suffering in hell has vanished from the mainstream of Western thought. Few, if any, give prolonged thought to the prospect that some people will be in hell. Fewer yet believe they themselves will be among that unfortunate number.

The Eclipse of Hell

For liberal Protestants, hell began to fade in the nineteenth century. The universalists believed God was too good to send anyone to hell, and the Unitarians concluded that man was too good to go there. United Church of Christ theologian Max Stackhouse said, "The prevailing opinion is that when you die you're dead but God still cares." Rabbi Terry Bard, director of pastoral services at Boston's Beth Israel hospital, sums up the view of many Jews: "Dead is dead," he says, "and what lives on are the children and the legacy of good works."

And what about evangelicals who believe in the complete trustworthiness of the Bible? University of Virginia sociologist James Hunter, who has written two books on contemporary evangelicalism, says, "Many evangelicals have a difficult time conceiving of people, especially virtuous nonbelievers, going to hell." He makes the point that according to evangelical theology, Ghandi should be in hell; but Hunter says that when evangelical students were asked about that, they became "extremely nervous." To say that good people who are not born again will be in hell is so difficult to accept that many evangelicals are now saying, "I think there is a hell, but I hope it will be soul-sleep."

At a symposium at Trinity Evangelical Divinity School in Deerfield, Illinois, in May 1989, a heated discussion arose as to whether those who disbelieved in eternal punishment could properly be called evangelicals. Though the denial of eternal hell is found among liberals and groups such as the Jehovah's Witnesses and Seventh Day Adventists, it has never been taught within mainstream Christianity. Yet it is now seeping into evangelicalism too. Though there was no denunciation of such views in the final draft of the conference (Evangelical Affirmatives '89), we must ask the question anew in this generation: Does the Bible teach that unbelievers will live forever in conscious torment or not?

Two Unbiblical Alternates

Two alternate, unbiblical views vie for acceptance in response to that question. The first is called universalism, claiming that in the end all will be saved. The other seeks to show that the Scriptures teach conditional immortality, that is, only the righteous live forever, whereas unbelievers are judged and then annihilated. They are thrown into the fire that consumes them.

All sensitive people cringe at the thought of multitudes in perpetual misery. No one wants to think that God would consign human beings to such punishment. If either of these views can be defended from the Bible we would most gladly accept such interpretation of the data. Let's consider these alternatives with an open mind, testing them by the only standard that matters, the Word of God.

UNIVERSALISM

Universalism teaches that since Christ died for all people without exception, it follows that all will eventually be saved. God will overcome every remnant of evil, and all rational creatures (some would even include Satan) will eventually be redeemed.

One of the earliest and most influential defenders of universalism was Origen, a scholar from North Africa (A.D. 185–254). He defended Christianity and expounded the Scriptures but was also the father of Arianism (the denial of Christ's deity) and of the belief that all would eventually be saved. He taught that even Satan would be reconciled to God.

Origen's teaching was condemned at the Council of Constantinople in 543 and was not taught in the church until several hundred years later when John Scotus Erigena (A.D. 810–877) embraced essentially the same teaching. He argued that since God was one, His will was one, and therefore all men were predestinated to salvation.

Scriptural support for universalism is found in passages that picture the final state as one of total subservience to God. Paul taught that in the fullness of time, there would be the "summing up of all things in Christ, things in the heavens and things upon the earth" (Ephesians 1:10). And it is God's intention to "reconcile all things to Himself, having made peace through the blood of His cross; through Him, I say, whether things on earth or things in heaven" (Colossians 1:20). The implication, we are told, is that everyone will eventually be brought into the family of God.

Unfortunately this attractive interpretation has serious weaknesses. If the universalist's interpretation were correct then Satan would also have to be redeemed, that is, reconciled to God. Yet it is clear that Christ did not die for him (Hebrews 2:16); therefore God would have no just grounds to pardon him, even if he repented.

What is more, the Scriptures explicitly teach that he along with the beast and the false prophet shall be "tormented day and night forever and ever" (Revelation 20:10). Here we have a clear statement that Satan shall never be redeemed but will exist in conscious eternal torment.

Yes, everything will be summed up in Christ, but that means that all things will be brought under Christ's direct authority. Christ has completed everything necessary to fulfill God's plan of salvation. The order of nature shall be restored, and justice will prevail throughout the whole universe. As we shall see later, that restoration does not negate the doctrine of hell but instead necessitates it.

Other passages are used to teach the eventual salvation of all men. Paul wrote, "So then as through one transgression there resulted condemnation to all men, even so through one act of righteousness there resulted justification of life to all men" (Romans 5:18). A similar passage is 1 Corinthians 15:22: "As in Adam all die, so also in Christ all shall be made alive." Universalists interpret these verses to mean that as all men are condemned for Adam's offense, so all men are justified by Christ's act of righteousness.

Unfortunately, that interpretation fails for two reasons: first, the texts must be interpreted in light of others that clearly teach the eternal misery of unbelievers in hell. We simply do not have the luxury of isolating passages of Scripture.

Second, we must realize that the Bible frequently uses the word *all* in a restricted sense, as pertaining to all in a certain category rather than all without exception. Examples are numerous. Matthew tells us that "all Judea" went out to hear John the Baptist (3:5–6). Luke records that a decree went out that "a census be taken of all the inhabited earth" (2:1). And the disciples of John the Baptist complained that "all men" were following Christ. In the passages written by Paul, it is clear that all who are in Adam die, whereas all who are in Christ shall be made alive. The *all* has limitations built into it by the context.

The final deathblow to universalism is in Matthew 12:32. Christ is speaking of the unpardonable sin: "It shall not be forgiven him, either in this age, or in the age to come." In Mark 3:29 it is called an "eternal sin," indicating that it begins in this age and is carried on for all eternity without hope of reversal. How could those who have committed this sin be reconciled to God when Scripture clearly says they shall never be forgiven?

The New Testament is so filled with warnings to those who do not turn to God in this life that universalism has never been widely accepted by those who take the Bible seriously. Obviously if this teaching were true, there would be no pressing reason to fulfill the Great Commission or to urge unbelievers to accept Christ in this life.

CONDITIONAL IMMORTALITY

Whereas universalism sought to take the "forever" out of hell, we now come to a theory that attempts to take the "hell" out of forever. Conditional immortality is more attractive to evangelicals than universalism. This teaching contends that all will not be saved, but neither will any be in conscious torment forever. God resurrects the wicked to judge them. Then they are thrown into the fire and consumed. The righteous are granted eternal life, while the unbelievers are granted eternal death. Hell is annihilation.

Clark Pinnock of McMaster University in Toronto, Canada, asks how one can imagine for a moment that the God who gave His Son to die on the cross would "install a torture chamber somewhere in the new creation in order to subject those who reject him in everlasting pain?" He observes that it is difficult enough to defend Christianity in light of the problem of evil and suffering without having to explain hell too.

Pinnock believes that the fire of God consumes the lost. Thus God does not raise the wicked to torture them but rather to declare judgment on them and condemn them to extinction, which is the second death. Everlasting punishment, according to Pinnock, means that God sentences the lost to final, definitive death.

Perhaps the most scholarly defense of this doctrine was written by Edward Fudge in his book *The Fire that Con-*

sumes. In it Fudge claims that only God has unqualified immortality. He had no beginning and has no end. As for souls, they have all been created and can be destroyed. Only the righteous are granted eternal life. The idea of the indestructibility of the soul comes from Plato, we are told, not from the New Testament. This belief was accepted by Christians, and thus it was natural to draw the conclusion that the souls of unbelievers are tormented forever. This popular medieval teaching was adopted by the Reformers and thus is associated with orthodoxy.

Obviously it is not possible to reproduce all of Dr. Fudge's arguments here. But in summary, his view turns on the interpretation of several phrases that are used in the Bible to refer to the end of the wicked. Specifically, Fudge says that whenever the word *eternal* is linked to words of action, it refers to the result of the action, not to the action itself. For example, the phrase "eternal judgment" does not mean that the judgment itself will go on eternally, though there will be consequences that will. "Eternal redemption" does not mean the the act of Christ goes on forever, though the consequences do.[3]

Now Fudge applies that theory to such passages as 2 Thessalonians 1:9, where Paul writes that when Christ comes He will deal out retribution to the wicked, who will "pay the penalty of eternal destruction, away from the presence of the Lord and from the glory of His power" (2 Thessalonians 1:9). The question is whether the phrase *eternal destruction* means conscious torment or annihilation. According to Fudge, eternal destruction is annihilation and will take place when Christ returns. It is eternal in the sense that the consequences (extinction) will go on forever. The phrase *eternal punishment* and the word *perish* are interpreted in the same way. The fire of hell consumes its victims and obliterates them.

Unfortunately, that interpretation will not survive careful analysis. Robert A. Morey, in his book *Death and the Afterlife,* points out that the word *destroyed* as used in the

Bible does not mean "to annihilate." The Greek word *apol-lumi* is used in passages such as Matthew 9:17; Luke 15:4; and John 6:12, 17. In none of those instances does it mean "to pass out of existence." Morey writes, "There isn't a single instance in the New Testament where *apollumi* means annihilation in the strict sense of the word."[4] Thayer's *Greek-English Lexicon* defines it as "to be delivered up to eternal misery."

Let's consider another text. Christ says that the lost will go into "eternal fire" that has been prepared for the devil and his angels. And then He adds, "And these will go away into eternal punishment, but the righteous into eternal life" (Matthew 25:46). Since the same word *eternal* describes both the destiny of the righteous and the wicked, it seems clear that Christ did not mean that their punishment would be swift and short. Eternal punishment implies that the wicked will experience it eternally. We must ask: In what sense would punishment be eternal if the wicked were annihilated? Clearly Christ taught that both groups will exist forever, albeit in different places. The same eternal fire that Satan and his hosts experience will be the lot of unbelievers.

The eternal conscious existence of unbelievers was already taught in the Old Testament. Daniel wrote, "And many of those who sleep in the dust of the ground will awake, these to everlasting life, but the others to disgrace and everlasting contempt" (12:2). The wicked will experience shame and contempt for as long as the righteous experience bliss.

If there should still be any doubt in anyone's mind whether the occupants of hell suffer eternal conscious misery, we can settle the matter by an appeal to two passages from the book of Revelation. Those who worship the beast and have received his mark are described as drinking the wine of the wrath of God which is mixed in full strength, and such will be

> tormented with fire and brimstone in the presence of the holy angels and in the presence of the Lamb. And the

smoke of their torment goes up forever and ever; and they have no rest day and night, those who worship the beast and his image, and whoever receives the mark of his name. (Revelation 14:10–11)

Notice that the fire does not annihilate the wicked but torments them. There, in the presence of the holy angels and the Lamb, there will be no periods of rest during which the wicked are unconscious of torment. They will never slip into peaceful nonexistence.

In Revelation 20, we have a similar scene. The beast and the false prophet were thrown into the lake of fire, and after a thousand years Satan is released to deceive the nations. At the end of that period, Satan is cast into the lake of fire. Notice carefully that *the beast and the false prophet have not been annihilated during those one thousand years in hell.* The fire has not consumed them: "And the devil who deceived them was thrown into the lake of fire and brimstone, where the beast and the false prophet are also; and they will be tormented day and night forever and ever" (20:10).

Hence, the teachings of universalism and annihilationism come to their deceptive end. Eternal, conscious torment is clearly taught—*there is no other honest interpretation of these passages.*

When we say that God should save everyone (as the universalists say) or that He is obligated to obliterate the wicked (as the annihilationists say), we make salvation a matter of justice. But the Bible teaches plainly that salvation is a matter of mercy, not justice. Thus if God wishes to bestow mercy on some and display His justice in the lives of others, He has that right.

Hell and the Justice of God

Read the literature of the universalists or annihilationists and you cannot help but suspect that their theories are believed not so much because the Bible supports them but because of the difficulty of harmonizing eternal punishment with the justice and love of God. Pinnock, you will recall, lamented that it was difficult enough to explain evil to the unbelieving world without having to explain hell, too. Sensitive Christians, he says, cannot believe in eternal, conscious punishment.

To us as humans, everlasting punishment is disproportionate to the offense committed. God appears cruel, unjust, sadistic, and vindictive. The purpose of punishment, we are told, is always redemptive. Rehabilitation is the goal of all prison sentences. The concept of a place where there will be endless punishment without any possibility of parole or reform seems unjust.

As far as we know, if He had so desired, God could have created a universe free from sin and the corruption of rebellion. If Adam and Eve had had natures that abhorred sin and loved obedience they could have made a voluntary choice to follow God's orders. Lucifer could have been either exterminated or confined to another planet. Even better, Lucifer himself could have been created with a nature that would have never desired to oppose God. Those are just some of the possibilities.

Yet the fact is that God set up a world in which there would be rebellion and the awful consequences of sin, a universe with both a heaven and a hell. Since we know that the Almighty works all things according to the counsel of His own will, we must believe that even the unbelievers in hell will bring honor to His name and magnify His attributes, among them His attribute of justice.

How can hell be just? The following observations may not answer all of our questions, but it is hoped that they will help us begin to see hell from God's perspective.

MAN IS JUDGED
ACCORDING TO HIS KNOWLEDGE

Men and women will be judged on the basis of knowledge. Christ taught, "And that slave who knew his master's will and did not get ready or act in accord with his will, shall receive many lashes, but the one who did not know it, and committed deeds worthy of a flogging, will receive but few. And from everyone who has been given much shall much be required; and to whom they entrusted much, of him they will ask all the more" (Luke 12:47–48).

Those who live without specific knowledge about Christ will be judged by the light of nature and their own conscience (Romans 1:20; 2:14–16). That does not mean that those who respond to general revelation will be automatically saved, for no one lives up to all that he knows. That is why a personal knowledge of Christ is needed for salvation. "And there is salvation in no one else; for there is no other name under heaven that has been given among men, by which we must be saved" (Acts 4:12).

But the light of God in nature and in the human conscience is still a sufficient basis for judgment. Whatever the degree of punishment, it will fit the offense exactly, for God is meticulously just. Those who believe in Christ experience mercy; those who do not (either because they have never heard of Him or they reject what they know of Him) will receive justice. Either way, God is glorified.

Man's responsibility is therefore based on knowledge and performance. That is why at the Great White Throne judgment where all unbelievers appear, the books are opened and the dead are judged "according to their deeds" (Revelation 20:13). Once again I emphasize that their deeds cannot save them, for by the works of the law no flesh can be justified in His sight. Yet their performance does determine their punishment.

Think of how accurately God will judge every unbeliever! Each day of every life will be analyzed in minute detail. The hidden thoughts and motives of each hour will be replayed, along with all actions and attitudes. The words spoken in secret will be made public, the intentions of the heart displayed for all to see. They will have no attorney to whom they may appeal, no loopholes by which they can escape. Nothing but bare, indisputable facts.

I believe that the balance of justice will be so accurate that a pornographer will wish he had never published such material; a thief will wish he had earned an honest living; and an adulterer will regret that he lived an immoral life. Faithfulness to his marriage vows would not have earned him a place in heaven, to be sure, but it would have made his existence in hell slightly more bearable.

Before God, no motives will be misinterpreted, no extenuating circumstances thrown out of court. The woman who seduced the man will receive her fair share of punishment, and the man who allowed himself to be seduced will receive his. All blame will be accurately proportioned.

We all agree that heaven is a comforting doctrine. What is often overlooked is that hell is comforting, too. Our newspapers are filled with stories of rape, child abuse, and a myriad of injustices. Every court case ever tried on earth will be reopened; every action and motive will be meticulously inspected and just retribution meted out. In the presence of an all-knowing God there will be no unsolved murders, no unknown child abductor, and no hidden bribe.

UNBELIEVERS ARE ETERNALLY GUILTY

Hell exists because unbelievers are eternally guilty. The powerful lesson to be learned is that no human being's suffering can ever be a payment for sin. If our suffering could erase even the most insignificant sin, then those in hell would eventually be freed after their debt was paid. But all human goodness and suffering from the beginning of time, if added together, could not cancel so much as a single sin.

> Could my tears forever flow,
> Could my zeal no respite know,
> All for sin could not atone;
> Thou must save and Thou alone.
> ("Rock of Ages")

Sir Francis Newport, who ridiculed Christianity, is quoted as saying these terrifying words on his deathbed:

> Oh that I was to lie a thousand years upon the fire that never is quenched, to purchase the favor of God, and be united to him again! But it is a fruitless wish. Millions and millions of years would bring me no nearer to the end of my torments than one poor hour. Oh, eternity, eternity! forever and forever! Oh, the insufferable pains of hell![5]

He was quite right in saying that a million years in hell could not purchase salvation. Tragically, he did not cast himself upon the mercy of God in Christ. Since no man's works or sufferings can save him, he must bear the full weight of his sin throughout eternity.

WE CANNOT COMPREHEND
THE SERIOUSNESS OF SIN

We must confess that we do not know exactly how much punishment is enough for those who have sinned against God. We may think we know what God is like, but we see through a glass darkly. The famous theologian Jonathan Edwards said that the reason we find hell so offensive is because of our insensitivity to sin.

What if, from God's viewpoint, the greatness of sin is determined by the greatness of the One against whom it is committed? Then the guilt of sin is infinite because it is a violation of the character of an infinite Being. What if, in the nature of God, it is deemed that such infinite sins deserve an infinite penalty, a penalty that no one can ever repay?

We must realize that God did not choose the attributes He possesses. Because He has existed from all eternity His attributes were already determined from eternity past. If God had not possessed love and mercy throughout all eternity, we might have been created by a malicious and cruel being who delighted in watching His creatures suffer perpetual torment. Fortunately, that is not the case. The Bible tells of the love and mercy of God; He does not delight in the death of the wicked. But it also has much to say about His justice and the fact that even the wicked in hell will glorify Him. To put it clearly, we must accept God as He is revealed in the Bible whether He suits our preferences or not.

When Paul was defending the doctrine of God's sovereignty in choosing a remnant of the Jewish nation for special favors, he knew that it would elicit loud objections from his readers. But he was undeterred by their protests and asserted that the clay did not have the right to question the potter. If God wanted to make His wrath and power known, He had the right to "[endure] with much patience vessels of wrath prepared for destruction" (Romans 9:22).

It is absurd in the extreme to say, "I don't want to be in heaven with a God who sends people to hell. . . . I would rather go to hell and defy Him." I can't exaggerate the foolishness of those who think they can oppose God to their own satisfaction or to His detriment! In Psalm 2 we read that God sits in the heavens and laughs at those who think they can defy Him. Like the mouse who thinks it can stand against the farmer's plow or the rowboat poised to thwart the path of an aircraft carrier, it is insanity for man to think that he can oppose the living God, who is angry with sinners and is bent on taking vengeance on those who oppose Him.

Even as we look at the suffering in the world today, we should not be surprised that God allows multitudes to live in eternal misery. Think of the vast amount of suffering (preventable suffering, if you please) that God has allowed on this earth. An earthquake in Mexico kills twenty thousand, a tidal wave in Bangladesh kills fifty thousand, and famines in the world cause twenty thousand deaths every single day! Who can begin to calculate the amount of emotional pain experienced by babies, children, and adults?

Yet we know that strengthening the earth's crust, sending rain, and withholding floods could all be accomplished by a word from the Almighty.

If God has allowed people to live in untold misery for thousands of years, why would it be inconsistent for Him to allow misery to continue forever? Charles Hodge asks, "If the highest glory of God and the good of the universe have been promoted by the past sinfulness and misery of men, why may not those objects be promoted by what is declared to be future?"[6]

If our concept of justice differs from God's, we can be quite sure that He will be unimpressed by our attempts to get Him to see things from our point of view. No one is God's counselor; no one instructs or corrects Him. He does not look to us for input on how to run His universe.

We now return to a study of the doctrine of hell, noting the Greek words used to describe it in the New Testament. Then we will glimpse its torments in a story told by Christ Himself.

Greek Words for Hell

The New Testament uses three different Greek words for *hell*. One is *tartarus*, used in 2 Peter 2:4 for the abode of evil angels who sinned during the time of Noah. "For . . . God did not spare angels when they sinned, but cast them into hell and committed them to pits of darkness, reserved for judgment." In Jude 6 the word *tartarus* is used similarly.

The second and most often used word for hell in the New Testament is *gehenna*, a word for hell already used by the Jews before the time of Christ. The word is derived from the Hebrew "valley of Hinnom" found in the Old Testament (Joshua 15:8; 2 Kings 23:10; Nehemiah 11:30). In that valley outside Jerusalem the Jews gave human sacrifices to pagan deities. There, too, the garbage of the city was thrown, where it bred worms. That explains why

Christ referred to hell as the place where "their worm does not die, and the fire is not quenched" (Mark 9:44, 46, 48).

This picture of an unclean dump where fires and worms never die became to the Jewish mind an appropriate description of the ultimate fate of all idolaters. Thus the word became applied to the ultimate *gehenna*. The Jews taught, and Christ confirmed, that the wicked would suffer there forever. Body and soul would be in eternal torment.

For years liberal scholars taught (and some sentimentalists still do) that Christ, who stressed the love of God, could never be party to the doctrine of hell. Yet significantly, of the twelve times the word *gehenna* is used in the New Testament, eleven times it came from the mouth of our Lord. Indeed, He spoke more about hell than about heaven.

The third word is *hades*, which is not a reference to hell but rather to the place where unbelievers presently go to await the Great White Throne judgment. The word, however, is translated "hell" in the King James Version of the Bible. Most other translations simply leave it untranslated as *hades* so that it might be properly distinguished from hell.

Purgatory has no basis in the New Testament but is an idea borrowed from mythologies about the existence of a place of temporary punishment from which one would finally be extricated. The reason it was incorporated into the teaching of the church during the Dark Ages is because it corresponded so directly with the defective view of justification that was prevalent at that time. Indeed, it is not too strong to say that the medieval understanding of justification necessitated purgatory.

Specifically, the belief was that God makes people righteous through their participation in the sacraments and their good works. But the people had no assurance that they had ever accumulated enough righteousness to gain God's approval. Purgatory was thus the place for temporal punishment of sins; they would be "purged" from sins so that they would become righteous enough to enter heaven. Later the notion arose that it was possible to pay a fee to the church for relatives so that their time in purgatory would be shortened.

Those abuses angered Luther, and his efforts at reformation were begun with the intention of basing theology on the Bible rather than on tradition and pagan mythologies. The New Testament doctrine of justification will be explained at the end of this chapter.

What will the suffering of hell be like? We must guard against undue speculation since the Scriptures do not describe the torments of hell in specifics. We must not fall into the error of the medievals who described hell with the vivid details of a guide taking tourists through the Vatican. Yet Jesus told a story that does give us a glimpse of hell, or more accurately, a glimpse of hades, which is a prelude to the final place of eternal punishment.

Characteristics of Hell

Often when Christ confronted the self-righteous Pharisees, He used a parable or a true story to awaken them to God's priorities over and against their own. On this occasion the topic was their love of money and disregard for the spiritual values of love and truth. To illustrate the fact that "that which is highly esteemed among men is detestable in the sight of God"(Luke 16:15), Christ told a story (it is not called a parable) of a rich man who ended up in hades in contrast to a poor man who was carried away by angels into Abraham's bosom (heaven). Christ's point was to show how the fortunes of the two men were reversed in the afterlife. The rich man was in torment; the poor man was in bliss.

> And in Hades he lifted up his eyes, being in torment, and saw Abraham far away, and Lazarus in his bosom. And he cried out and said, "Father Abraham,

have mercy on me, and send Lazarus, that he may dip the tip of his finger in water and cool off my tongue; for I am in agony in this flame."

But Abraham said, "Child, remember that during your life you received your good things, and likewise Lazarus bad things; but now he is being comforted here, and you are in agony. And besides all this, between us and you there is a great chasm fixed, in order that those who wish to come over from here to you may not be able, and that none may cross over from there to us."

And he said, "Then I beg you, Father, that you send him to my father's house—for I have five brothers—that he may warn them, lest they also come to this place of torment."

But Abraham said, "They have Moses and the Prophets; let them hear them."

But he said, "No, Father Abraham, but if someone goes to them from the dead, they will repent!"

But he said to him, "If they do not listen to Moses and the Prophets, neither will they be persuaded if someone rises from the dead." (Luke 16:23–31)

What can we say about the rich man's experience in hades? Let me remind you once again that he was not yet —indeed he *is* not yet—in hell. Though hell will be far worse than hades, this story does give a telling glimpse of what the fate of unbelievers will be.

A PLACE OF TORMENT

Usually when we think of hell, we think of fire since Christ spoke of the "fire of hell." In Revelation we read of "the lake of fire and brimstone."

There is no reason the torments of hell could not include physical fire, since the bodies of those present will have been re-created and made indestructible. Unlike our present bodies, those of the resurrected dead will not burn up or be extinguished. Literal fire is a possibility.

However, there is another kind of fire that will be in hell, a fire that may be worse than literal fire. That is the fire of unfulfilled passion, the fire of desires that are never satisfied. Perpetually burning lusts never subside, and the tortured conscience burns but is never sedated or appeased. There will be increased desire with decreased satisfaction.

In hades the rich man experiences a preview of the torments of hell. Notice that in the story his physical desires were still active; he was thirsty, wishing for a drop of water to cool his tongue. Let us remember that the people in hell will be the same people they were on earth, with the same desires, aspirations, and feelings. Yet their needs will not be met.

In Proverbs we read of the insatiable desires of the netherworld and a man's lusts. "Sheol and Abaddon are never satisfied, nor are the eyes of man ever satisfied" (27:20). An alcoholic will thirst for a drop of liquor in hell but will not get it; a drug addict will crave a shot of heroin; the immoral man will burn with sexual desire but will never be gratified. The body will be aflame with lusts, but the fire will never be quenched. It's as if God is saying, "On earth you did not let Me satisfy you but turned to your own lusts; now you will find that those lusts can only drive you to despair."

Hell, then, is the raw soul joined to an indestructible body, exposed to its own sin for eternity. Hell is the place of unquenchable, raging, unmet emotional needs, without painkillers or sedation.

A PLACE OF ABANDONMENT

The rich man was permitted to speak to Abraham, but there could be no direct, intimate communication with those in heaven. The rich man's request for a drop of water to cool his tongue was denied because he was getting his just deserts, and furthermore, between them was an unbridgeable chasm.

Does that mean that there will be some form of communication between those in heaven and the occupants of hell? Not necessarily. There is evidence in the New Testament that "Abraham's bosom" was transferred directly into the presence of Christ at the Ascension. Even more important, however, the Scriptures teach that hades shall be thrown into hell, the lake of fire, after the final judgment. "And the sea gave up the dead which were in it, and death and Hades gave up the dead which were in them; and they were judged, every one of them according to their deeds" (Revelation 20:13).

However, those who are in hell will be tormented in the presence of Christ and the holy angels (Revelation 14:10). It is generally believed that the righteous shall behold the terrors of hell, and part of the suffering of the unbelievers will be to see a friend or relative in eternal bliss. Though that is not expressly stated, God often invites righteous people or angels to behold the judgment He inflicts upon the wicked (Psalm 46:8–9; Isaiah 66:23–24; Revelation 19:17–21). Famous British preacher Charles Haddon Spurgeon wrote, "If there be one thing in hell worse than another, it will be seeing the saints in heaven. . . . Husband, there is your wife in heaven and you are among the damned. And do you see your father? Your child is before the throne, and you accursed of God and man are in hell!"

If believers do witness these events, we can be sure that they will agree completely with the justice displayed by God, for then they shall see all things from His point of view. Thus, the righteous can enjoy the bliss of heaven knowing full well the fate of the wicked in hell.

Will there be communication among those who occupy hell? We cannot say, for the Scriptures are silent. C. S. Lewis believed there would not be, stating that hell is a place of solitude. Jonathan Edwards believed that if unbelievers are next to one another they will only add to each other's agony through expressions of hatred, accusations, and curses. Of one thing we can be absolutely certain: no comfort will be derived from the presence of others. Consumed with the torment of raging, unforgiven sin, those in hell will never find comfort again.

Though Dante added many of his own ideas to the superstitions of his day when he wrote *The Inferno*, the sign he read in the vestibule of hell does portray the biblical teaching of hopelessness and abandonment.

> I am the way to the city of woe.
> I am the way to a forsaken people.
> I am the way into eternal sorrow.
>
> Sacred justice moved my architect.
> I was raised here by divine omnipotence,
> Primordial love and ultimate intellect.
>
> Only those elements time cannot wear
> Were made before me, and beyond time I stand.
> Abandon all hope ye who enter here.

Jonathan Edwards pointed out that those in hell will have no reason for entertaining any secret hope that after being in the flames many ages God will take pity on them and release them. God, says Edwards, will not be any more inclined to release them after a million ages than He was at the very first moment. Little wonder, Edwards said, that any description we give of hell can be but a faint representation of the reality!

A PLACE OF AN ACTIVE CONSCIENCE AND A GOOD MEMORY

The rich man asked Abraham to let Lazarus return to his (the rich man's) house to warn his five brothers that they might not come to the same place of torment. There in hades he expressed concern for those whom he loved; he remembered who he was and what happened on earth. The similarity between who he had been on earth and who he was now in hades should not escape us.

Incredibly, this man became interested in missions! He would like Lazarus to return from the dead to dramatize to his brothers the need to prepare for the life to come.

This man who lived in luxury on earth and saw no special need for God now suddenly saw that one's relationship with God is of highest priority. Apparently he knew more about the way to God then we might have expected. He specifically asked Abraham to return and preach *repentance* to his brothers.

Abraham's answer is instructive: "They have Moses and the Prophets; let them hear them."

The rich man replied, "No, Father Abraham, but if someone goes to them from the dead, they will repent!"

Abraham replied, "If they do not listen to Moses and the Prophets, neither will they be persuaded if someone rises from the dead."

How true! When Christ told this story, He had not yet been put to death and resurrected. But today, even after His resurrection, many men and women do not believe. Yet Christ taught that His own resurrection was the only sign He would give to the world. "A man convinced against his will is of the same opinion still."

Far from thinking that the presence of his brothers would give him some much needed company in hades, this man was more than willing not to see them again if only they would be in a place of comfort rather than torment! Those in hell will be the same people they were on earth with the same memories, identity, and feelings.

A PLACE OF ETERNITY

We have already established the fact that the Bible teaches that hell is unending. But now we must pause to try to understand what that means. How long is eternity?

Visualize a bird coming to earth every million years and taking one grain of sand with it to a distant planet. At that rate it would take thousands of billions of years before the bird had carried away a single handful of sand. Now let's expand that illustration and think how long it would take the bird to move the Oak Street Beach in Chicago and then the other thousands of beaches around the world. After that the bird could begin on the mountains and the earth's crust.

By the time the bird transported the entire earth to the far-off planet, eternity would not have officially begun. Strictly speaking one cannot begin an infinite series, for a beginning implies an end. In other words, we might say that after the bird has done his work, those in eternity will not be one step closer to having their suffering alleviated. There is no such thing as half an eternity.

The most sobering thought that could ever cross our minds is the fact that the rich man in hades referred to above has not *yet* received the drop of water for which he so desperately longed. Today, as you read this chapter, he is still there awaiting the final judgment of the lake of fire. Eternity endures, and it endures *forever*.

A PLACE OF EASY ACCESS BUT NO EXIT

We could wish that the signs along the pathway to hell were clearly marked: "Turn Left for Eternal Destruction," or, "Follow These Truths to Everlasting Blessedness." Such signs, if accurate, would be of help in our journey through life. Regrettably, the way is a bit more difficult.

Christ in effect taught that for many people *the path to hell is labeled as the path to heaven.* There are two roads, He said: a wide one that leads to everlasting destruction and a narrow one that leads to eternal life. Many who are on the broad way are actually confident that they will arrive at the right destination. A recent poll showed that about three out of four Americans believe that their chances of getting to heaven are good or excellent.

Jonathan Edwards, whom we have already quoted, gave more consideration to the doctrine of hell than any other theologian. His sermon "Sinners in the Hands of an Angry God" kept audiences spellbound, stripping from them any objections or excuses they might have had against the doctrine of hell. He made the point that there are some people now living for whom God has more anger than some who are in hades (he called it hell) who have already died. Therefore it was only the mercy of God that kept them from plunging into the abyss:

> There is nothing that keeps wicked men at any one moment out of hell, but the mere pleasure of God. . . . There is no want in God's power to cast wicked men into hell at any moment. . . . They deserve to be cast into hell, so divine justice never stands in the way. . . . They are now the objects of that very same anger and wrath that is expressed in the torments of hell . . . yea God is a great deal more angry with great numbers that are now on the earth, yea doubtless with some who re-read this book, who it may be are at ease, than he is with many of those who are now in the flames of hell.
> Unconverted men walk over the pit of hell on a rotten covering, and there are innumerable places in this covering so weak that they will not bear their weight, and these places are not seen. . . . There is the dreadful pit of the glowing flames of the wrath of God; there is hell's wide gaping mouth open; and you have nothing to stand upon, nor anything to take hold of, there is nothing between you and hell but air; it is only the power and mere pleasure of God that holds you up. . . . His wrath burns against you like fire; he looks upon you as worthy of nothing else than to be thrown into the fire . . . you hang by the slender thread, with the flames of divine wrath flashing about it and ready every moment to singe it, and burn it asunder.[7]

Edwards concluded his sermon with an appeal to men to take advantage of the mercy of God in Christ. Just think, he said, of what those who are in hell would give for one single hour of opportunity to respond to God's saving grace!

Just as there have been believers who have already seen glimpses of heaven before they died, so some unbelievers have already described the torments of hades as they slipped from this world into the next. The skeptic Robert Ingersoll said, "You do not have to tell me there is no hell, for I already feel its flames." Others have confessed to seeing demons waiting to escort them into that fearful abyss.

Let me ask, Which path are you on? Who is qualified to tell us which signposts are accurate and which ones are erected by deceivers who snare the wary into a false hope? Obviously you and I are not in a position to resolve such issues, since they fall outside the scope of human knowledge. What we need is someone who has the authority to speak for God, someone who is not limited to human inclinations and observations.

The one man—the only man—with such impressive credentials is Christ. He came down from heaven as the second member of the Trinity to reveal God the Father and to give His life as a sacrifice for sins. He spoke about the hereafter with confidence—referring to hell more often than to heaven.

First of all we must see that Christ alone is the way to God the Father: "I am the way, and the truth, and the life; no one comes to the Father, but through Me" (John 14:6).

Second, we must understand that Christ is the only one who is qualified to lead us to God because His death was a sacrifice for sinners. He satisfied God's just requirements so that sinners could be declared righteous—so righteous that they can go to heaven immediately at death without the need for purgatory.

Christ bore our hell so that we would not have to bear it ourselves. Sin demands an infinite payment; only Christ who is Himself God could make such a payment.

How do we receive these benefits? We must acknowledge our sinfulness and helplessness, confessing our inability to save ourselves. Then we must willfully transfer all of our trust to Christ alone for our acceptance before God. "But as many as received Him, to them He gave the right to become children of God, even to those who believe in His name" (John 1:12).

Let me warn you not to trust in your baptism, the sacraments, or any other ritual. Only those who are born again of the Holy Spirit will enter the kingdom of heaven (John 3:5).

Many years ago a father and his daughter were walking through the grass on the Canadian prairie. In the distance they saw a prairie fire which eventually, they realized, would engulf them. The father knew that there was only one way of escape: they would build a fire right where they were and burn a large area of grass. When the huge fire drew near, the child was terrified, but the father assured her that they would not be burned because *they were standing where the fire had already been.*

The fire of God's wrath fell on Christ so that we might be shielded from His wrath. Faith placed personally and exclusively in Christ can exempt us from punishment. Only those who flee to Him will escape the flames.

It is a fearful thing to fall into the hands of the living God unprepared.

Notes

1. "Universalism—Is It Heretical?" *Scottish Journal of Theology*, June 1949, 155.
2. Percy Dearmer, *The Legend of Hell* (London: Cassell, 1929), 74–75.
3. Edward Fudge, *The Fire That Consumes* (Houston, Texas: Providential, 1982), 48–49.
4. Robert Morey, *Death and the Afterlife* (Minneapolis: Bethany, 1984), 90.
5. Walter B. Knight, *Knight's Master Book of New Illustrations* (Grand Rapids: Eerdmans, 1956), 159.
6. Charles Hodge, *Systematic Theology*, vol. 3, pt. 4 (Grand Rapids: Eerdmans, reprint, 1982), 879.
7. Warren Wiersbe, *Treasury of the World's Great Sermons* (Grand Rapids: Kregel, 1977), 198–205.

CHAPTER 10

What Will
Heaven Be Like?

In the Middle East a fable is told of a Baghdad merchant who sent his servant to the marketplace to run an errand. When he had completed his assignment and was about to leave the marketplace, he turned a corner and unexpectedly met Lady Death. The look on her face so frightened him that he left the marketplace and hurried home. He told his master what had happened and requested his fastest horse so that he could get as far from Lady Death as possible—a horse that would take him all the way to Sumera before nightfall.

Later that same afternoon the merchant himself went to the marketplace and met Lady Death. "Why did you startle my servant this morning?" he asked.

"I didn't intend to startle your servant—it was I who was startled," replied Lady Death. "I was surprised to see your servant in Baghdad this morning, because I have an appointment with him in Sumera tonight."

You and I have an appointment. Perhaps it will be in London, Taipei, or Chicago. Wherever, it is one appointment we will not miss. As C. S. Lewis observed, the statistics on death are impressive—so far, it is one out of one!

Of course believers can be confident that we die in God's time. When Christ was told that His friend Lazarus was sick, He stayed away two extra days so that Lazarus would already be dead and buried by the time He arrived in Bethany. The sisters individually voiced their complaint, "If only You had been here, my brother would not have died." Yet Christ wanted them to understand that Lazarus had died within the will of God; he died according to the divine schedule.

In recent days I have conducted two funerals. The first was that of a Christian woman who had distinguished herself by a life of sacrificial service for Christ. The triumph of the family was striking; there was irrepressible joy mixed with the sorrow.

The second was that of an apparent unbeliever who was killed in a highway accident. The grief of the relatives was marked by desperation and hopelessness. They refused to be comforted.

We all are following those two people to the grave. Unless Christ should return in our lifetime, we will all pass through that iron gate described by Hamlet as "the undiscover'd country from whose bourn no traveler returns" (III, i, 80–81). The question is: Where will we be five minutes after we die?

I'm told that there is a cemetery in Indiana that has an old tombstone bearing this epitaph:

> Pause, Stranger, when you pass me by
> As you are now, so once was I
> As I am now, so you will be
> So prepare for death and follow me

An unknown passerby read those words and underneath scratched this reply:

> To follow you I'm not content
> Until I know which way you went

The way we go is determined in this life. At death our destiny is unalterably fixed. For those who have admitted their sinfulness and received the free gift of eternal life through Jesus Christ, death leads to the realm called heaven, the abode of God.

Why is the contemplation of heaven so important for each of us? First, because it gives us perspective. Visualize a measuring tape extending from the earth to the farthest star. Our stay here would just be a hairline; it would be almost invisible compared to the length of the tape. Eternity is even longer, of course, and when that becomes our measuring rod the longest life is but a dot of time. That's why Paul says that the suffering of this present life cannot be compared with the glory that shall be revealed in us. Eternity gives perspective to time.

Second, the contemplation of heaven is crucial because we must use our time and resources to lay up treasures in heaven where moth and rust do not corrupt and where thieves do not break through and steal. Every one of us wants to make wise investments, to get the "biggest bang for our buck," as the saying goes. The best investments are those that are safe and permanent. Although entrance into heaven is a free gift, the extent of our inheritance will be determined by our faithfulness here on earth.

Imagine spending time redecorating a room of a house that is on fire! Why waste effort on that which is so temporary? Yet all that we have will be destroyed. Nothing we can see is forever. Why not send on ahead investments that will have permanent value and reward?

Recently I was browsing in the Travel section of a bookstore. Potential travelers choose from a dozen different books on Hawaii or Europe. They will be saving their money and making other sacrifices to prepare for their vacation, and though it will last but a few weeks they learn as much as they can about their destination. Some even try to learn the language of the country they intend to visit.

With heaven as our final destination, we should be learning all we can about that eternal home. The daughter of a fine Christian man who eventually died of cancer was heard to remark, "In Dad's final weeks he spent more time in heaven than he did on earth." And why not? The sufferings of this life often make us anxious to get on with the life to come. The certainty of heaven helps us cope with the uncertainties of earth.

A knowledge of heaven takes the sting out of death. A dying woman told her children, "Don't give me any further treatment. . . . Don't interfere with God's plan for my glorification." That represents the strong faith of one who walked with God for many years. There is no reason we cannot face death with the same degree of confidence. The apostle Paul looked forward to death, saying that he was ready to be offered, for the time of his departure had come.

Those of us who have close relatives who have died find another reason to learn what heaven will be like. We wonder what our friends are now doing; we try to visualize what it will be like to meet them someday. Paul taught that we have every right to know what God has revealed about the afterlife so that we will not grieve as those who have no hope. All believers will meet again. That gives comfort to the sorrowing.

How certain is heaven for the Christian? When Paul wanted to list all of the aspects of our salvation he wrote, "For whom He foreknew, He also predestined to become conformed to the image of His Son, that He might be the first-born among many brethren; and whom He predestined, these He also called; and whom He called, these He also justified; and whom He justified, these He also glorified" (Romans 8:29–30).

Notice that we are *already* glorified. In effect, our arrival in heaven has taken place. Those whom God chooses to be His—that is, those whom He foreknows and predestinates—are guaranteed a safe passage into their heavenly home. None is lost en route; in God's mind they have already arrived with their new bodies. For God "calls into being that which does not exist" (Romans 4:17).

In order to understand heaven, let us consider five new possessions we will experience in the life to come.

A New Body

We are a spiritual and physical unity. Our destiny includes the entirety of our being—body, soul, and spirit. In heaven we shall be the same people we are here on earth—the same body, soul, and spirit, though those three aspects will be adapted for heavenly existence. On the Mount of Transfiguration the disciples conversed with Moses and Elijah—the real Moses and Elijah. No replicas, no stand-ins.

THE CONTINUITY OF THE BODY

Some Christians assume that God will create new bodies for us out of nothing. But if that were so, there would be no need for the doctrine of resurrection. Paul's point in 1 Corinthians 15 is that our present physical bodies will be raised. "It is sown a perishable body, it is raised an imperishable body; it is sown in dishonor, it is raised in glory; it is sown in weakness, it is raised in power; it is sown a natural body, it is raised a spiritual body" (1 Corinthians 15:42–44). There is continuity between our earthly and our heavenly bodies.

Our future body will be like Christ's resurrection body. "We know that, when He appears, we shall be like Him, because we shall see Him just as He is" (1 John 3:2). Just think of the implications.

The continuity between Christ's earthly and heavenly body was clear to see—for example, the nail prints were in His hands. The disciples recognized Him instantly, and He even ate fish with them at the seashore. But there were also radical changes. He was able to travel from one place to another without physical effort and went through doors without opening them.

Evidently we too shall be able to travel effortlessly. Just as Christ could be in Galilee and then suddenly appear in Judea, so we shall be free from the limitations of terrestrial travel. That does not mean, of course, that we will be omnipresent as God is; we will be limited to one place at one time. But travel will be swift and effortless.

We can also expect that we shall have increased mental powers. "For now we see in a mirror dimly, but then face to face; now I know in part, but then I shall know fully just as I also have been fully known" (1 Corinthians 13:12). Again, we must remind ourselves that we shall not be omniscient, for the knowledge of all things is the special prerogative of God. But our minds will have keen perception without the limitations of a failing memory or fragmented comprehension. Like Adam before the Fall, our mental ability will operate at a high level.

There is good reason to expect that we shall continue learning in heaven. Our appreciation of God and His grace will grow throughout the ages. The famous Puritan writer Jonathan Edwards believed that the saints in heaven would begin by contemplating God's providential care of the church on earth and then move on to other aspects of the divine plan and thus "the ideas of the saints shall increase to eternity."

THE INTERMEDIATE STATE

Several views have arisen in the history of the church regarding the present status of the saints in heaven since they do not as yet have their permanent bodies. In about the seventh century the Roman Catholic church began teaching the doctrine of purgatory, a temporary residence where people's sins were worked out.

Martin Luther, while studying the book of Romans, came to understand that justification means that God declares us to be as righteous as Christ despite our present imperfections. Thus souls go directly to heaven, accepted by God on the basis of the complete merit of Christ. That teaching put the doctrine of salvation on a firm footing and also explains why the thief on the cross was assured fellowship with Christ in paradise on that very day. The doctrine of purgatory must be rejected.

Others, such as Seventh Day Adventists, teach that the soul sleeps until the resurrection of the body. Those who die in the Lord are at this moment unconscious. They shall be awakened when the Lord shall come with the sound of a trumpet and the dead in Christ are raised.

The teaching of soul sleep is based on those passages where the word *sleep* is used to refer to those who have died (John 11:11; Acts 7:60; 1 Corinthians 15:51). However, we must realize that in each instance those Scriptures refer to the sleep of the body, not the sleep of the soul. The body sleeps until the resurrection, but the soul is conscious. That is proved by many Scriptures teaching that believers are immediately taken to heaven at death and are conscious in His presence (Luke 23:43; Philippians 1:23).

That leads us to a question that has puzzled theologians: Since the resurrection of the body is future, are the present saints in heaven disembodied spirits? Or do they have some kind of a temporary "intermediate" body that will be discarded on the day of resurrection—the day when we all receive our permanent, glorified bodies?

The point of disagreement is over Paul's words in 2 Corinthians 5:1, "For we know that if the earthly tent which is our house is torn down, we have a building from God, a house not made with hands, eternal in the heavens." The question is: To what period in the future does he refer when he speaks of our having "a building of God . . . eternal in the heavens"? Do we have that building at death, or do we receive it at the future resurrection? Paul shrinks from the idea that his soul would live through a period of nakedness, a time when it would exist without a body.

Some scholars teach that the saints who have died already now have bodies, temporary bodies that will be replaced by their eternal bodies at the time of resurrection. This view is attractive because it explains how the redeemed in heaven can relate to Christ and to one another. If departed believers can sing the praises of God and communicate to one another, it seems that they must have a body in which to do so. What is more, at the point of transition between life and death some have actually testified that they have already seen departed relatives awaiting their arrival. That points to the conclusion that the saints in heaven already have recognizable bodies.

On the Mount of Transfiguration, Moses and Elijah appeared in some kind of body. Admittedly, Elijah was taken up to heaven and therefore may not have needed to await the resurrection—he may have his permanent body already. But Moses was buried on Mount Nebo and was awaiting a future resurrection. Though he has as yet not received that eternal resurrection body, he already appeared with Christ two thousand years ago, recognizable to the disciples and communicating with them. The rich man who died and went to hades evidently had a body, since he was able to use human speech and wanted his tongue cooled with water.

However, we must ask ourselves, if the saints already have bodies in heaven (albeit temporary ones), why does Paul place such an emphasis on the resurrection in his writings? He does imply that the saints in heaven today are incomplete; they are in an unnatural state.

So a second plausible explanation might be that the souls of the departed dead may in some ways have the functions of a body. If that is the case, it would explain how they can communicate with one another and have a visible presence in heaven. These capabilities of the soul are implied in Revelation 6:9–10. "And when He broke the fifth seal, I saw underneath the altar the *souls* of those who had been slain because of the word of God, and because of the testimony which they had maintained; and they cried out with a loud voice, saying, 'How long, O Lord, holy and true, wilt Thou refrain from judging and avenging our blood on those who dwell on the earth?'" (italics added). We then read that they were even given white robes to wear as they waited for God to avenge them.

Admittedly the word *psychas* (translated "souls") has a broad meaning and can also be translated "lives" or "persons." But the word is often translated *soul* as distinguished from the body. If that is what John meant, it would give credence to the view that souls can take upon themselves shape and bodily characteristics. If that seems strange to us, it may well be that our concept of the soul is too limited.

We cannot be sure about which of those views is correct. Of this much we may be certain: believers go directly into the presence of Christ at death. They are conscious and in command of all of their faculties. As D. L. Moody said before he died, "Soon you will read in the papers that Moody is dead . . . don't believe it . . . for in that moment I will be more alive than I have ever been."

THE AGE OF THE BODY

What about infants who have died? Since there is continuity between the earthly and heavenly body, will they be infants forever?

Parents who have lost a child rightly wonder whether their child has made a safe arrival in heaven. The answer, I believe, is yes, though we must be clear as to why we believe they will be saved. Contrary to popular opinion, children will not be in heaven because they are innocent. Paul taught clearly that children are born under the condemnation of Adam's sin (Romans 5:12). Indeed, it is because they are born sinners that they experience death.

Nor should we make a distinction between children who are baptized and those who are not, as if such a ritual can make one a child of God. The idea of infant baptism arose in North Africa years after the New Testament was written. Even if it can be justified theologically as a sign of the covenant (a debatable proposition), there is no evidence whatever that it can give to children the gift of eternal life.

If children are saved (and I believe they shall be) it can only be because God credits their sin to Christ; because they are too young to believe, the requirement of personal faith is waived. We do not know at what age they are held personally accountable. It is impossible to suggest an age, since that may vary, depending on the child's capacity and mental development.

Though the Bible is not clear on the subject, there are strong indications that children who die are with the Lord. David lost two sons for whom he grieved deeply. For Absalom, his rebellious son, he wept uncontrollably and refused comfort, for he was uncertain about the young man's destiny. But when the child born to Bathsheba died, he washed, anointed himself, and came into the house of the Lord to worship. He gave this explanation to those who asked about his behavior: "Now he has died; why should I fast? Can I bring him back again? I shall go to him, but he will not return to me" (2 Samuel 12:23).

Christ saw children as being in close proximity to God and the kingdom of heaven. "See that you do not despise one of these little ones, for I say to you, that their angels in heaven continually behold the face of My Father who is in heaven" (Matthew 18:10). Children are close to the heart of God.

Will a baby always be a baby in heaven? James Vernon McGee has made the interesting suggestion that God will resurrect the infants as they are and that the mothers' arms that have ached for them will have the opportunity of holding their little ones. The father who never had the opportunity of holding that little hand will be given that privilege. Thus the children will grow up with their parents.

Whether that will be the case, we do not know. But of this we can be confident: a child in heaven will be complete. Either the child will look as he would have if he were full grown, or else his mental and physical capacities will be enhanced to give him full status among the redeemed. Heaven is not a place for second-class citizens; all handicaps are removed. Heaven is a place of perfection.

The death of an infant, however, causes all of us to struggle with the will and purpose of God. It seems strange that God would grant the gift of life and then cause it to be snuffed out before it could blossom into a stage of usefulness. But we can be sure that there is a purpose in such a life, even if it is not immediately discernable.

James Vernon McGee again says that when a shepherd seeks to lead his sheep to better grass up the winding, thorny mountain paths, he often finds that the sheep will not follow him. They fear the unknown ridges and the sharp rocks. The shepherd will then reach into the flock and take a little lamb in one arm and another on his other arm. Then he starts up the precipitous pathway. Soon the two mother sheep begin to follow and afterward the entire flock. Thus they ascend the tortuous path to greener pastures.

So it is with the Good Shepherd. Sometimes He reaches into the flock and takes a lamb to Himself. He uses the experience to lead His people, to lift them to new heights of commitment as they follow the little lamb all the way home.

A little girl died in a hotel where she was staying with her father. Since her mother was already dead, just two followed the body to the cemetery—the father and the minister. The man grieved uncontrollably as he took the key and unlocked the casket to look upon the face of his child one last time. Then he closed the casket and handed the key to the keeper of the cemetery. On the way back the minister quoted Revelation 1:17b–18 to the brokenhearted

274   MATTERS OF LIFE AND DEATH

man. "'Do not be afraid; I am the first and the last, and the living One; and I was dead, and behold, I am alive forevermore, and I have the keys of death and of Hades.'

"You think the key to your little daughter's casket is in the hands of the keeper of the cemetery," the minister said. "But the key is in the hands of the Son of God, and He will come some morning and use it."

The words comforted the heart of the grieving father, for he understood the meaning of the resurrection.

In heaven we shall experience our new resurrection bodies, perfect in beauty and power. We shall be able to use our bodies and minds to serve the Savior and to express to Him our eternal adoration. Let me quote once more John's incredible words: "We know that, when He appears, we shall be like Him, because we shall see Him just as He is" (1 John 3:2b).

A New Home

Though a glorified body can live quite comfortably in this world (as Christ did after the resurrection), God has prepared a new home for the redeemed of all ages. Christ assured the disciples that the place He was preparing had "many dwelling places." There would be plenty of room for all of the redeemed.

John gives us this description: "And I saw a new heaven and a new earth; for the first heaven and the first earth passed away, and there is no longer any sea. And I saw the holy city, new Jerusalem, coming down out of heaven from God, made ready as a bride adorned for her husband" (Revelation 21:1–2).

This city is new—that is, re-created—just as our resurrected bodies are re-created from our earthly bodies. The previous heavens (the atmospheric heavens) and the earth, tainted by sin, will have been dissolved by fire to make room for the new order of creation (2 Peter 3:7–13).

This city came out of heaven. It originates from heaven because it is part of the heavenly realm. This is the most detailed description of what heaven will be like. Let's consider some features of this beautiful permanent home.

THE SIZE OF THE CITY

The dimensions are given as a cube, 1,500 miles square. "And the city is laid out as a square, and its length is as great as the width; and he measured the city with the rod, fifteen hundred miles; its length and width and height are equal" (Revelation 21:16).

If we take that literally, heaven will be composed of 396,000 stories (at twenty feet per story) each having an area as big as one half the size of the United States! Divide that up into separate condominiums, and you have plenty of room for all who have been redeemed by God since the beginning of time. The Old Testament saints, Abraham, Isaac, and Jacob—they will be there. Then we think of the New Testament apostles and all the redeemed throughout two thousand years of church history—heaven will be the home for all of them. Unfortunately, however, the majority of the world's population will likely not be there. Heaven, as Christ explained, is a special place for special people.

You need not fear that you will be lost in the crowd; nor need you fear being stuck on the thousandth floor when all of the activity is in the downstairs lounge. All that you will need to do is to decide where you would like to be, and you will be there! Each occupant will receive individualized attention. The Good Shepherd who calls His own sheep by name will have a special place prepared for each of His lambs. As someone has said, there will be a crown awaiting us that no one else can wear, a dwelling place that no one else can enter.

THE MATERIALS OF THE CITY

The details can be written, though hardly imagined. In John Bunyan's *Pilgrim's Progress*, as Christian and Hopeful finally see the City of God, there was such beauty that they fell sick with happiness, crying out, "If you see my Beloved, tell Him I am sick with love." The city was so glorious that they could not yet look upon it directly but had to use an instrument made for that purpose. This, after all, is the dwelling place of God.

John wrote in Revelation that the city had the glory of God. "Her brilliance was like a very costly stone, as a stone of crystal-clear jasper" (21:11). It is interesting that the city shares some features of the earthly Jerusalem, but we are more impressed with the contrasts. The new Jerusalem is a city of unimaginable beauty and brilliance.

First, there is a wall with twelve foundation stones that encompasses the city. "And the wall of the city had twelve foundation stones, and on them were the twelve names of the twelve apostles of the Lamb" (21:14).

As for the foundation stones on which the wall is built, each is adorned with a different kind of precious stone—the list is in 21:19–20. The jewels roughly parallel the twelve stones in the breastplate of the high priest (Exodus 28:17–20).

The height of the wall is given as seventy-two yards, not very high in comparison to the massive size of the city. But high enough to provide security and to make sure that it is accessible only through proper entrances.

Second, we notice the twelve gates, each a single pearl (Revelation 21:12, 21). That is a reminder that entrance to the city is restricted; only those who belong are admitted "and nothing unclean and no one who practices abomination and lying, shall ever come into it, but only those whose names are written in the Lamb's book of life" (v. 27).

John gives a further description of those who are outside the city walls. "Outside are the dogs and the sorcerers and the immoral persons and the murderers and the idolaters, and everyone who loves and practices lying" (22:15). There is a sentinel angel at each gate, evidently to make sure that only those who have their names written in the book are admitted.

The twelve gates are divided into four groups, thus three gates face each of the four directions. "There were three gates on the east and three gates on the north and three gates on the south and three gates on the west" (21:13). That is a reminder that the gospel is for all men, and all the tribes of the earth will be represented.

Notice that the saints of the Old Testament and the New are both included. The names of the twelve sons of Israel are written on the gates of the city, and the New Testament apostles have their names inscribed on the foundation stones. Thus the unity of the people of God throughout all ages is evident.

As for the street of the city it is "pure gold, like transparent glass" (v. 21). It is illuminated by the glory of God, and the Lamb is the lamp.

Now we can better understand why Bunyan said that the pilgrims must see the city through a special instrument. Its beauty is simply too much for us to comprehend. We need a transformed body and mind to behold it with unrestricted admiration.

When Christ said He was preparing a home for us with many mansions, He did not imply, as some have suggested, that He needed plenty of time to do the building. God is able to create the heavenly Jerusalem in a moment of time. But Christ did emphasize that we would be with Him, and we know that His presence will even be more marvelous than our environment.

A New Occupation

It's been estimated that there are at least 40,000 different occupations in the United States. Yet, for all that; only a small percentage of the population is completely satisfied with their responsibilities. Personnel problems, the lack of adequate pay, and wearisome hours of routine tasks are only some of the reasons. Few, if any, are truly satisfied.

But those problems will be behind us forever in heaven. Each job description will entail two primary responsibilities. First, there will be the worship of God; second, there will be the serving of the Most High in whatever capacity that is assigned to us.

THE WORSHIP OF GOD

Let's try to capture the privilege of worship.

Heaven is first and foremost the dwelling place of God. It is true, of course, that God's presence is not limited to heaven, for He is omnipresent. Solomon perceptively commented, "Behold, heaven and the highest heaven cannot contain Thee, how much less this house which I have built!" (1 Kings 8:27).

Yet in heaven God is localized. John saw God seated upon a throne with twenty-four other thrones occupied by twenty-four elders who worship the King. "And from the throne proceed flashes of lightning and sounds and peals of thunder" (Revelation 4:5). And what is the nature of the activity around that throne? There is uninhibited joy and spontaneous worship.

Needless to say the saints on earth are imperfect. They are beset by quarrels, carnality, and doctrinal deviations. Read a book on church history and you will marvel that the church has survived these two thousand years.

Have you ever wondered what it would be like to belong to a perfect church? That is precisely what John saw when he peered into heaven. Free from the limitations of the flesh and the opposition of the devil, the perfect church is found singing the praises of Christ without self-consciousness or mixed motives.

Repeatedly John sees worship taking place in heaven. Even after the judgment of God is heaped upon unrepentant sinners, the saints join with other created beings to chant the praises of God:

And a voice came from the throne, saying, "Give praise to our God, all you His bond-servants, you who fear Him, the small and the great." And I heard, as it were, the voice of a great multitude and as the sound of many waters and as the sound of mighty peals of thunder, saying, "Hallelujah! For the Lord our God, the Almighty, reigns." (Revelation 19:5–6)

If we want to prepare for our final destination, we should begin to worship God here on earth. Our arrival in heaven will only be a continuation of what we have already begun. Praise is the language of heaven and the language of the faithful on earth.

SERVICE TO THE LORD

Though worship shall occupy much of our time in heaven, we will also be assigned responsibilities commensurate with the faithfulness we displayed here on earth: "And His bond-servants shall serve Him; and they shall see His face, and His name shall be on their foreheads" (Revelation 22:3b–4).

That word *servant* is found frequently in the book of Revelation, for it pictures a continuation of the relationship we even now have with Christ. However, the word *serve* used here is used primarily in the New Testament for service that is carried on within the temple or church (Matthew 4:10; Luke 2:37; Acts 24:14). Thus we shall serve Him in that special, intimate relationship available only to those who are included within the inner circle of the redeemed. David Gregg gives his conception of what that kind of work will be like:

It is work as free from care and toil and fatigue as is the wing-stroke of the jubilant lark when it soars into the sunlight of a fresh, clear day and, spontaneously and for self-relief, pours out its thrilling carol. Work up there is a matter of self-relief, as well as a matter of obedience to the ruling will of God. It is work according to one's tastes and delight and ability. If tastes vary there, if abilities vary there, then occupations will vary there.[1]

What responsibilities will we have? Christ told a parable that taught that the faithful were given authority over cities. Most scholars believe that will be fulfilled during the millennial kingdom when we shall rule with Christ here on earth. But it is reasonable to assume that there is continuity between the earthly kingdom and the eternal heavenly kingdom. In other words, it may well be that our faithfulness (or unfaithfulness) on earth may have repercussions throughout eternity.

Yes, everyone in heaven will be happy and fulfilled. Everyone will be assigned a place in the administration of the vast heavenly kingdom. But just as there are varied responsibilities in the palace of an earthly king, so in heaven some will be given more prominent responsibilities than others.

Of this we may be certain: heaven is not a place of inactivity or boredom. It is not, as a Sunday school pupil thought, an interminable worship service where we begin on page one of the hymnal and sing all the way through. God will have productive work for us to do. We will increase our knowledge of Him and His wondrous works. Will not Christ show us the Father that we might be forever satisfied? Will we not then learn to love the Lord our God in ways that we have never been able to do on earth?

We do not know, as some have speculated, whether we shall explore other worlds. Others have suggested that we shall be able to complete many projects begun on earth. Whatever our activity, we can be sure that our infinite heavenly Father will have infinite possibilities.

A New Family

We were created for the pleasure of God. His purpose was that at least some human beings would be in fellowship with Him forever.

In Eden, Adam walked with God in the cool of the day.

After the tabernacle was built, the Shekinah glory settled in the Holy of Holies and among the people to give visible evidence that God was dwelling among them.

In this church age, the presence of God has been transferred to believers as they meet together in the name of Christ. Even more specifically, our bodies are the "temple of the Holy Spirit."

In heaven all of those relationships will be changed so that we will be in the presence of Christ without the limitations of sin. The barriers that hide the face of God will be lifted, and we shall "see Him as he is."

We often wonder whether the family relationships of earth will still be in existence in heaven. The Sadducees, who did not believe in the resurrection of the body, came to Christ with this puzzle: If a man is married on earth and his wife dies and he chooses to remarry, and the pattern repeats itself seven times—who will his wife be at the resurrection? Christ chided them, saying they knew neither the Scriptures nor the power of God. In heaven the marriage relationship does not exist.

That does not mean that in heaven we will be sexless (i.e., neither male nor female). Your mother will still be known as your mother in heaven; your father will be known as he was here on earth. Christ is simply saying that in heaven there is no marriage—there will be no babies born. Just as the angels are not reproduced by procreation, so the sexual relationship will no longer be a part of the divine order.

Will we still have a special relationship with family members? Think of it this way: The intimacy you now enjoy with your family will be expanded to include all the other saints that are present. Even in the Old Testament there was a recognition that saints would know one another in the life beyond. When a man died it was said, "He was gathered to his people."

One day some of Christ's friends sent word that His mother and brothers were looking for Him. Christ responded, "Who are My mother and My brothers?" And looking around Him, He said, "Behold, My mother and My brothers! For whoever does the will of God, he is My brother and sister and mother" (Mark 3:33–35).

Think of the implications: we will be just as close to Christ as we are to any member of our present family. Indeed, He is not ashamed to call us His brothers! There will be extended family with greater intimacy than we have known on earth.

Archbishop Whately has an excellent description of the kind of friendship we can expect in heaven:

> I am convinced that the extension and perfection of friendship will constitute a great part of the future happiness of the blest. . . . A wish to see and personally know, for example, the apostle Paul, or John, is the most likely to arise in the noblest and purest mind. I should be sorry to think such a wish absurd and presumptuous, or unlikely ever to be gratified. The highest enjoyment doubtless to the blest will be the personal knowledge of their great and beloved Master. Yet I cannot but think that some part of their happiness will consist in an intimate knowledge of the greatest of His followers also; and of those of them in particular, whose peculiar qualities are, to each, the most peculiarly attractive.[2]

Think of the joys of such a family! And of the infinite time to become better acquainted.

A New Order of Reality

Fortunately heaven will not have everything. In fact, John lists many different experiences and realities known on earth that will be absent there.

No more sea. Throughout the Bible the word *sea* stands for the nations of the world, usually the rebellious nations. Heaven means that the strife between nations and the seething turmoil that accompanies those struggles will vanish. No broken treaties, no wars, no scandals.

No more death. The hearse will have made its last journey. Today we look at death as a thief that robs us of our earthly existence. It is simply the final act in the deterioration of the human body. As such it is almost universally feared; no one can escape its terrors. Even Christians who have conquered it in Christ may tremble at its fearsome onslaught. But death shall not enter heaven. No funeral services, no tombstones, no tearful good-byes.

No more sorrow. Read the newspaper, and sorrow is written on every page. An automobile accident takes the life of a young father; a child is raped by a madman; a flood in Bangladesh kills 20,000. No one can fathom the amount of emotional pain borne by the inhabitants of this world in any single moment. In heaven there will be uninterrupted joy and emotional tranquillity.

No more crying. No one could possibly calculate the buckets of tears that are shed every single moment in this hurting world. From the child crying because of the death of a parent to the woman weeping because of a failed marriage—multiply those tears by a million, and you will realize that we live in a crying world.

In heaven, He who wiped away our sins now wipes away our tears. This comment has raised the question of why there would be tears in heaven in the first place. And does the Lord come with a handkerchief and literally wipe away each tear? That is possible. But I think that John means more than that. He wants us to understand that God will give us an explanation for the sorrow we experienced on earth so that we will not have to cry anymore. If that were not so, then the tears might return after He has wiped them away. But being able to view the tearful events of earth from the perspective of heaven will dry up our tears forever.

The question is often asked how we can be happy in heaven if one or more of our relatives is in hell. Can a child, for example, enjoy the glories of eternity knowing that a father or a mother will always be absent from the celebration? Or can a godly mother serve and worship with joy knowing that her precious son will be in torment forever? That question has so vexed the minds of theologians that some have actually asserted that in heaven God will blank out a part of our memory. The child will not know that his parents are lost in hell; the mother will not remember that she had a son.

However, it is unlikely that we will know less in heaven than we do on earth. It is not characteristic of God to resolve a problem by expanding the sphere of human ignorance. That is especially true in heaven, where we will have better mental faculties than on earth. In heaven we shall be comforted, not because we know less than we did on earth but because we know more.

It is more likely that God will wipe away all tears by explaining His ultimate purposes. We will look at heaven and hell from His viewpoint and say that He did all things well. If God can be content knowing that unbelievers are in hell, so will we.

I expect that all who are in heaven will live with the knowledge that justice was fully served and that God's plan was right. And with such an explanation and perspective, our emotions will mirror those of our heavenly Father. Jonathan Edwards said that heaven will have no pity for hell, not because the saints are unloving but because they are perfectly loving. They will see everything in conformity with God's love, justice, and glory. Thus with both head and heart we will worship the Lord without regret, sorrow, or misgivings about our Father's plan.

No more pain. Come with me as we walk down the corridors of a hospital. Here is a young mother dying of cancer; a man is gasping for breath, trying to overcome the terror of a heart attack. In the next ward an abused child has just been admitted with burns inflicted by an angry father. For those and countless other emergencies, scientists have prepared painkillers to help people make it through life, one day at a time.

In heaven pain, which is the result of sin, is banished forever. No headaches, slipped discs, or surgery. And no more emotional pain because of rejection, separation, or abuse.

No temple. Some have been puzzled by that assertion because elsewhere John says that there is a temple in heaven (Revelation 11:19). Wilbur M. Smith points out that the apparent contradiction can be resolved when we realize that the temple and its angelic messengers "continue in action during the time of man's sin and the outpouring of the wrath of God, but after the old earth has disappeared, the temple has no longer any function."[3] The worship in heaven is now carried on directly; God Himself is the Shrine, the Temple. The former patterns of worship give way to a new, unrestricted order.

No more sun or moon. Those planets created by God to give light to the earth have outlived their purpose. God Himself is the light of heaven. "And the city has no need of the sun or of the moon to shine upon it, for the glory of God has illumined it, and its lamp is the Lamb" (Revelation 21:23). Again we read, "And there shall no longer be any night; and they shall not have need of the light of a lamp nor the light of the sun, because the Lord God shall illumine them; and they shall reign forever and ever" (22:5).

That means that the Holy City is interpenetrated with light. Joseph Seiss explains it this way:

> That shining is not from any material combustion, not from any consumption of fuel that needs to be replaced as one supply burns out; for it is the uncreated light of Him who is light, dispensed by and through the Lamb as the everlasting Lamp, to the home, and hearts, and understandings of His glorified saints.[4]

No abominations. The nations shall bring the honor and glory of God into the city, but we read, "Nothing unclean and no one who practices abomination and lying, shall ever come into it, but only those whose names are written in the Lamb's book of life" (21:27). John lists others who will be excluded: immoral people, murderers, idolaters, and the like.

No more hunger, thirst, or heat. Those burdens borne by the multitudes of this present world will vanish forever. In their place will be the Tree of Life and the beauty of the paradise of God.

Those things that cast such a pall of gloom over the earth today will be replaced by indescribable happiness in the presence of Divine Glory.

> Just think of stepping on shore
> And finding it heaven
> Of clasping a hand
> And finding it God's
> Of breathing new air
> And finding it celestial
> Of waking up in glory
> And finding it home.[5]

Checking Your Passport

Those of us who have traveled in foreign countries know the importance of a passport. Regardless of your status and charisma, that document is what qualifies you for entry and acceptance among the people in a different land.

There is nothing quite like coming home to the land of your own citizenship. If you are an American there is no fear in returning to America—you know that your entry is assured.

We have a passport to get into heaven, the country where we claim citizenship. In fact we have already established residence there, for all believers are "seated with Christ in the heavenlies." That means we will not have a hassle at the border but are guaranteed entry. Only those who are prepared to die are prepared to live.

What is Christ's attitude toward our homecoming? Repeatedly in the New Testament Christ is spoken of as sitting "at the right hand of God." But there is one reference to Christ's leaving His seat and standing; He is welcoming one of His servants home. As Stephen was being stoned, we read that "being full of the Holy Spirit, he gazed intently into heaven and saw the glory of God, and Jesus standing at the right hand of God" (Acts 7:55).

Thus the seated Son of God stood to welcome one of His own into the heavenly realm. A believer's death may be unnoticed on earth, but it is front-page news in heaven. The Son of God takes note.

No one can enter heaven without God's specific approval. Each one must have a passport signed by His own Son. Those who receive it may enter those gates; all others must stay outside. Those who have the passport need not fear saying good-bye to earth, for they are assured a welcome in heaven.

D. L. Moody at death caught a glimpse of heaven. Awakening from sleep he said, "Earth recedes, Heaven opens before me. If this is death, it is sweet! There is no valley here. God is calling me and I must go!"

Remember the words of Hamlet in Shakespeare's play? In a moment of deep contemplation he mused, "To be, or not to be, that is the question" (III, i, 57). He was contemplating suicide because life had become unbearable. Yet when he thought of where that might lead him, he continued, "In that sleep of death what dreams may come when we have shuffled off this mortal coil" (III, i, 67–68). He wondered whether his existence on the other side might be even more intolerable than life.

Compare that with the words of Paul, "But I am hardpressed from both directions, having the desire to depart and be with Christ, for that is very much better; yet to remain on in the flesh is more necessary for your sake" (Philippians 1:23–24).

Hamlet says, "Live or die, I lose!" Paul says, "Live or die, I win!"

Knowing Christ makes the difference.

Notes

1. David Gregg, *The Heaven-Life* (New York: Revell, 1895), 62.
2. Richard Whately, *A View of the Scripture Revelations Concerning a Future State,* 3d ed. (Philadelphia: Lindsay & Blakiston, 1857), 214–15.
3. Wilbur M. Smith, *Biblical Doctrine of Heaven* (Chicago: Moody, 1968), 253.
4. Joseph Seiss, *Lectures on the Apocalypse* (New York: Charles C. Cook, 1901), 3:412–13. Quoted in Smith, 249.
5. "Finally Home," reprinted with permission of Benson Company, Inc. Copyright 1971 by Singspiration Music.

Moody Press, a ministry of the Moody Bible Institute,
is designed for education, evangelization, and edification.
If we may assist you in knowing more about Christ
and the Christian life, please write us without obligation:
Moody Press, c/o MLM, Chicago, Illinois 60610.